MICROSOFT® OFFICE WORD 2007

QuickSteps

MARTY MATTHEWS
CAROLE MATTHEWS

New York Chicago San Francisco
Lisbon London Madrid Mexico City
Milan New Delhi San Juan
Seoul Singapore Sydney Toronto

The McGraw·Hill Companies

Cataloging-in-Publication Data is on file with the Library of Congress

McGraw-Hill books are available at special quantity discounts to use as premiums and sales promotions or for use in corporate training programs. For more information, please write to the Director of Special Sales, Professional Publishing, McGraw-Hill, Two Penn Plaza, New York, NY 10121-2298, or contact your local bookstore.

Microsoft®, Windows®, FrontPage®, and PowerPoint® are registered trademarks of Microsoft Corporation in the United States and other countries.

Information has been obtained by McGraw-Hill from sources believed to be reliable. However, because of the possibility of human or mechanical error by our sources, McGraw-Hill, or others, McGraw-Hill does not guarantee the accuracy, adequacy, or completeness of any information and is not responsible for any errors or omissions or the results obtained from the use of such information.

MICROSOFT® OFFICE WORD 2007 QUICKSTEPS

1234567890 CCI CCI 01987

ISBN-13:   978-0-07-148299-8
ISBN-10:   0-07-148299-7

SPONSORING EDITOR / Roger Stewart

EDITORIAL SUPERVISOR / Patty Mon

PROJECT MANAGER / Samik Roy Chowdhury (International Typesetting and Composition)

ACQUISITIONS COORDINATOR / Carly Stapleton

SERIES CREATORS AND EDITORS / Marty and Carole Matthews

TECHNICAL EDITOR / John Cronan

COPY EDITOR / Lisa McCoy

PROOFREADER / Joette Lynch

INDEXER / Valerie Perry

PRODUCTION SUPERVISOR / Jim Kussow

COMPOSITION / International Typesetting and Composition

ILLUSTRATION / International Typesetting and Composition

ART DIRECTOR, COVER / Jeff Weeks

COVER DESIGN / Pattie Lee

SERIES DESIGN / Bailey Cunningham

Wilma O'Nan...

A kind and gentle lady, who is also a prize-winning gardener and a wonderful dessert-maker. We have been most honored to call her our friend for the last 21 years.

—Carole and Marty

About the Authors

Carole and Marty Matthews have used computers for over 30 years, from some of the early mainframe computers to recent personal computers. They have done this as programmers, systems analysts, managers, and company executives. As a result, they have firsthand knowledge of not only how to program and use a computer, but also how to make the best use of all that can be done with one.

Over 27 years ago, Carole and Marty wrote their first computer book on how to buy mini-computers. Over 23 years ago, they began writing books as a major part of their occupation. In the intervening years, they have written over 70 books, including ones on desktop publishing, Web publishing, Microsoft Office, and Microsoft operating systems from MS-DOS through Windows Vista. Recent books published by McGraw-Hill include *Windows Vista QuickSteps, Microsoft Office PowerPoint 2007 QuickSteps, Microsoft Office Outlook 2007 QuickSteps*, and *QuickSteps to Winning Business Presentations*.

Marty and Carole live on an island in Puget Sound, where, on the rare moments when they can look up from their computers, they look west across seven miles of water and the main shipping channel to the snow-capped Olympic Mountains.

Acknowledgments

This book is a team effort of truly talented people. Among them are:

Lisa McCoy, copy editor, added greatly to the readability and understandability of the book while always being a joy to work with. Thanks, Lisa!

Valerie Perry, indexer, who adds so much to the usability of the book, and does so quickly and without notice. Thanks, Valerie!

Patty Mon, editorial supervisor and **Samik Roy Chowdhury**, project manager, who greased the wheels and straightened the track to make a very smooth production process. Thanks, Patty and Sam!

Roger Stewart, sponsoring editor, believed in us enough to sell the series, and continues to stand behind us as we go through the second edition. Thanks, Roger!

Contents at a Glance

Contents

Chapter 3 **Formatting a Document** 43

Chapter 4 **Customizing a Document** 71

5

6

9

10

Introduction

QuickSteps books are recipe books for computer users. They answer the question "How do I..." by providing a quick set of steps to accomplish the most common tasks with a particular operating system or application.

The sets of steps are the central focus of the book. QuickSteps sidebars show how to quickly perform many small functions or tasks that support the primary functions. QuickFacts sidebars supply information that you need to know about a subject. Notes, Tips, and Cautions augment the steps; they are presented in a separate column so as not to interrupt the flow of the steps. The introductions are minimal rather than narrative, and numerous illustrations and figures, many with callouts, support the steps.

QuickSteps books are organized by function and the tasks needed to perform that function. Each function is a chapter. Each task, or "How To," contains the steps needed for accomplishing the function, along with the relevant Notes, Tips, Cautions, and screenshots. You can easily find the tasks you need through:

- The table of contents, which lists the functional areas (chapters) and tasks in the order they are presented

- A How To list of tasks on the opening page of each chapter

- The index, which provides an alphabetical list of the terms that are used to describe the functions and tasks

- Color-coded tabs for each chapter, or functional area, with an index to the tabs in the Contents at a Glance section (just before the table of contents)

Conventions Used in This Book

Microsoft Office Word 2007 QuickSteps uses several conventions designed to make the book easier for you to follow:

- A ⚙ in the table of contents and in the How To list in each chapter references a QuickSteps sidebar in a chapter, and a ⬡ references a QuickFacts sidebar.

- **Bold type** is used for words or objects on the screen that you are to do something with—for example, "click **Start** and click **Computer**."

- *Italic type* is used for a word or phrase that is being defined or otherwise deserves special emphasis.

- Underlined type is used for text that you are to type from the keyboard.

- SMALL CAPITAL LETTERS are used for keys on the keyboard, such as ENTER and SHIFT.

- When you are expected to enter a command, you are told to press the key(s). If you are to enter text or numbers, you are told to type them.

How to...

Chapter 1
Stepping into Word

Microsoft Word is the most widely used of all word-processing programs. Most personal computers (PCs) have some version of Word installed, and most people with PCs probably have Word available to them, as well as some experience in its use. Word is both simple to use and highly sophisticated, offering many features that commonly go unused. It is a "sleeper" product, one that delivers a high degree of functionality even when only a small percentage of its capabilities are used. The purpose of this book is to acquaint you with many of those features that can enhance your experience with Word.

In this chapter you will become familiar with Word; see how to start and exit it; use Word's windows, panes, ribbon, toolbars, and menus; learn how to get help; and find out how to customize Word.

Start and Exit Word

How you start Word depends on how Word was installed and what has happened to it since its installation. In this section you'll see a surefire way to start Word and some alternatives. You'll also see how to exit Word.

Use the Start Menu to Start Word

If no other icons for or shortcuts to Word are available on your desktop, you can always start Word using the Start menu.

1. Start your computer if it is not already running, and log on to Windows if necessary.
2. Click **Start**. The Start menu opens.
3. Click **All Programs**, click **Microsoft Office**, and click **Microsoft Office Word 2007**, as shown in Figure 1-1.

Start Word in Different Ways

In addition to using All Programs on the Start menu, Word can be started in several other ways.

USE THE START MENU ITSELF

The icons of the programs you use most often are displayed on the left side of the Start menu. If you frequently use Word, its icon will appear there. To use that icon to start Word:

1. Click **Start**. The Start menu opens.
2. Click the **Word** icon on the left of the Start menu.

PIN WORD TO THE TOP OF THE START MENU

The Start menu's contents and sequence of items will differ based on how often you use the various programs. If you think that you may use other programs more frequently, you can keep Word at the top of the Start menu by "pinning" it there.

Figure 1-1: *The foolproof way to start Word is via the Start menu.*

1. Click **Start** to open the Start menu.
2. Right-click (click the right mouse button) the **Word** icon, and click **Pin To Start Menu**.

CREATE A DESKTOP SHORTCUT

An easy way to start Word is to create a shortcut icon on the desktop and use it to start the program.

1. Click **Start**, click **All Programs**, and click **Microsoft Office**.
2. Right-click **Microsoft Office Word 2007**, click **Send To**, and click **Desktop (Create Shortcut)**.

USE THE QUICK LAUNCH TOOLBAR

The Quick Launch toolbar is a small area on the taskbar next to the Start button. You can put a Word icon on the Quick Launch toolbar and use it to start Word. If your Quick Launch toolbar is not visible, open it and put a Word icon there.

1. Right-click a blank area of the taskbar, click **Toolbars**, and click **Quick Launch**. The Quick Launch toolbar is displayed.
2. Click **Start**, click **All Programs**, click **Microsoft Office**, and drag **Microsoft Office Word 2007** icon to where you want it on the Quick Launch toolbar.
3. Click the icon on the Quick Launch toolbar to start Word.

Explore Word

Word uses a wide assortment of windows, ribbon tabs, toolbars, menus, and special features to accomplish its functions. Much of this book explores how to find and use all of those items. In this section you'll learn to use the most common features of the default Word window, including the parts of the window, the tabs on the ribbon, and the task pane.

Explore the Word Window

The Word window has many features to aid you in creating and editing documents. The view presented to you when you first start Word is shown in Figure 1-2. You can see the primary parts of the ribbon in Figure 1-3.

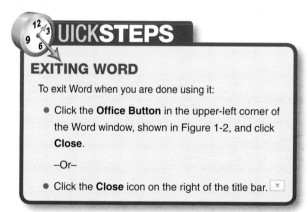

UICKSTEPS

EXITING WORD

To exit Word when you are done using it:

- Click the **Office Button** in the upper-left corner of the Word window, shown in Figure 1-2, and click **Close**.

–Or–

- Click the **Close** icon on the right of the title bar.

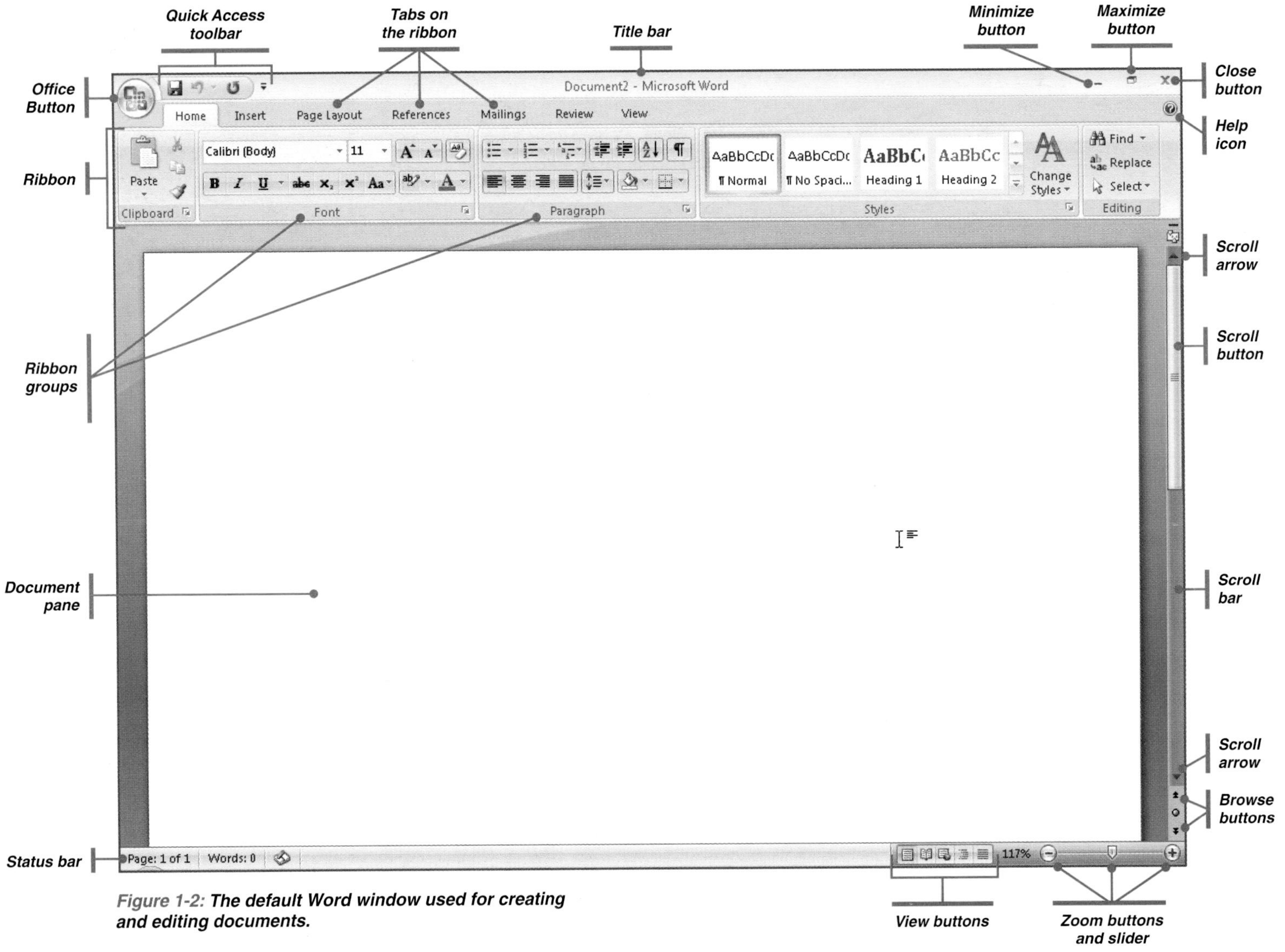

Quick Access toolbar

Tabs on the ribbon

Title bar

Minimize button

Maximize button

Office Button

Close button

Document2 - Microsoft Word

Home   Insert   Page Layout   References   Mailings   Review   View

Help icon

Ribbon

Calibri (Body)   11

B *I* U   abe x₂ x² Aa

AaBbCcDc   AaBbCcDc   **AaBbC**   **AaBbCc**   Change Styles

Find
Replace
Select

Paste

Clipboard   Font   Paragraph   ¶ Normal   ¶ No Spaci...   Heading 1   Heading 2   Styles   Editing

Scroll arrow

Ribbon groups

Scroll button

Document pane

Scroll bar

Scroll arrow

Browse buttons

Status bar

Page: 1 of 1   Words: 0

117%   ⊖   ⊕

Figure 1-2: *The default Word window used for creating and editing documents.*

View buttons

Zoom buttons and slider

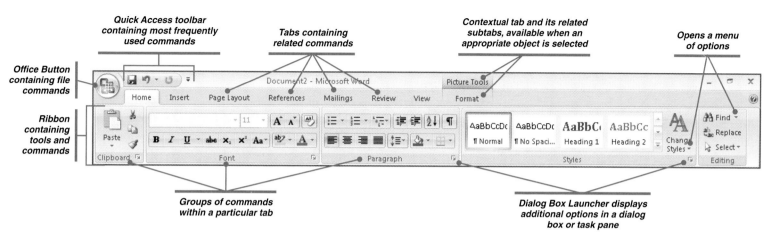

Office Button containing file commands

Ribbon containing tools and commands

Quick Access toolbar containing most frequently used commands

Tabs containing related commands

Contextual tab and its related subtabs, available when an appropriate object is selected

Opens a menu of options

Groups of commands within a particular tab

Dialog Box Launcher displays additional options in a dialog box or task pane

Figure 1-3: *Organized into tabs and then groups, the commands and tools on the ribbon are how you create, edit, and otherwise work with documents.*

UNDERSTANDING THE RIBBON

So where are the familiar toolbars and menus from previous versions of Word? They're gone, not unlike black-and-white televisions and 40-MB hard drives. The original menu structure used in earlier Office products (File, Edit, Format, Window, Help, and other menus) was designed to accommodate fewer tasks and features. That menu structure has simply outgrown its usefulness. Microsoft's solution to the increased number of feature enhancements is the *ribbon*, the container at the top of most Office program windows that holds the tools and features you are most likely to use (see Figure 1-3). The ribbon collects tools for a given function into *groups*—for example, the Font group provides the tools to work with text. Groups are then organized into tabs for working on likely tasks. For example, the Insert tab contains groups for adding components, such as tables, links, and charts to your document (or spreadsheet or slide presentation).

Continued . . .

The principal features of the Word window, including the various ribbon tabs, are described further in this and other chapters of this book.

Use the Mouse

A *mouse* is any pointing device—including trackballs, pointing sticks, and graphic tablets—with two or more buttons. This book assumes you are using a two-button mouse. Moving the mouse moves the pointer on the screen. You *select* an object on the screen by moving the pointer so that it is on top of the object and then pressing the left button on the mouse.

You may control the mouse with either your left or right hand; therefore, the buttons may be switched. (See *Windows Vista QuickSteps*, published by McGraw-Hill/Osborne, for how to switch the buttons.) This book assumes the right hand controls the mouse and the left mouse button is "*the* mouse button." The right button is always called the "right mouse button." If you switch the buttons, you must change your interpretation of these phrases.

UNDERSTANDING THE RIBBON

(Continued)

Each Office program has a default set of tabs, with additional *contextual* tabs that appear as the context of your work changes. For instance, when you select a picture, a Format tab containing shapes and drawing tools that you can use with the particular object appears beneath the defining tools tab (such as the Picture Tools tab); when the object is unselected, the Format tab disappears. The ribbon contains labeled buttons you can click to use a given command or tool. Depending on the tool, you are then presented with additional options in the form of a list of commands, a dialog box or task pane, or galleries of choices that reflect what you'll see in your work. Groups that contain several more tools than can be displayed in the ribbon include a *Dialog Box Launcher* icon that takes you directly to these other choices. The ribbon also takes advantage of new Office 2007 features, including a live preview of many potential changes (for example, you can select text and see it change color as you point to various colors in the Font Color gallery). See the accompanying sections and figures for more information on the ribbon and other elements of the Word window.

TIP

To gain working space in the document pane, you can minimize the size of the ribbon. To do this, double-click the active tab name. Click it again to restore the size of the ribbon. You can also press **CTRL+F1** to toggle the size of the ribbon.

Five actions can be accomplished with the mouse:

- **Point** at an *object* on the screen (a button, an icon, a menu or one of its options, or a border) to highlight it. To *point* means to move the mouse so that the tip of the pointer is on top of the object.

- **Click** an object on the screen to *select* it, making that object the item that your next actions will affect. Clicking will also open a menu, select a menu option, or activate a button or "tool" on a toolbar or the ribbon. *Click* means to point at an object you want to select and quickly press and release the left mouse button.

- **Double-click** an object to open or activate it. *Double-click* means to point at an object you want to select, and then press and release the left mouse button twice in rapid succession.

- **Right-click** an object to open a context menu containing commands used to manipulate that object. *Right-click* means to point at an object that you want to select, and then quickly press and release the right mouse button. For example, right-clicking text opens this context menu:

- **Drag** an object to move it on the screen to where you want it moved within the document. *Drag* means to point at an object you want to move and then hold down the left mouse button while moving the mouse. The object is dragged as you move the mouse. When the object is where you want it, release the mouse button.

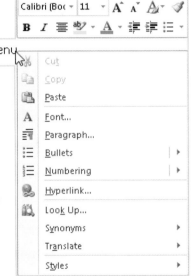

Use Tabs and Menus

Tabs are displayed at the top of the ribbon or a dialog box. Menus are displayed when you click a down arrow on a button on the ribbon, a dialog box, or a toolbar. You can use tabs and menus in the following ways:

- To open a tab or menu with the mouse, click the tab or menu.

QUICKSTEPS

USING THE MINI TOOLBAR IN WORD

When you select (highlight) text, a mini toolbar is displayed that allows you to perform an action directly on that text, such as making it bold or centering a paragraph. This toolbar contains a subset of the tools contained in the Fonts and Paragraph groups of the Home tab.

DISPLAY THE TEXT TOOLBAR

1. Select text by clicking it or dragging over the text.

2. Place the pointer over the text, and a vague image of the mini toolbar is displayed. Place your pointer over it to clarify the image.

–Or–

Right-click the selected text and click the mini toolbar to remove the context menu.

USE A TEXT TOOL

Click the button or icon on the mini toolbar that represents the tool you want to use.

HIDE THE MINI TOOLBAR

You can hide the mini toolbar by changing the default which is to show it.

1. Click the **Office Button**, and click the **Word Options** button.

2. Click the **Popular** option.

3. Click **Show Mini Toolbar On Selection** to remove the check mark.

4. Click **OK** to finalize the choice.

- To open a tab or menu with the keyboard, press **ALT** and the underlined letter in the tab or menu name. For example, press **ALT+F** to open the Office Button menu.

- To select a tab or menu command, click the tab or menu to open it, and then click the option.

- A number of menu options have a right-pointing arrow on their right to indicate that a submenu is associated with that option. To open the submenu, move the mouse pointer to the menu option with a submenu. After the submenu appears, move the mouse pointer to the submenu, and click the desired option.

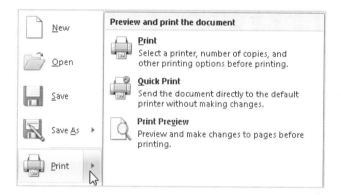

Use Views in Word

Word presents text in several views, allowing you to choose which one facilitates the task you are doing. To access a view, click the **View** tab, and then click a Document Views group button:

- **Print Layout** displays the text as it looks on a printed page.

- **Full Screen Reading** replaces the ribbon with a Full Screen toolbar. Click **View Options** to select options for displaying and using this screen view, such as whether to allow typing, tracking changes, displaying one or two pages, enlarging text, showing comments, and so on. Click **Close** to return to Normal view.

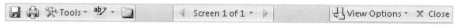

- **Web Layout** shows how the text will look as a Web page. Creating Web layout pages is discussed in Chapter 9.

- **Outline** displays the text in outline form, with a contextual Outlining tab on the ribbon, shown in Figure 1-4. You can use this view to promote and demote levels of text and rearrange levels, as shown in the Outline Tools group. With the Show Document button, you can toggle commands to extend your ability to create, insert, link, merge, split, and lock the document. Click **Close Outline View** to return to Normal view. Outlining is discussed further in Chapter 4.

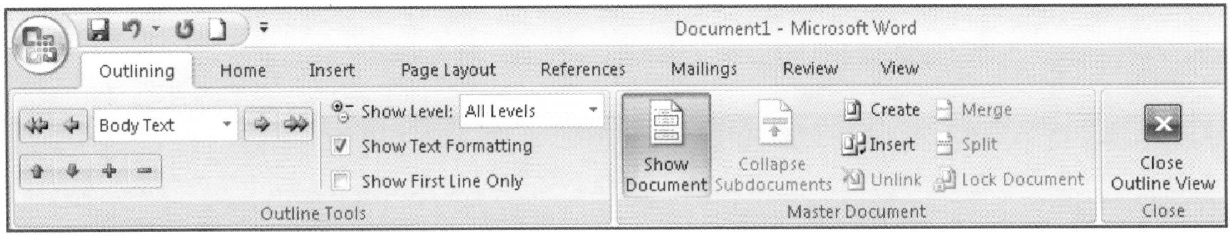

*Figure 1-4: **The Outline view allows you to rearrange and manipulate the document in various ways using a special Outlining tab.***

- **Draft** displays the text of the document in draft status for quick and easy editing. Headings and footings may not be visible.

Personalize and Customize Word

You can personalize Word, or make it your own, by changing the personal default settings Word has for options such as the tools available on the Quick Access toolbar or your user name and initials. You can customize Word by changing the general default settings with regards to editing, proofing, display, and other options. Many of these options are discussed in the other chapters. Here we will look at the Quick Access toolbar, display, and other popular options.

TIP

The mini toolbar becomes clearer when you place the pointer directly over it.

Work with the Quick Access Toolbar

The Quick Access toolbar can become a "best friend" if you modify it so that it fits your personal way of working.

ADD TO THE QUICK ACCESS TOOLBAR

The Quick Access toolbar contains the commands most commonly used. The default tools are Save, Undo, and Redo. You can add additional commands to it if you want.

1. Click the **Office Button**, and click the **Word Options** button.

2. Click the **Customize** option, and you will see the dialog box shown in Figure 1-5.

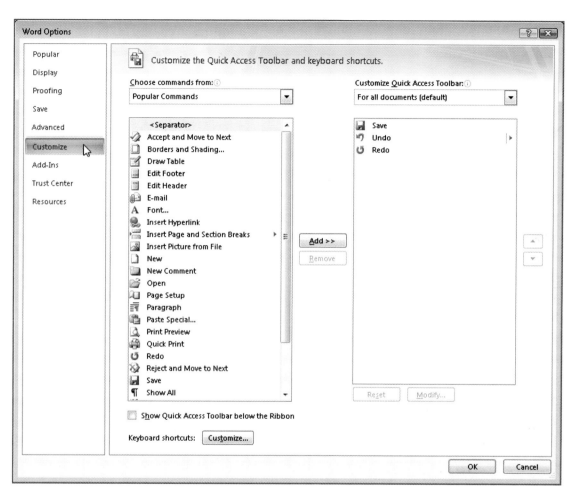

*Figure 1-5: **You can customize the Quick Access toolbar by adding to and removing from it commands for easy and quick access.***

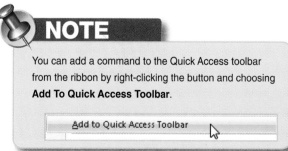

NOTE

You can add a command to the Quick Access toolbar from the ribbon by right-clicking the button and choosing **Add To Quick Access Toolbar**.

3. Open the drop-down list box, and select the type of command you want from the available options.

4. In the leftmost list box, find and click the command you want to add to the toolbar, and then click **Add** to move its name to the list box on the right. Repeat this for all the commands you want in the toolbar.

5. Click **OK** when you are finished.

QUICKSTEPS

CHANGING THE WINDOW COLOR

You can change the background color of the Word window, which is set to blue by default, to black or silver instead.

1. Click the **Office Button**, and click **Word Options**.

2. Click the **Popular** tab.

3. Click the **Color Scheme** down arrow, and click the color you want.

4. Click **OK** to save the change.

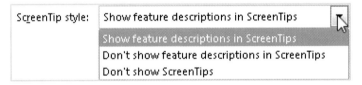

| Blue | Silver | Black |

MOVE THE QUICK ACCESS TOOLBAR

To move the Quick Access toolbar beneath the main toolbar, right-click the Quick Access toolbar, and click **Show Quick Access Toolbar Below The Ribbon**.

Show or Hide ScreenTips

When you hold your pointer over a command or tool, a ScreenTip is displayed. The tip may be just the name of the tool or command, or it may be enhanced with a small description. You can hide the tips or change whether they are enhanced or not.

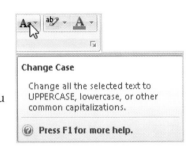

1. Click the **Office Button**, and click the **Word Options** button.

2. Click the **Popular** option.

3. Open the **ScreenTip Style** drop-down list, and choose the option you want.

4. Click **OK** to finalize the choice.

Add Identifying Information to Documents

You can add identifying information to a document to make it easier to organize your documents and to find them quickly during searches, especially in a shared environment (see Chapter 9 for more on removing this document information).

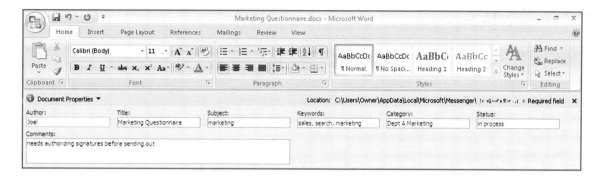

Figure 1-6: *A Document Information panel beneath the ribbon allows you to more easily locate a document using search tools if you add identifying data.*

1. Click the **Office Button**, click **Prepare** on the left, and click **Properties** in the right pane. A Document Information panel containing standard identifiers displays under the ribbon, as shown in Figure 1-6.

2. Type identifying information, such as title, subject, and keywords (words or phrases that are associated with the document).

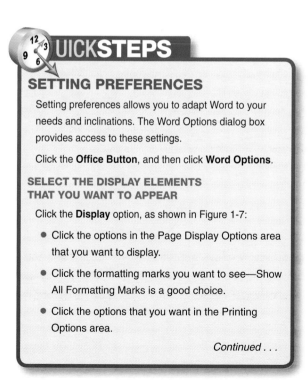

QUICKSTEPS

SETTING PREFERENCES

Setting preferences allows you to adapt Word to your needs and inclinations. The Word Options dialog box provides access to these settings.

Click the **Office Button**, and then click **Word Options**.

SELECT THE DISPLAY ELEMENTS THAT YOU WANT TO APPEAR

Click the **Display** option, as shown in Figure 1-7:

- Click the options in the Page Display Options area that you want to display.

- Click the formatting marks you want to see—Show All Formatting Marks is a good choice.

- Click the options that you want in the Printing Options area.

Continued . . .

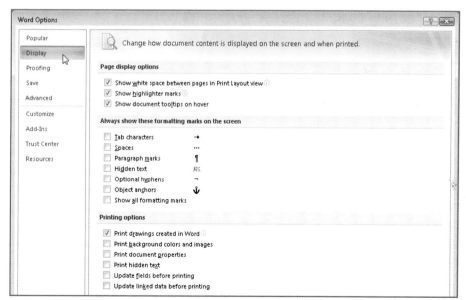

Figure 1-7: *The Display options in the Word Options dialog box provides page display, formatting, and printing preferences.*

QUICKSTEPS

SETTING PREFERENCES *(Continued)*

SET GENERAL POPULAR OPTIONS

1. Click the **Popular** option (see Figure 1-8):

   • Review and click the check marks that are relevant for your situation. Earlier in this chapter, you saw how to disable the mini toolbar, show and hide ScreenTips, and change the color scheme of the Word window. If you are unsure about other options, keep the default and see how well those settings work for you.

   • Type the user name you want displayed in documents revised using the Track Changes feature.

   • Type the initials associated with the user name that will be displayed in comments you insert into a document.

   • Click **Language Settings** to select the languages you'll be using in Office.

2. When you have set the Popular and Display options as you want, click each of the other options, review the settings and making any applicable changes. These are discussed further in the relevant chapters.

3. When you have finished selecting your preferences, click **OK** to close the Word Options dialog box.

NOTE

If you are not connected to the Internet, a limited Help feature is also available offline.

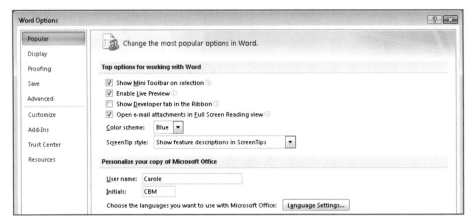

Figure 1-8: *Many basic preferences used in Word are set in the Popular Options dialog box.*

3. To view more information about the document, click the **Document Properties** down arrow in the panel's title bar, and click **Advanced Properties**. Review each tab in the Properties dialog box to see the information available and make any changes or additions. Close the Properties dialog box when you are finished.

4. When you are finished with the Document Information panel, click the X at the rightmost end of the panel's title bar to close it.

Get Help

Help can be accessed from online Microsoft servers. A different kind of help, which provides the Thesaurus and Research features, is also available.

Open Help

The Word Help system is maintained online at Microsoft. It is easily accessed.

Click the **Help** icon 🔘, and the Word Help window will open, shown in Figure 1-9.

• Find the topic you want, and click it.

   –Or–

• Type keywords in the Search text box, and click **Search**.

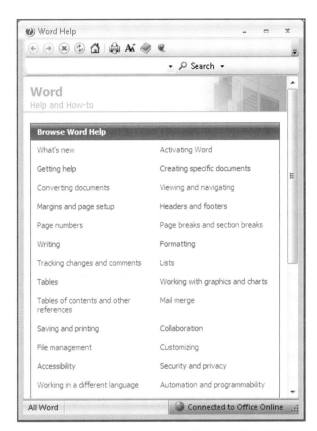

Figure 1-9: *When you click the Help icon, the Word Help dialog box appears, where you can click the topic you want or search for specific keywords.*

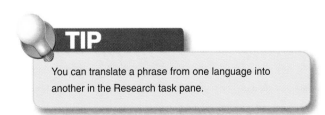
Use the Help Toolbar

On the toolbar at the top of the Word Help window are several options for navigating through the topics and printing one out, as seen in Figure 1-10.

Conduct Research

You can conduct research on the Internet using Word's Research command. Clicking this command displays a Research task pane that allows you to enter your search criteria and specify references to search.

1. Click the **Review** tab, and in the Proofing group, click the **Research** down arrow. You may be asked for the language you are using. Click it, and the Research task pane will appear on the right of the document pane, as shown in the example in Figure 1-11.

2. Type your search criteria in the Search For text box.

3. To change the default reference (All Reference Books), click the down arrow to open the drop-down list, and click a reference to be searched.

4. Click the green arrow to the right of the Search For box to start the search. The results will be displayed in the task pane.

5. Click **Close** to close the task pane.

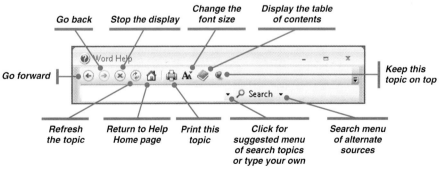

Figure 1-10: *Use the Help toolbar to navigate through the topics and print them out.*

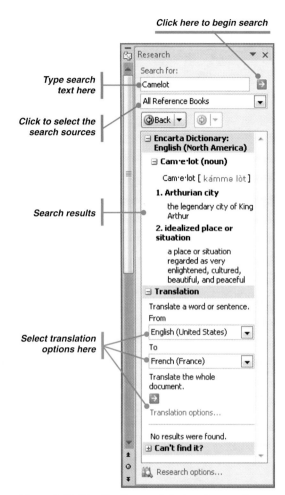

Click here to begin search

Type search text here

Click to select the search sources

Search results

Select translation options here

Figure 1-11: *Use the Research feature to search a dictionary, a thesaurus, an encyclopedia, and several other sources.*

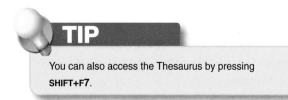

TIP

You can also access the Thesaurus by pressing **SHIFT+F7**.

Use the Thesaurus

You can find synonyms for words using the Thesaurus feature.

1. To use the Thesaurus, first select the text that you want to use for the search.

2. Click the **Review** tab, and in the Proofing group, click **Thesaurus**. The Research task pane will appear with the most likely synonyms listed:

   - Click a listed word to search for its synonyms.
   - Click the word down arrow to insert, copy, or look up the word.

3. Click **Close** to close the task pane.

Translate a Document

To translate a whole document from one language to another:

1. Click the **Review** tab, and in the Proofing group, click **Translate**. The Search task pane will appear with the translation as its source reference.

2. Click the **From** and **To** down arrows, and click the relevant languages.

3. Click the green arrow to begin the translation. A Translate Whole Document message will appear, informing you that your document will be sent over the Internet to a special service, WorldLingo, to be translated perhaps for a fee.

4. Click **Yes** to start the translation. Your translated document will appear in a browser window, as shown in Figure 1-12.

Figure 1-12: *You can translate an entire document using WorldLingo.*

NOTE

You can translate just a word or phrase by highlighting the text and then right-clicking the selection. Click **Translate** from the context menu, and then select the language into which the selected text is to be translated. Place the pointer over the selected text, and the translation will appear.

measure
['meʒər]
1. *noun (step)* mesure *féminin,* **we've had a measure of** **success** nous avons eu un certain succès
2. *transitive verb & intransitive verb* mesurer

measure

ACCESSING MICROSOFT RESOURCES

Microsoft maintains a resource center online that you can easily access. This resource center allows you to communicate with Microsoft about Office and Word subjects.

1. Click the **Office Button**, and click the **Word Options** button.

2. Click the **Resources** option. Select from the following, shown in Figure 1-13:

   ● Click **Get Updates** to find out if updates are available for Microsoft Office. (See "Update Word.")

   Continued . . .

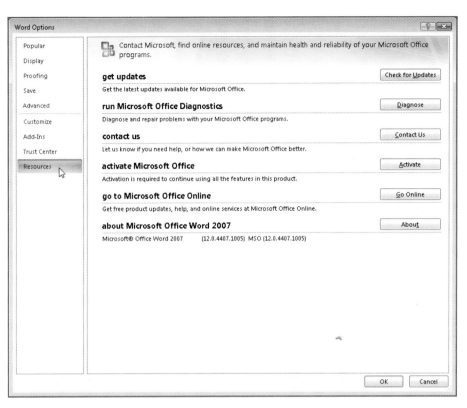

*Figure 1-13: **The Resources page in the Word Options dialog box facilitates communication with Microsoft.***

Update Word

Microsoft periodically releases updates for Office and Word (these are almost always problem fixes and not enhancements). You can check on available updates, download them, and install them from Word.

1. Click the **Office Button**, and click **Word Options**. The Word Options dialog box appears. Click **Resources**.

2. On the Resources page, next to Get Updates, click the **Check For Updates** button. Your Web browser opens and connects to the Microsoft Online Web site, as shown in Figure 1-14.

ACCESSING MICROSOFT RESOURCES *(Continued)*

- Click **Run Microsoft Office Diagnostics** to run a diagnostic program if Microsoft Office seems to be operating incorrectly. The program will automatically capture data and send it to Microsoft to be diagnosed.

- Click **Contact Us** to send a message to Microsoft experts. You may be seeking advice for a problem or making suggestions for improvements to the product.

- Click **Activate Microsoft Office** if you cannot access all features within Word. If you have already activated Office, a message will be displayed telling you so.

- Click **Go To Microsoft Office Online** to access new product information, tips for using products, downloads (for product updates, free demos, and third-party downloads), clip art, templates, and so on.

- Click **About Microsoft Office Word 2007** to open the About Microsoft Office Word dialog box, which gives the version, licensing information, and so on.

3. Click **Check For Updates**. Your system will be checked for any necessary updates, and you will be given the opportunity to download and install them if you choose. When you have downloaded the updates you want, close your Web browser.

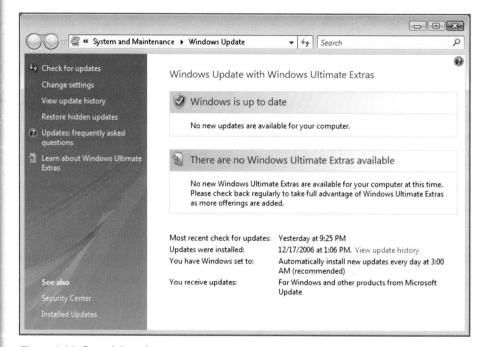

Figure 1-14: ***One of the primary reasons to check for and download Office and Windows updates is to get needed security patches.***

How to...

- Create a New Document
- Use a Unique Template
- Locate an Existing Document
- Search for an Existing Document
- Entering Special Characters
- Import a Document
- Enter Text
- Determine Where Text Will Appear
- Insert Text or Type Over It
- Insert Line or Page Breaks
- Select Text
- Using the Office Clipboard
- Copy and Move Text
- Delete Text
- Move Around in a Document
- Find and Replace Text
- Check Spelling and Grammar
- Using Wildcards
- Saving a Document
- Save a Document for the First Time
- Save a Document Automatically

Chapter 2
Working with Documents

Microsoft Office Word 2007 allows you to create and edit *documents*, such as letters, reports, invoices, plays, and books. The book you are reading now was written in Word. Documents are printed on one or more pages, and are probably bound by anything from a paper clip to stitch binding. In the computer, a document is called a *file*, an object that has been given a name and is stored on a disk drive. For example, the name given to the file for this chapter is Chap02.doc. "Chap02" is the file name, and ".doc" is the file extension. Most files produced by previous editions of Word used the .doc extension. Documents saved with Word 2007 are, by default, saved with the .docx extension.

In this chapter you'll see how to create new documents and edit existing ones. This includes ways to enter, change, and delete text, as well as ways to find, select, copy, and move text.

Create a New Document

In the days before computers, creating a new document was termed "starting with a clean sheet of paper." Today, it is "starting with a blank screen"—actually, a blank area within a window on the screen, as shown in Figure 2-1. You can create a new document in two ways: using the default (or "normal") document template or using a unique template.

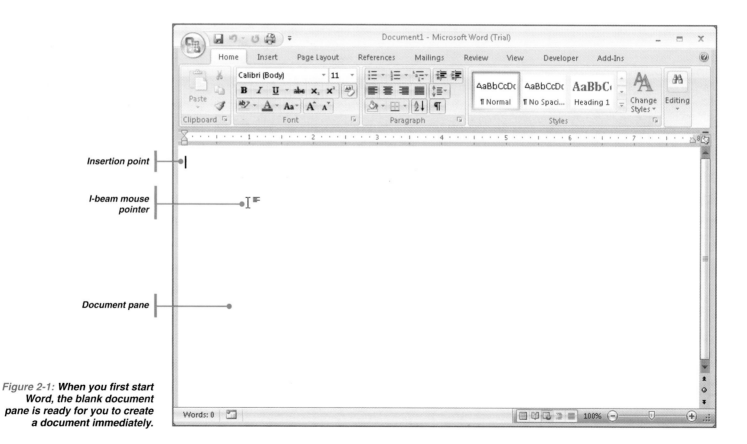

Insertion point

I-beam mouse pointer

Document pane

*Figure 2-1: **When you first start Word, the blank document pane is ready for you to create a document immediately.***

NOTE

The remainder of this chapter assumes that Word has been started and is open on your screen.

NOTE

You can also create and use your own templates, as described in Chapter 4.

Create a New Document

Simply starting Word opens up a blank document pane into which you can start typing a new document immediately. The blinking bar in the upper-left corner of the document pane, called the *insertion point*, indicates where the text you type will appear.

- To start Word, use one of the ways described at the beginning of Chapter 1.

Use a Unique Template

A template is a special kind of document that is used as the basis for other documents you create. The template is said to be "attached" to the document, and every Word document must have a template attached to it. The template acts as the framework around which you create your document. The document that is opened automatically when you start Word 2007 uses a default template called Normal.dotm (previous versions used Normal.dot). This is referred to as "the Normal template" and contains standard formatting settings. Other templates can contain boilerplate text, formatting options for the types of document they create, and even automating procedures. Word is installed on your computer with a number of templates that you can use, and you can access other templates through Office Online.

USING A TEMPLATE ON YOUR COMPUTER

With Word open on your computer:

1. Click the **Office Button**, and then click **New**. The New Document dialog box appears, as shown in Figure 2-2.

2. In the Templates pane, you have the following options:
   - **Blank And Recent:** To use a new blank template or templates you have used recently.
   - **Installed Templates:** To use templates stored on your computer.
   - **My Templates:** To use custom templates you have created.

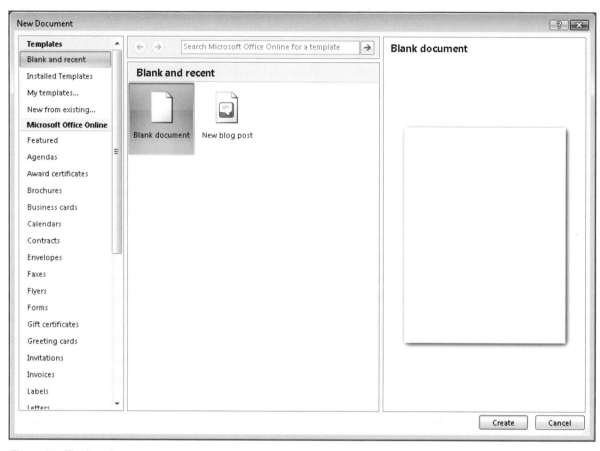

Figure 2-2: The New Document dialog box gives you choices for how to start a document.

- **New From Existing:** To use templates you can copy from existing documents.
- **Microsoft Office Online:** To use template categories that can be obtained from Microsoft's online resources.

3. Click **Installed Templates**. The dialog box shown in Figure 2-3 appears. Click the template you want, and then, on the bottom of the right pane, next to Create New, click **Document**. A document with the selected template will open.

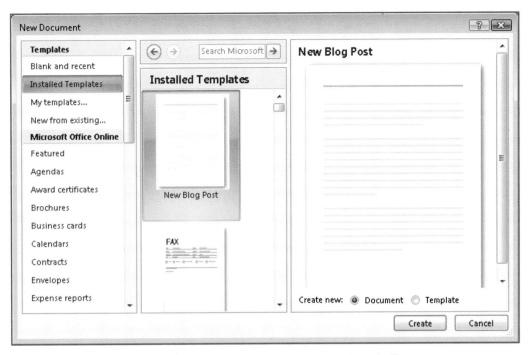

Figure 2-3: Word installs a number of templates on your computer automatically.

USING AN OFFICE ONLINE TEMPLATE

With Word open on your computer:

1. Click the **Office Button**, and then click **New**. The New Document dialog box will appear.

2. In the Templates pane, located beneath Microsoft Office Online, is a list of categories of templates. Click the category you want, and you'll see the possibilities related to it, as seen the example in Figure 2-4.

3. Find the template you want, and click **Download** in the right pane. A new document is opened with the template attached.

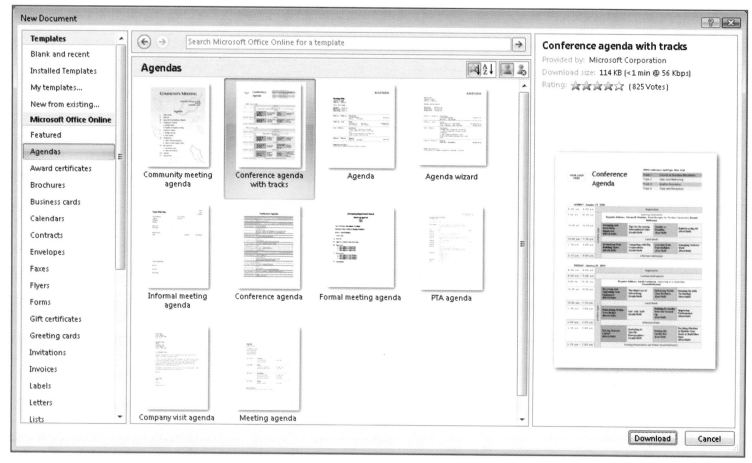

Figure 2-4: *Microsoft offers many templates online, both for Word and its other Office products.*

NOTE

Not all documents created in other programs can be opened by Word, although many can be. See "Import a Document later in this chapter."

Open an Existing Document

After creating and saving a document, you may want to come back and work on it later. You may also want to open and work on a Word document created by someone else (or created in a different program). To do this, you must first locate the document and then open it in Word. You can locate the document either directly from Word or search for it in either Word or Windows.

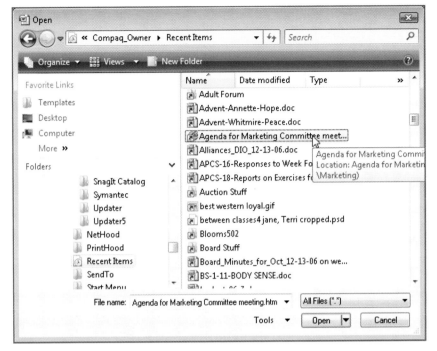

Figure 2-5: *When you hold the mouse pointer over a document name, you see additional information about the document.*

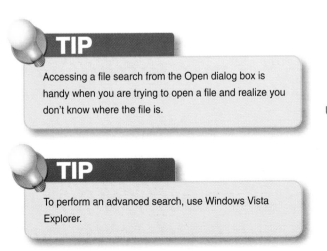

TIP

Accessing a file search from the Open dialog box is handy when you are trying to open a file and realize you don't know where the file is.

TIP

To perform an advanced search, use Windows Vista Explorer.

Locate an Existing Document

With Word open on your screen:

1. Click the **Office Button**, and click **Open**. The Open dialog box appears.

2. Double-click the folder or sequence of folders you need to open in order to find the document.

3. When you have found the document you want to open (see Figure 2-5), double-click it. It will appear in Word, ready for you to begin your work.

Search for an Existing Document

If you have a hard time finding a document using the direct approach described in the previous section, you can search for it either in Word or in Windows.

SEARCH FOR A DOCUMENT IN WORD

A document search performed in Word looks for a piece of text that is contained within the document or within some property of the document, such as the name of the author, the creation date, or the name of the file. The basic search looks for text within the document.

1. Click the **Office Button**, and click **Open**. The Open dialog box appears. Locate the folder or drive that you want to search.

2. Begin to enter the text you want to search for (see Figure 2-6). As you type, the search will begin. The results are listed in the right pane of the dialog box, beneath the search text.

3. Double-click the file you want, or select it and click **Open** to open it in Word.

USE THE SEARCH AND SORT FEATURES

You can sort the files within the search results list using the column headings. Doing this allows you to sort files by some special property, such as name, date, folder type, author, or tag.

1. Display the Open dialog box (see the preceding set of steps), locate the folder containing the file you want, and type your search text. The search results will be listed below as you type.

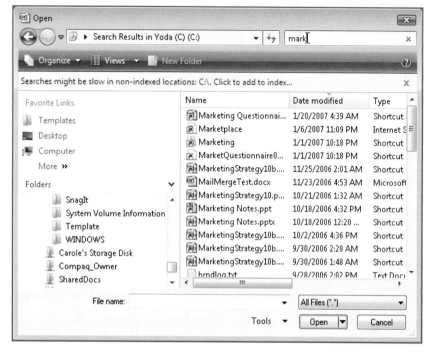

Figure 2-6: *As you type the text you want to search for, the search automatically begins and the results are listed beneath the search text.*

TIP

To quickly find a folder that you have previously used, click the **Recent Pages** down arrow to the left of the folder name.

2. Point to a column heading by which you want to sort the results, and click the down arrow.

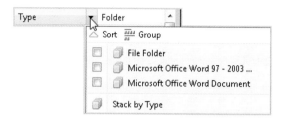

3. Click the sort option again, and the files will be resorted to their default order.

USE ADVANCED FILTERS IN WINDOWS

Window Explorer allows you to modify searches with filters for files, including Word documents. In Windows Vista:

1. Click **Start** to open the Start menu, click **All Programs**, and then click **Computer**.

2. Click **Organize**, click **Layout**, and click **Search Pane**. A search bar will be displayed below the folder name.

3. Click **Document** in the search bar to restrict the search to document files.

4. Click the **Advanced Search** down arrow on the right end of the search bar. The Advanced Search pane will open, as seen in Figure 2-7. (Clicking Advanced Search again will close it.)

5. You have these filter options:

- **Date** filters by the date the file was last modified or created. Click the down arrow, and then click the option you want. Click the next down arrow to the right to choose whether the date is equal to, before, or after a date entered in the calendar box to the right.

- **Size** filters by file size. Click the down arrow to the right to choose whether the size is equal to, larger than, or smaller than the file size entered in the text box to the right.

- **Name** filters by file name. Type the file name in the Name text box.

- **Tags** filters by tags. Type the tag in the Tag text box.

- **Authors** filters by author name. Type the author in the Authors text box.

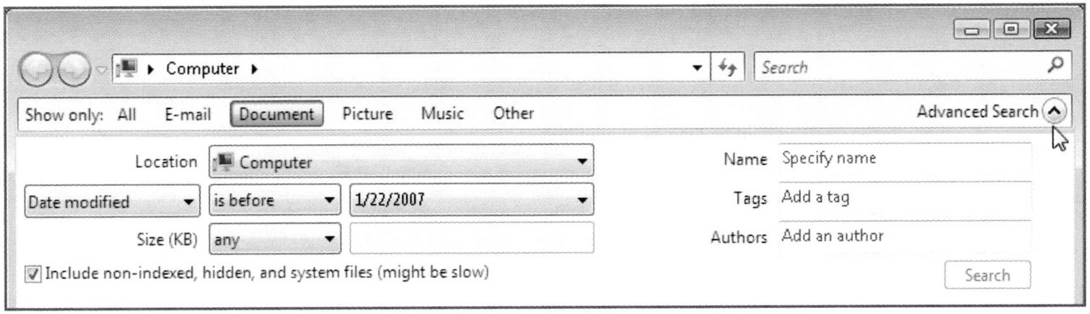

Figure 2-7: *Using Windows Vista, you can use advanced filters to narrow your search for a specific file or files.*

6. Click the **Include Non-Indexed, Hidden, And System Files** check box to show these types of files in the search.

7. Click **Search**.

Import a Document

If you have a word-processing document created in a program other than Word, you can most likely open it and edit it in Word.

1. Click the **Office Button**, and click **Open**. The Open dialog box appears.

2. Find the folder or sequence of folders you need to open in order to find the document.

3. Click the down arrow on the right of the File Type drop-down list box to display the list of files that you can directly open in Word, as shown next (see Table 2-1 for a complete list).

QUICKSTEPS

ENTERING SPECIAL CHARACTERS

Entering a character that is on the keyboard takes only a keystroke, but many other characters and symbols exist beyond those that appear on the keyboard. For example: ©, £, Ã, Ω, ♪, and •. You can enter these characters using either the Symbol dialog box or a sequence of keys (also called a keyboard shortcut).

SELECT SPECIAL CHARACTERS FROM THE SYMBOL DIALOG BOX

1. Move the insertion point to where you want to insert the special character(s).

Continued . . .

FILE TYPE	EXTENSION
Plain text files	.txt
Rich text format file	.rtf
Web page files	.htm, .html, .mht, .mhtml
Word 97 to 2003 files	.doc
Word 97 to 2003 template files	.dot
Word 2007 document files (macro-enabled)	.docx (.docm)
Word 2007 template files	.dotx
WordPerfect 5.x and 6.x files	.doc, .wpd
Works 6.0 to 9.0 files	.wps
XML files	.xml

Table 2-1: *File Types That Word Can Open Directly*

UICKSTEPS

ENTERING SPECIAL CHARACTERS
(Continued)

2. Click the **Insert** tab, and then click **Symbol** in the Symbols group. A Symbol menu will open containing the symbols you most commonly use. If the symbol you want is on the list, click it, and the symbol will be inserted in the document.

3. If the symbol you want is not on the menu, click **More Symbols**. The Symbol dialog box will appear:

    • Click the **Symbols** tab for characters within font styles.

    • Click the **Special Characters** tab for common standard characters, as shown in Figure 2-8.

4. Click the character you want, click **Insert**, and then click **Close**. You should see the special character or symbol where the insertion point was.

ENTER SPECIAL CHARACTERS FROM THE KEYBOARD

You can use keyboard shortcuts to enter symbols and special characters. The numeric part of the shortcut must be entered on the numeric keypad.

1. Move the insertion point to where you want to insert the special characters.

2. Press **NUM LOCK** to put the numeric keypad into numeric mode.

Continued . . .

4. Click the file type that you want to open. The Open dialog box will list only files of that type.

5. Double-click the file that you want to open. Depending on the file, you may get one of several messages.

Write a Document

Whether you create a new document or open an existing one, you will likely want to enter and edit text. Editing, in this case, includes adding and deleting text, as well as selecting, moving, and copying it.

Enter Text

To enter text in a document that you have newly created or opened, simply start typing. The characters you type will appear in the document pane at the insertion point and in the order that you type them.

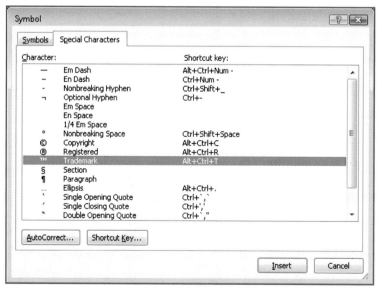

*Figure 2-8: **The Symbol dialog box contains special characters, as well as several complete alphabets and symbol sets.***

CHARACTER	NAME	SHORTCUT KEYS
•	Bullet	ALT+0149
©	Copyright	ALT+CTRL+C
™	Trade Mark	ALT+CTRL+T
®	Registered	ALT+CTRL+R
¢	Cent	CTRL+/ , C
£	Pound	ALT+0163
€	Euro	ALT+CTRL+E
–	En dash	CTRL+NUM-
—	Em dash	ALT+CTRL+NUM-

Table 2-2: Shortcut Keys for Common Characters

NOTE

In Table 2-2, the comma (,) means to release the previous keys and then press the following key(s). For example, for a ¢, press and hold **CTRL** while pressing **/**, then release **CTRL** and press **C**. In addition, "NUM" means to press the following key on the numeric keypad. So, "NUM-" means to press "-" in the upper-right corner of the numeric keypad.

NOTE

When you click a common symbol or special character in the Symbol dialog box, you'll see the shortcut keys for the character.

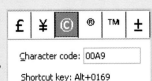

Determine Where Text Will Appear

The *insertion point*, the blinking vertical bar shown earlier in Figure 2-1, determines where text that you type will appear. In a new document, the insertion point is obviously in the upper-leftmost corner of the document pane. It is also placed there by default when you open an existing document. You can move the insertion point within or to the end of existing text using either the keyboard or the mouse.

MOVE THE INSERTION POINT WITH THE KEYBOARD

When Word is open and active, the insertion point moves every time you press a character or directional key on the keyboard (unless a menu or dialog box is open or the task pane is active). The directional keys include **TAB**, **BACKSPACE**, and **ENTER**, as well as the four arrow keys, and **HOME**, **END**, **PAGE UP**, and **PAGE DOWN**.

MOVE THE INSERTION POINT WITH THE MOUSE

When the mouse pointer is in the document pane, it appears as an I-beam, as you saw in Figure 2-1. The reason for the I-beam is that it fits between characters on the screen. You can move the insertion point by moving the I-beam mouse pointer to where you want the insertion point `Insertion|Point` and then clicking.

Insert Text or Type Over It

When you press a letter or a number key with Word in its default mode (as it is when you first start it), the insertion point and any existing text to the right of the insertion point is pushed to the right and down on a page. This is also true when you press the **TAB** or **ENTER** key. This is called *insert* mode: new text pushes existing text to the right.

TIP

You can insert multiple special characters in sequence by selecting one after another in the Symbol dialog box.

TIP

The AutoCorrect As You Type feature, which is discussed in Chapter 4, also provides a quick way of entering commonly used special characters, such as copyright, trademark, and registered symbols and en and em-dashes.

CAUTION

In Word 2007, there is no "OVR" in the status bar to indicate that you are in overtype mode.

NOTE

In both insert and overtype modes, the directional keys move the insertion point without regard to which mode is enabled.

NOTE

Section breaks are used to define columns within a page and to define different types of pages, as you might have with differently formatted left and right pages. The use of section breaks, columns, and different types of pages are described in Chapter 4.

In previous versions of Word, if you press the **INSERT** (or **INS**) key, Word is switched to *overtype* mode, and the OVR indicator is enabled in the status bar. In Word 2007, this capability is turned off by default, and the **INSERT** (or **INS**) key does nothing. The reason is that more often than not, the **INSERT** (or **INS**) key gets pressed by mistake, and you don't find out about this until after you have typed over a lot of text you didn't want to type over. You can turn on this capability by clicking the **Office Button**, clicking **Advanced**, and, under Editing Options, clicking **Use The Insert Key To Control Overtype Mode**.

In overtype mode, any character key you press types over (replaces) the existing character to the right of the insertion point. Overtype mode does not affect the **ENTER** key, which continues to push existing characters to the right of the insertion point and down. The **TAB** key does replace characters to the right, *unless* it is pressed at the beginning of the line—in which case, it is treated as an indent and pushes the rest of the line to the right.

Insert Line or Page Breaks

If you are used to typing on a typewriter, you have learned to press **RETURN** at the end of each line to go to the next line. In Word, as in all word-processing programs, you simply keep typing and the text will automatically wrap around to the next line. Only when you want to break a line before it would otherwise end must you manually intervene. There are four instances where manual line breaks are required:

- At the **end of a paragraph**—to start a new paragraph, press **ENTER**.
- At the **end of a short line** within a paragraph—to start a new line, press **SHIFT+ENTER**.
- At the **end of a page**—to force the start of a new page, press **CTRL+ENTER**.
- At the **end of a section**—to start a new section, press **CTRL+SHIFT+ENTER**.

You can also enter a page break using the mouse:

With the insertion point placed where you want the break, click the **Insert** tab, and click **Page Break** in the Pages group. A page break will be  inserted in the text.

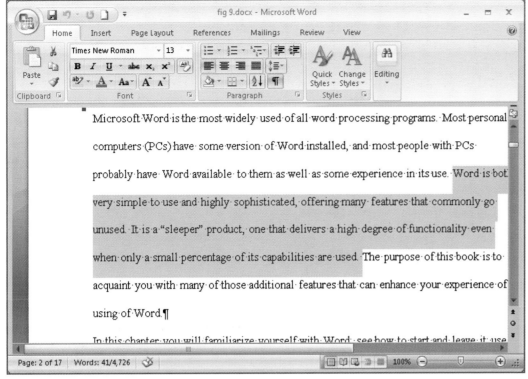

Figure 2-9: **You will always know what you are moving, copying, or deleting because it is highlighted on the screen.**

Select Text

In order to copy, move, or delete text, you first need to select it. *Selecting text* means to identify it as a separate block from the remaining text in a document. You can select any amount of text, from a single character up to an entire document. As text is selected, it is highlighted with a colored background, as you can see in Figure 2-9. You can select text with both the mouse and the keyboard.

SELECT TEXT WITH THE MOUSE

You can select varying amounts of text with the mouse:

* **Select a single word** by double-clicking that word.

* **Select a single line** by clicking on the far left of the line when the I-beam mouse pointer becomes an arrow (this area on the left where the mouse pointer becomes an arrow is called the *selection bar*).

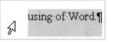

* **Select a single sentence** by holding down **CTRL** while clicking in the sentence.

* **Select a single paragraph** by double-clicking in the selection bar opposite the paragraph.

* **Select an entire document** by holding **CTRL+SHIFT** while clicking in the selection bar anywhere in the document.

* **Select one or more characters** in a word, or select two or more words by clicking:

    1. Click to place the insertion point to the left of the first character.

    2. Hold **SHIFT** while clicking to the right of the last character. The selected text will be highlighted.

TIP

After selecting one area using the keyboard, the mouse, or the two together, you can select further independent areas by holding **CTRL** while using any of the mouse selection techniques described here.

QUICKSTEPS

USING THE OFFICE CLIPBOARD

As mentioned, the Office Clipboard is shared by all Office products. You can copy objects and text from any Office application and paste it to another. The Office Clipboard contains up to 24 items. The 25th item will overwrite the first one.

OPEN THE CLIPBOARD

To display the Office Clipboard, click the **Home** tab, and then click the **Clipboard Dialog Box Launcher** in the Clipboard group. The Clipboard task pane will open.

ADD ITEMS TO THE CLIPBOARD

When you cut or copy text with the Clipboard task pane open, it is automatically added to the Office Clipboard.

PASTE ITEMS FROM THE CLIPBOARD

To paste one item:

1. Click to place the insertion point in the document or text box where you want the item from the Office Clipboard inserted.

Continued . . .

- **Select one or more characters** in a word, or to select two or more words by dragging:

  1. Move the mouse pointer to the left of the first character.

  2. Hold down the mouse button while dragging the mouse pointer to the right of the last character. The selected text will be highlighted.

SELECT TEXT WITH THE KEYBOARD

Use the arrow keys to move the insertion point to the left of the first character you want to select:

- Hold down **SHIFT** while using the arrow keys to move the insertion point to the right of the last character you want to select.

  - To select a line, place the pointer at the beginning of a line. Hold **SHIFT** and press **END**.

  - To select the entire document using the keyboard, press **CTRL+A**.

Copy and Move Text

Copying and moving text are similar actions. Think of copying text as moving it and leaving a copy behind. Both copying and moving are done in two steps.

1. Selected text is copied or cut from its current location to the Clipboard.

2. The contents of the Clipboard are pasted to a new location, as identified by the insertion point.

USE THE CLIPBOARD

The *Clipboard* is a location in the computer's memory that is used to store information temporarily. Two Clipboards can actually be used:

- The **Windows Clipboard** can store one object, either text or a picture, and pass that object within or among other Windows programs. Once an object is cut or copied to the Windows Clipboard, it stays there until another object is cut or copied to the Clipboard or until the computer is turned off. The Windows Clipboard is used by default.

QUICKSTEPS

USING THE OFFICE CLIPBOARD

(Continued)

2. Click the item on the Clipboard to be inserted.

–Or–

1. With the Clipboard item selected but no insertion point placed, right-click where you want the item.

2. Click **Paste** from the context menu.

To paste all items:

1. Click to place the insertion point in the text box or placeholder where you want the items from the Office Clipboard inserted.

2. Click **Paste All** on the Clipboard.

DELETE ITEMS ON THE CLIPBOARD

To delete all items, click **Clear All** on the Clipboard task pane.

To delete a single item, click the down arrow next to the item, and click **Delete**.

SET CLIPBOARD OPTIONS

1. On the Clipboard task pane, click **Options** on the bottom. A context menu is displayed.

2. Click an option to select or clear it:

- **Show Office Clipboard Automatically** always shows the Office Clipboard when copying.

Continued . . .

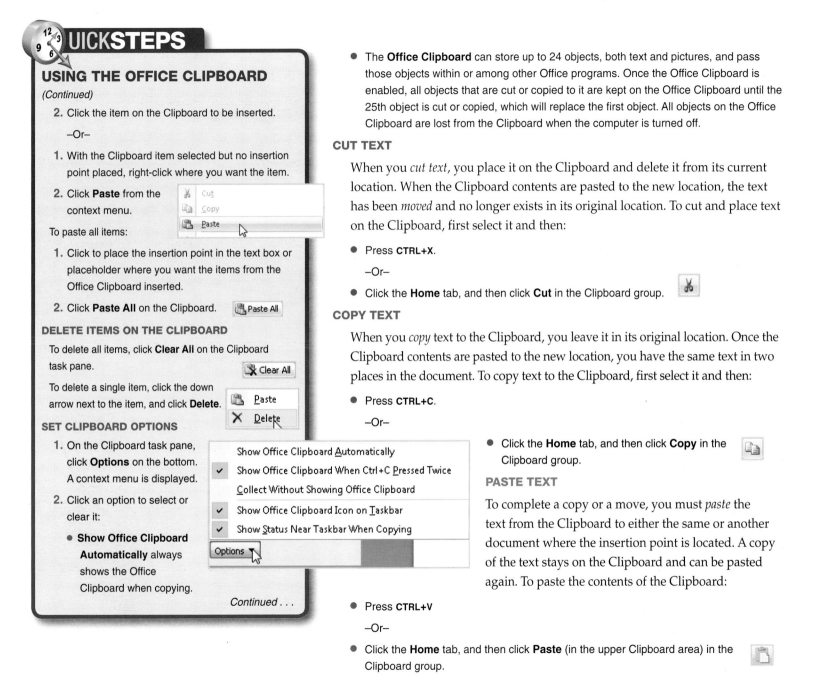

- The **Office Clipboard** can store up to 24 objects, both text and pictures, and pass those objects within or among other Office programs. Once the Office Clipboard is enabled, all objects that are cut or copied to it are kept on the Office Clipboard until the 25th object is cut or copied, which will replace the first object. All objects on the Office Clipboard are lost from the Clipboard when the computer is turned off.

CUT TEXT

When you *cut text*, you place it on the Clipboard and delete it from its current location. When the Clipboard contents are pasted to the new location, the text has been *moved* and no longer exists in its original location. To cut and place text on the Clipboard, first select it and then:

- Press **CTRL+X**.

  –Or–

- Click the **Home** tab, and then click **Cut** in the Clipboard group.

COPY TEXT

When you *copy* text to the Clipboard, you leave it in its original location. Once the Clipboard contents are pasted to the new location, you have the same text in two places in the document. To copy text to the Clipboard, first select it and then:

- Press **CTRL+C**.

  –Or–

- Click the **Home** tab, and then click **Copy** in the Clipboard group.

PASTE TEXT

To complete a copy or a move, you must *paste* the text from the Clipboard to either the same or another document where the insertion point is located. A copy of the text stays on the Clipboard and can be pasted again. To paste the contents of the Clipboard:

- Press **CTRL+V**

  –Or–

- Click the **Home** tab, and then click **Paste** (in the upper Clipboard area) in the Clipboard group.

USING THE OFFICE CLIPBOARD
(Continued)

- **Show Office Clipboard When CTRL+C Pressed Twice** shows the Office Clipboard when you press **CTRL+C** twice to make two copies (in other words, copying two items to the Clipboard will cause the Clipboard to be displayed).

- **Collect Without Showing Office Clipboard** copies items to the Clipboard without displaying it.

- **Show Office Clipboard Icon On Taskbar** displays the icon on the right of the Windows taskbar when the Clipboard is being used.

- **Show Status Near Taskbar When Copying** displays a message about the items being added to the Clipboard as copies are made.

To close the Office Clipboard and revert to the Windows Clipboard, click **Close** at the top of the task pane. The items you placed on the Office Clipboard while it was open will stay there until you shut down Word, but only the last item you cut or copied after closing the Office Clipboard will be displayed.

TIP

Place your pointer over the Clipboard icon in the taskbar to see how many items are currently on it.

USE THE PASTE OPTIONS SMART TAG

The Paste Options smart tag appears when you paste text. It asks you if you want to keep source formatting (the original formatting of the text), match destination formatting (change the formatting to that of the surrounding text), or keep text only (remove all formatting from the text). The Set Default Paste option displays the Word Options dialog box so that you can set defaults for pasting text during a cut or copy action. The Paste Options smart tag is most valuable when you can see that the paste operation has resulted in formatting that you don't want.

UNDO A MOVE OR PASTE ACTION

You can undo a move or paste action by:

- Pressing **CTRL+Z**

  –Or–

- Clicking **Undo** on the Quick Access toolbar

REDO AN UNDO ACTION

You can redo many actions you have undone by:

- Pressing **CTRL+Y**

  –Or–

- Clicking **Redo** on the Quick Access toolbar

Delete Text

Deleting text removes it from its current location *without* putting it in the Clipboard. To delete a selected piece of text:

- Press **DELETE** or **DEL**.

  –Or–

- On the Home tab, click **Cut** in the Clipboard group.

NOTE

Under certain circumstances, especially while formatting, the Redo option becomes the Repeat option.

NOTE

You can recover deleted text using the Undo command in the same way that you can reverse a cut or paste action.

NOTE

You select a picture by clicking it. Once selected, a picture can be copied, moved, and deleted from a document in the same ways as text, using either the Windows or Office Clipboards. See Chapter 7 for further discussion about working with pictures.

NOTE

Some of the ways used to move around in a document move the insertion point as you go; some only change what you are looking at within the document, moving your view to a new location. In the latter case, if you find that you want the insertion point where you are looking, click there or use one of the arrow keys to move the insertion point. The insertion point will appear.

Edit a Document

After entering all the text into a document, most people want to edit it and, possibly, revise it at a later date. You'll want to be able to move around the document, quickly moving from location to location, to do this.

Move Around in a Document

Word provides a number of ways to move around in a document using the mouse and the keyboard.

USE THE MOUSE

You can easily move the insertion point by clicking in your text anywhere on the screen, but how do you move to some place you cannot see? You have to change what you are looking at. Word provides two sets of tools for use with the mouse to do just that: the scroll bars and the browse buttons, as shown in Figure 2-10.

USE THE SCROLL BARS

There are two scroll bars: one for moving vertically within the document and one for moving horizontally. These are only displayed when your text is too wide or too long to be completely displayed on the screen. Each scroll bar contains four controls for getting you where you want to go. Using the vertical scroll bar, you can:

- **Move upward one line** by clicking the upward-pointing scroll arrow.
- **Move upward or downward** by dragging the scroll button in the corresponding direction.
- **Move up or down the screen's height** by clicking in the scroll bar above the scroll button to move toward the beginning of the document or by clicking below the scroll bar to move toward the end of the document.
- **Move downward by one line** by clicking the downward-pointing scroll arrow.

The horizontal scroll bar has similar controls, only these are used for moving in a horizontal fashion.

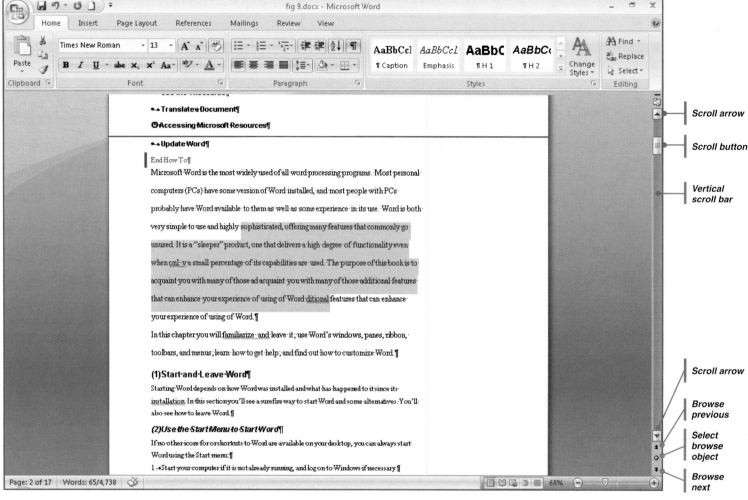

Figure 2-10: *The scroll bars and browse buttons allow you to move easily to different locations within your document.*

USE THE BROWSE BUTTONS

The browse buttons (the three buttons below the vertical scroll bar) allow you to specify the type of object by which you want to browse through the document. The most obvious browse object—and the default one—is a page. With that as the object, you can browse through a document going forward or backward a page at a time.

Clicking the **Select Browse Object** button in the center opens a menu of objects from which you can select. By selecting one of these objects—such as a page, a heading, a comment, or an edit—you can move through the document, going from one chosen object to the next. Often overlooked, this feature can be quite handy. Place the pointer over the options to find out what the picture or icon represents.

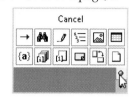

USE THE KEYBOARD

The following keyboard commands, used for moving around in your document, also move the insertion point:

- Press the **LEFT** or **RIGHT ARROW** key to move one character to the left or right.
- Press the **UP** or **DOWN ARROW** key to move one line up or down.
- Press **CTRL+LEFT ARROW** or **CTRL+RIGHT ARROW** to move one word to the left or right.
- Press **CTRL+UP ARROW** or **CTRL+DOWN ARROW** to move one paragraph up or down.
- Press **HOME** or **END** to move to the beginning or end of a line.
- Press **CTRL+HOME** or **CTRL+END** to move to the beginning or end of a document.
- Press **PAGE UP** or **PAGE DOWN** to move one screen up or down.
- Press **CTRL+PAGE UP** or **CTRL+PAGE DOWN** to move to the previous or next instance of the current browse object.
- Press **CTRL+ALT+PAGE UP** or **CTRL+ALT+PAGE DOWN** to move to the top or bottom of the window.

GO TO A PARTICULAR LOCATION

The Go To command opens the Go To tab in the Find And Replace dialog box, shown in Figure 2-11. This allows you to go immediately to the location of some object, such as a page, a footnote, or a table. You can open the dialog box by:

- Pressing the **F5** key
- Pressing **CTRL+G**
- Clicking the **Home** tab, clicking **Find** in the Editing group, and clicking the **Go To** tab

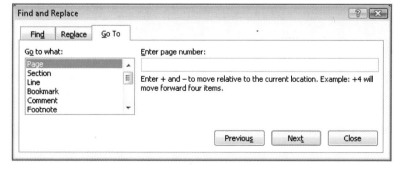

Figure 2-11: The Go To command allows you to go to a particular page, as well as to locate other items within a document.

You can also move a certain number of items relative to your current position by typing a plus sign (+) or a minus sign (–) and a number. For example, if Page is selected and you type –3, you will be moved backwards three pages.

TIP

If you want your search to find just the word "ton" and not words like "Washington" or "tonic," you can either put a space at both the beginning and end of the word in Find What (" ton "), or click **More** in the Find And Replace dialog box, and then click **Find Whole Words Only**. The latter is the preferred way to do this, because putting a space after the word would not find the word followed by a comma or a period, for example.

TIP

If you find that the Find And Replace dialog box is getting in the way after finding the first occurrence of a word or phrase, you close the dialog box and use **SHIFT+F4** to find the remaining occurrences. Also, once you have used the Find command, you can close the Find And Replace dialog box and use the Find Next or Previous Browse buttons at the bottom of the vertical scroll bar to browse using Find. You can also press **CTRL+PAGE DOWN** or **CTRL+PAGE UP** to move quickly from one instance of the search term to the next.

- Clicking **Select Browse Object** beneath the vertical scroll bar, and then clicking **Go To**
- Double-clicking the left end of the status bar in the Page X Of Y area

After opening the dialog box, select the object you want to go to from the list on the left, and then enter the number or name of the object in the text box on the right. For example, click **Page** on the left and type 5 on the right to go to page 5 in your document.

Find and Replace Text

Often, you may want to find something that you know is in a document, but you are not sure where, or even how many times, that item occurs. This is especially true when you want to locate names or words that are sprinkled throughout a document. For example, if you had repeatedly referred to a table on page 4 and, for some reason or another, the table had moved to page 5, you would need to search for all occurrences of "page 4" and change them to "page 5." In this example, you not only want to *find* "page 4," but you also want to *replace* it with "page 5." Word allows you to do a simple search for a word or phrase, as well as to conduct an advanced search for parts of words, particular capitalization, and words that sound alike.

FIND TEXT WITH A SIMPLE SEARCH

If you just want to search for a word or phrase:

1. Click the **Home** tab, and click **Find** in the Editing group. The Find And Replace dialog box appears.

2. Enter the word or phrase for which you want to search in the Find What text box.

3. Click **Find Next**. The first occurrence in the document below the current insertion point will be highlighted, as you can see in Figure 2-12.

4. To find additional occurrences, continue to click **Find Next** or press **SHIFT+F4**. When you are done (you will be told when the entire document has been searched), click **Close**.

Figure 2-12: *When you search for a word or phrase, the Find command can highlight individual occurrences or all occurrences at once.*

NOTE

Instead of repeatedly clicking **Find Next** to highlight each occurrence of an item, in the Find And Replace dialog box, you can click **Reading Highlight** and click **Highlight All**. Then click **Find In**, click **Main Document**, and click **Find Next**. This will highlight all occurrences of what you are searching for and will allow you to observe them, but as soon as you click anywhere in the document, the highlights will all go away. If you press **SHIFT+F4, CTRL+PAGE UP, CTRL+PAGE DOWN**, or one of the browse buttons, you will select the next occurrence, but all occurrences will remain highlighted.

FIND TEXT WITH AN ADVANCED SEARCH

By clicking **More** in the Find And Replace dialog box, you will find that Word provides a number of features to make your search more sophisticated (see Figure 2-13). These include specifying the direction of the search, as well as additional search options:

- **Match Case:** Find a specific capitalization of a word or phrase

- **Find Whole Words Only:** Find whole words only, so when searching for "equip," for example, you don't get "equipment."

- **Use Wildcards:** Find words or phrases that contain a set of characters by using wildcards to represent the unknown part of the word or phrase (see the "Using Wildcards" QuickSteps).

- **Sounds Like:** Find words that sound alike but are spelled differently (homonyms).

- **Find All Word Forms:** Find a word in all its forms—noun, adjective, verb, or adverb (for example, ski, skier, and skiing).

- **Match Prefix Or Match Suffix:** Find words containing a common prefix or suffix.

- **Ignore Punctuation Characters:** Find words, regardless of punctuation. This is especially useful when a word might be followed by a comma or period.

- **Ignore White-Space Characters:** Find characters regardless of spaces, tabs, and indents.

- **Format:** Find specific types of formatting, such as for fonts, paragraphs, etc.

- **Special:** Find special characters, such as paragraph marks, em-dashes (—), or nonbreaking spaces (can't be the first or last character in a line).

REPLACE TEXT

Sometimes, when searching for a word or phrase, you might want to replace it with something else. Word lets you use all the features of Find and then replace what is found.

1. Click the **Home** tab, and click **Replace** in the Editing group. The Find And Replace dialog box appears.

2. Enter the word or phrase for which you want to search in the Find What text box.

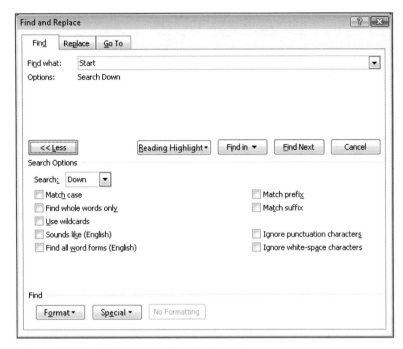

Figure 2-13: *Word offers a number of advanced ways to search a document.*

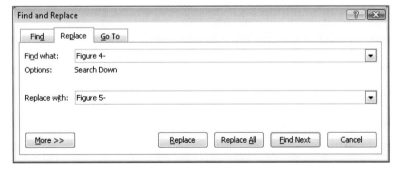

Figure 2-14: *You can replace words and phrases either individually or all at once.*

3. Enter the word or phrase you want to replace the found item(s) with in the Replace With text box, as you can see in Figure 2-14.

4. Click **Find Next**. The first occurrence in the document below the current insertion point will be highlighted.

5. Choose one of the following options:

- Click **Replace** if you want to replace this instance with the text you entered. Word replaces this instance and automatically finds the next one.

- Click **Find Next** if you don't want to replace the text that was found and want to find the next occurrence.

- Click **Replace All** if you want to replace all occurrences of the word you found.

6. When you are done, click **Close**.

Complete and Save a Document

When you have completed working in a document, or if you feel that you have done enough to warrant saving it and putting it aside for a while, you should go though a completion procedure that includes checking the spelling and grammar, determining where to save the document, and then actually saving it.

Check Spelling and Grammar

By default, Word checks spelling and grammar as you type, so it might be that these functions have already been performed. You can tell if Word is checking the spelling and grammar by noticing if Word automatically places a wavy red line under words it thinks are misspelled and if a wavy green line appears beneath words and phrases whose grammar is questioned. You can

when only a small percentage

QUICKFACTS

USING WILDCARDS

Wildcards are characters that are used to represent one or more characters in a word or phrase when searching for items with similar or unknown parts. You must select the **Use Wildcards** check box, and then type the wildcard characters, along with the known characters in the Find What text box. For example, typing page ? will find both "page 4" and "page 5." The "?" stands for any single character.

Find what:	page ?
Options:	Search Down, Use Wildcards

Word has defined the following characters as wildcard characters when used with the Find command to replace one or more characters, as shown in Table 2-3.

NOTE

When searching using wildcards, both Find Whole Words Only and Match Case are turned on automatically and cannot be turned off.

CHARACTER	USED TO REPLACE	EXAMPLE	WILL FIND	WON'T FIND
?	A single character	Page ?	Page 4 or Page 5	Page1
*	Any number of characters	Page *	Page 4 and Page 5	Pages 1-5
<	The beginning of a word	<(corp)	Corporate	Incorporate
>	The end of a word	(ton)>	Washington	Toner
\	A wildcard character	What\?	What?	What is
[cc]	One of a list of characters	B[io]b	Bib or Bob	Babe
[c-c]	One in a range of characters	[l-t]ook	look or took	Book
[!c-c]	Any character except one in the range	[!k-n]ook	book or took	Look
{n}	n copies of the previous character	Lo{2}	Loo or Look	Lot
{n,}	n or more copies of the previous character	Lo{1,}	Lot or Look	Late
{n,m}	n to m copies of the previous character	150{1,3}	150 to 1500	15
@	Any number of copies of the previous character	150@	15, 150, or 1500	1400

Table 2-3: Wildcard Characters Used with the Find Command

turn off the automatic spelling and grammar checker. You can also have these features run using an array of options. You can ask Word to perform a spelling and/or grammar check whenever you want—most importantly, when you are completing a document.

CONTROL THE SPELLING AND GRAMMAR CHECKER

Word provides a number of settings that allow you to control how the spelling and grammar check is performed.

1. Click the **Office Button**, click **Word Options**, and click the **Proofing** option on the left. The dialog box shown in Figure 2-15 will appear.

2. If you wish to turn off the automatic spelling checker, clear **Check Spelling As You Type**.

3. If you wish to turn off the automatic grammar checker, clear **Mark Grammar Errors As You Type**.

4. Click **Settings** under Grammar to set the rules by which the grammar check is done.

5. Click **OK** twice to close both the Grammar Settings and Options dialog boxes.

INITIATE SPELLING AND GRAMMAR CHECK

To manually initiate the spelling and grammar check:

1. Click the **Review** tab, and click **Spelling And Grammar** in the Proofing group. The Spelling And Grammar dialog box will appear and begin checking your document. When a word is found that Word believes might not be correct, the dialog box will display both the perceived error and one or more suggestions for its correction (see Figure 2-16).

2. You have these options for handling flagged spellings:

   • If you wish not to correct the perceived error, click **Ignore Once** for this one instance, or click **Ignore All** for all instances.

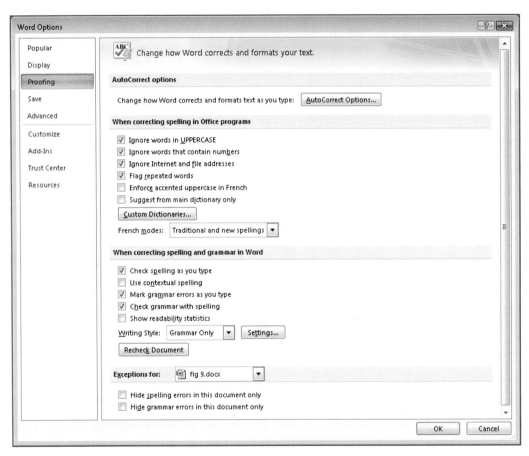

Figure 2-15: *By default, Word checks spelling and grammar as you type, but you can disable those utilities in the Word Options dialog box.*

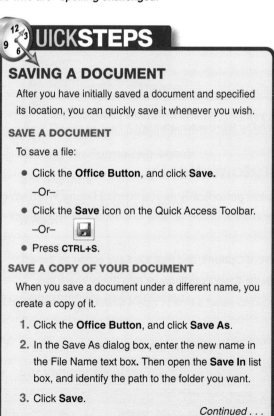

Figure 2-16: *The spelling checker is a gift to those of us who are "spelling challenged!"*

QUICKSTEPS

SAVING A DOCUMENT

After you have initially saved a document and specified its location, you can quickly save it whenever you wish.

SAVE A DOCUMENT

To save a file:

- Click the **Office Button**, and click **Save.**

  –Or–

- Click the **Save** icon on the Quick Access Toolbar.

  –Or–

- Press **CTRL+S**.

SAVE A COPY OF YOUR DOCUMENT

When you save a document under a different name, you create a copy of it.

1. Click the **Office Button**, and click **Save As**.

2. In the Save As dialog box, enter the new name in the File Name text box. Then open the **Save In** list box, and identify the path to the folder you want.

3. Click **Save**.

Continued . . .

- Click **Change** for this one instance, or click **Change All** for all instances if you want to replace the perceived error with the highlighted suggestion. If one of the other suggestions is a better choice, click it before clicking **Change** or **Change All**.

- Click **Add To Dictionary** if you want Word to add your spelling of the word to the dictionary to be used for future documents. If you want Word to automatically correct this misspelling with the selected correction every time you type the incorrect word, click **AutoCorrect**. (See Chapter 4 for more information on AutoCorrect.)

- Click **Options** to display the Word Options Proofing dialog box, where you can reset many of the spelling and grammar checking rules.

- Click **Undo** to reverse the last action.

3. When Word has completed checking the spelling and grammar, you'll see a message to that effect. Click **OK**.

Save a Document for the First Time

The first time you save a document, you have to specify where you want to save it—that is, the disk drive and the folder or subfolder in which you want it saved. If this is your first time saving the file, the Save As dialog box will appear so that you can specify the location and enter a file name.

1. Click the **Office Button**, and click **Save As**.

2. Click the icon on the left for the major area (for example, Favorite Links or Folders) in which the file is to be saved.

3. If you want to store your new document in a folder that already exists in the major area, double-click that folder to open it.

4. If you want to store your new document in a new folder, click the **New Folder** icon in the toolbar, type the name of the new folder, and click **OK**. The new folder will open. (You can create yet another new folder within that folder using the same steps.)

5. When you have the folder(s) open in which you want to store the document, enter the name of the document, as shown in Figure 2-17, and then click **Save**.

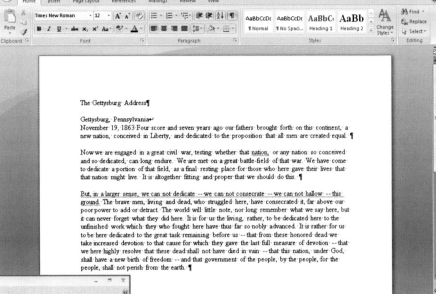

Figure 3-1: Formatting makes text both more readable and more pleasing to the eye.

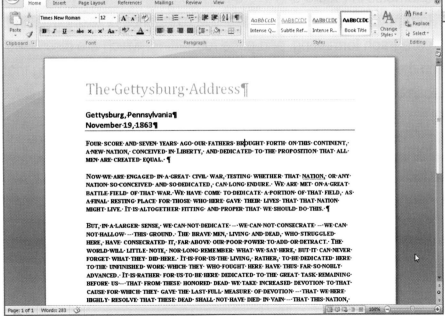

Format Text

Text formatting is the formatting that you can apply to individual characters, and includes the selection of fonts, font size, color, character spacing, and capitalization.

Apply Character Formatting

Character formatting can be applied using keyboard shortcuts, the Home tab on the ribbon, and a Formatting dialog box. Of these, clicking the **Home** tab and clicking the **Font Dialog Box Launcher** to open the Font dialog box (see Figure 3-2) provides a comprehensive selection of character formatting and

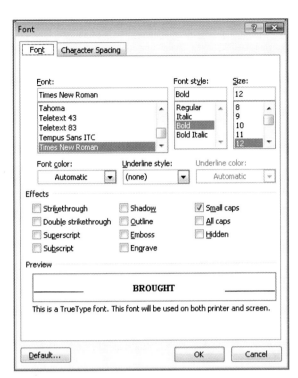

Figure 3-2: *The Font dialog box provides the most complete set of character-formatting controls.*

spacing alternatives. In the sections that follow this one, the Font dialog box may be used to accomplish the task being discussed. Keyboard shortcuts and the Font and Paragraph groups on the Home tab (see Figure 3-3) often provide a quicker way to accomplish the same task, and keyboard shortcuts (summarized in Table 3-1) allow you to keep your hands on the keyboard.

USE THE MINI TOOLBAR

When you right-click text in Word 2007, you see both a context menu and a mini toolbar. This toolbar has several of the buttons available in the Home tab's Font and Paragraph groups. In the next sections, when we point out that you can use the Home tab Font group to accomplish a function, it is likely that you can do the same function with the mini toolbar. However, to reduce repetition, using the mini toolbar to carry out these tasks will not be included.

SELECT A FONT

A *font* is a set of characters that share a particular design, which is called a *typeface*. When you install Windows, and again when you install Office, a number of fonts are automatically installed on your computer. You can see the

NOTE

Prior to applying formatting, you must select the text to be formatted. Chapter 2 contains an extensive section on selecting text.

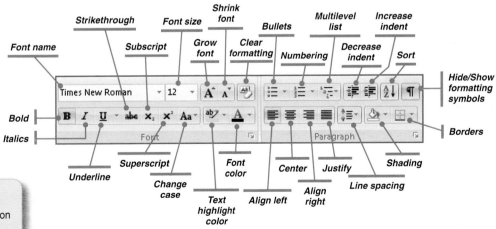

Figure 3-3: *The Font and Paragraph groups on the Home tab provide fast formatting with the mouse.*

APPLY FORMATTING	SHORTCUT KEYS	APPLY FORMATTING	SHORTCUT KEYS
Align left	CTRL+L	Indent paragraph	CTRL+M
Align right	CTRL+R	Italic	CTRL+I
All caps	CTRL+SHIFT+A	Justify paragraph	CTRL+J
Bold	CTRL+B	Line space—single	CTRL+1
Bulleted list	CTRL+SHIFT+L	Line space—1.5 lines	CTRL+5
Center	CTRL+E	Line space—double	CTRL+2
Change case	SHIFT+F3	Normal style	CTRL+SHIFT+N
Copy format	CTRL+SHIFT+C	Paste format	CTRL+SHIFT+V
Decrease font size	CTRL+SHIFT+<	Reset character formatting	CTRL+SPACEBAR
Increase font size	CTRL+SHIFT+>	Reset paragraph formatting	CTRL+Q
Decrease font size one point	CTRL+[	Small caps	CTRL+SHIFT+K
Increase font size one point	CTRL+]	Subscript	CTRL+=
Open font dialog box	CTRL+D	Superscript	CTRL+SHIFT+=
Font name	CTRL+SHIFT+F	Symbol font	CTRL+SHIFT+Q
Hang paragraph	CTRL+T	Un-hang paragraph	CTRL+SHIFT+T
Heading level 1	ALT+CTRL+1	Un-indent paragraph	CTRL+SHIFT+M
Heading level 2	ALT+CTRL+2	Underline (continuous)	CTRL+U
Heading level 3	ALT+CTRL+3	Underline (double)	CTRL+SHIFT+D
Hidden character	CTRL+SHIFT+H	Underline (word)	CTRL+SHIFT+W

*Table 3-1: **Formatting Shortcut Keys***

fonts available by clicking the down arrow next to the font name in the Home tab Font group and then scrolling through the list (your most recently used fonts are at the top, followed by all fonts listed alphabetically). You can also see the list of fonts in the Font dialog box, where you can select a font in the Font list and see what it looks like in the Preview area at the bottom of the dialog box.

By default, the Calibri font is used for body text in all new documents using the default Normal template. To change this font:

1. Select the text to be formatted (see Chapter 2).
2. Click the **Home** tab, and click the **Font** down arrow in the Font group. Scroll through the list until you see the font that you want, and then click it.

APPLY BOLD OR ITALIC STYLE

Fonts come in four styles: regular (or "roman"), bold, italic, and bold-italic. The default is, of course, regular, yet fonts such as Arial Black and Eras Bold appear bold. To make fonts bold, italic, or bold-italic:

1. Select the text to be formatted (see Chapter 2).
2. Press **CTRL+B** to make it bold, and/or press **CTRL+I** to make it italic.

   –Or–

   Click the **Bold** icon in the Font group, and/or click the **Italic** icon. **B** *I*

CHANGE FONT SIZE

Font size is measured in *points*, which is the height of a character, not its width. For most fonts, the width varies with the character, the letter "i" taking up less room than "w." (The Courier New font is an exception, with all characters having the same width.) There are 72 points in an inch. The default font size is 11 points for body text, with standard headings varying from 11 to 14 points. The 8-point type is common for smaller print; below 6 point is typically unreadable. To change the font size of your text:

1. Select the text to be formatted (see Chapter 2).
2. On the Home tab, click the **Font Size** down arrow in the Font group, scroll through the list until you see the font size you want, and then click it.

   –Or–

   Press **CTRL+SHIFT**+< to decrease the font size, or press **CTRL+SHIFT**+> to increase the font size.

UNDERLINE TEXT

Several forms of underlining can be applied.

1. Select the text to be formatted (see Chapter 2).

2. Click the **Underline** down arrow in the Home tab Font group, and click the type of underline you want.

   –Or–

   Press **CTRL+U** to apply a continuous underline to the entire selection (including spaces).

   –Or–

   Press **CTRL+SHIFT+W** to apply an underline to just each word in the selection.

   –Or–

   Press **CTRL+SHIFT+D** to apply a double underline to the entire selection.

USE FONT COLOR

To change the color of text:

1. Select the text to be formatted (see Chapter 2).

2. Click the **Home** tab, and click **Font Color** in the Font group to apply the currently selected color.

   –Or–

   Click the **Font Dialog Box Launcher** for the Font dialog box. Click the **Font Color** down arrow, click the color you want, and click **OK**.

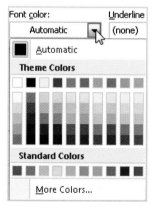

3. If, in selecting a color from either the Home tab Font group or the Font dialog box, you do not find the color you want within the 40-color palette, click **More Colors** to open the Colors dialog box. In the Standard tab, you can pick a color from a 145-color palette, or you can use the Custom tab to choose from an almost infinite range of colors by clicking in the color spectrum or by entering the RGB (red, green, and blue) values, as you can see in Figure 3-4, or the HSL (hue, saturation, and luminescent) values.

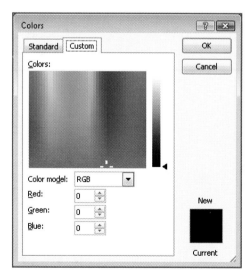

Figure 3-4: You can create any color you want in the Custom tab of the Colors dialog box.

RESET TEXT

Figure 3-5 shows some of the formatting that has been discussed. All of those can be reset to the plain text or the default formatting. To reset text to default settings:

Select the text to be formatted (see Chapter 2).

- Click **Clear Formatting** in the Home tab, Font group.

 –Or–

- Press **CTRL+SPACEBAR**. (This will not reset a font size change if it is the only difference with the default.)

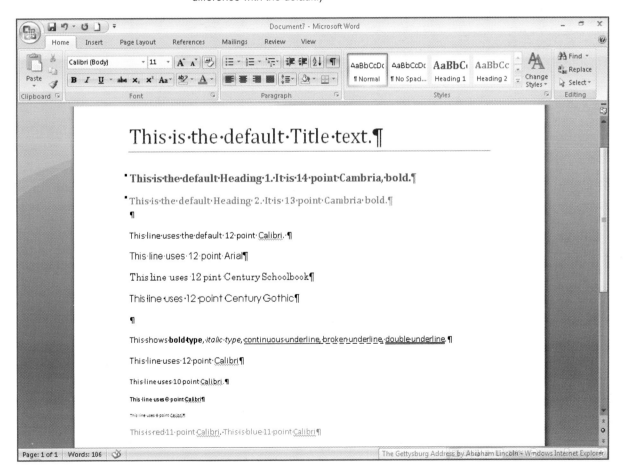

Figure 3-5: Character formatting must be applied judiciously, or it will detract from the appearance of a document.

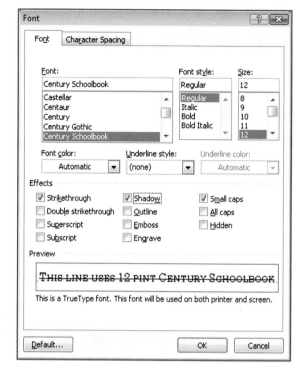

QUICKSTEPS

USING THE FONT DIALOG BOX

Although you can apply many effects using the Fonts group in the Home tab—such as superscript, emboss, and small caps,—you have an alternative way to make these changes. You can use the Font dialog box, shown in Figure 3-6, to change text effects.

1. Click the **Home** tab, and click the **Font Dialog Box Launcher** in the Font group to open the Font dialog box. If it isn't already selected, click the **Font** tab.

2. In the Effects area, click the options that you want to apply (some are mutually exclusive, such as superscript and subscript).

3. Check the results in the Preview area. When you are satisfied, click **OK**.

NOTE

Character spacing, especially kerning, is predominantly used when you are creating something like a brochure, flyer, or newspaper ad in which you want to achieve a typeset look.

Figure 3-6: The Font dialog box is an alternative way to add text effects, such as strikethrough, shadow, and small caps.

Set Character Spacing

Character spacing, in this case, is the amount of space between characters on a single line. Word gives you the chance to increase and decrease character spacing, as well as to scale the size of selected text, raise and lower vertically the position of text on the line, and determine when to apply kerning (how much the space for certain characters such as "A" and "V" can overlap) in the Character Spacing tab of the Font dialog box. To apply character spacing:

1. Select the text to be formatted, click the **Home** tab, click the **Font Dialog Box Launcher** to open the Font dialog box, and click the **Character Spacing** tab. You have these options:

   • **Scale:** Select the percentage scale factor that you want to apply. (This is not recommended. It is better to change the font size so as not to distort the font).

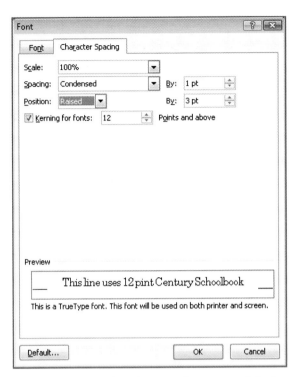

*Figure 3-7: **The spacing of text can have as much to do with its appearance as the choice of font.***

- **Spacing:** Select the change in spacing (expanded or condensed) that you want and the amount of that change.
- **Position:** Select the change in position (raised or lowered) that you want and the amount of that change.
- **Kerning For Fonts:** Determine if you want to apply kerning rules and the point size at which you want to do that.

2. Check the results in the Preview area, an example of which is shown in Figure 3-7. When you are satisfied, click **OK**.

Change Capitalization

You can, of course, capitalize a character you are typing by holding down **SHIFT** while you type. You can also press **CAPS LOCK** to have every letter that you type be capitalized and then press **CAPS LOCK** again to turn off capitalization. You can also change the capitalization of existing text:

1. Select the text whose capitalization you want to change.

2. In the Home tab Font group, click **Change Case**. Select one of these options:

- **Sentence Case** capitalizes the first word of every selected sentence.
- **Lowercase** displays all selected words in lowercase.
- **UPPERCASE** displays all selected words in all caps. All the characters of every selected word will be capitalized.
- **Capitalize Each Word** puts a leading cap on each selected word.
- **tOGGLE cASE** changes all lowercase words to uppercase and all uppercase words to lowercase.

Create a Drop Cap

A *drop cap* is an enlarged capital letter at the beginning of a paragraph that extends down over two or more lines of text. To create a drop cap:

1. Select the character or word that you want to be formatted as a drop cap.

2. Click the **Insert** tab, and click **Drop Cap** in the Text group. A context menu will open. You have these choices:

- Click **Dropped** to have the first lettered dropped within the paragraph text.
- Click **In Margin** to set the capital letter off in the margin.
- Click **Drop Cap Options** to see further options. You can change the font, specify how many lines will be dropped (3 is the default), and specify how far from the text the dropped cap will be placed.

3. Click **OK** to close the Drop Cap dialog box.

The paragraph will be reformatted around the enlarged capital letter. Here are the two examples of putting the dropped cap in the paragraph or in the margin:

NOTE

To remove a drop cap, select the character or word, click **Drop Cap** in the Insert tab Text group, and click **None** on the context menu.

Format a Paragraph

Paragraph formatting, which you can apply to any paragraph, is used to manage alignment, indentation, line spacing, bullets or numbering, and borders. In Word, a paragraph consists of a paragraph mark (created by pressing **ENTER**) and any text or objects that appear between that paragraph mark and the previous paragraph mark. A paragraph can be empty, or it can contain anything from a single character to as many characters as you care to enter.

Set Paragraph Alignment

Four types of paragraph alignment are available in Word (see Figure 3-8): left aligned, centered, right-aligned, and justified. Left-aligned, right-aligned, and centered are self-explanatory. Justified means that the text in a paragraph is spread out between the left and right margins. Word does this by adding space between words, except for the last line of a paragraph. To apply paragraph alignment:

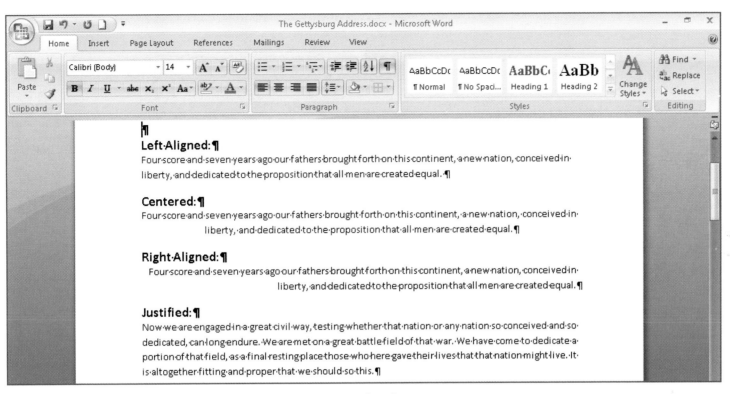

*Figure 3-8: **Paragraph alignment provides both visual appeal and separation of text.***

1. Click in the paragraph you want to align. (You don't need to select the entire paragraph.)

2. For left alignment, press **CTRL+L**; for right alignment, press **CTRL+R**; for centered, press **CTRL+E**; and for justified, press **CTRL+J**.

   –Or–

   In the Home tab Paragraph group, click the **Align Left**, **Center**, **Align Right**, or **Justify** button, depending on what you want to do.

   –Or–

USING INDENTATION

A good question might be "Why use indentation"? There are at least four good reasons:

- To organize and group pieces of text so they can be viewed as elements within a given topic. Bulleted and numbered lists fall into this category.

- To separate and call attention to a piece of text. An ordinary indented paragraph, either just on the left or on both the left and right, is done for this reason.

- To provide a hierarchical structure. An outline uses this form of indentation.

- To indicate the start of a new paragraph by indenting the first line of the paragraph.

Indentation is a powerful formatting tool when used correctly. Like other formatting, it can also be overused and make text hard to read or to understand. Ask yourself two questions about indentation: 1.) Do I have a good reason for it? and 2.) Does it improve the readability and/or understanding of what is being said?

In the Home tab Paragraph group, click the **Paragraph Dialog Box Launcher** to open the Paragraph dialog box. On the Indents And Spacing tab, click the **Alignment** down arrow, click the type of alignment you want, and click **OK**.

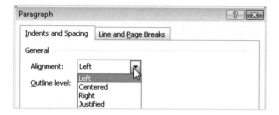

Indent a Paragraph

Indenting a paragraph in Word means to:

- Move the left or right edge (or both) of the paragraph inward toward the center

- Move the left side of the first line of a paragraph inward toward the center

- Move the left side of the first line of a paragraph leftward, away from the center, for a *hanging indent*

Figure 3-9 shows the various types of indenting styles available to you.

CHANGE THE LEFT INDENT

To move the left edge of an entire paragraph to the right:

1. Click in the paragraph to select it.

2. In the Home tab Paragraph group, click **Increase Indent** one or more times to indent the left edge a half-inch each time.

   –Or–

   Press **CTRL+M** one or more times to indent the left edge a half-inch each time.

   –Or–

   On the Page Layout tab Paragraph group, click the **Left Indent** spinner.

   –Or–

   In the Home tab Paragraph group, click the **Paragraph Dialog Box Launcher** to open the Paragraph dialog box. On the Indents And Spacing tab, under Indentation, click the **Left** spinner's up arrow up until you get the amount of indentation you want, and then click **OK**.

Indentation

Left: 0.6"

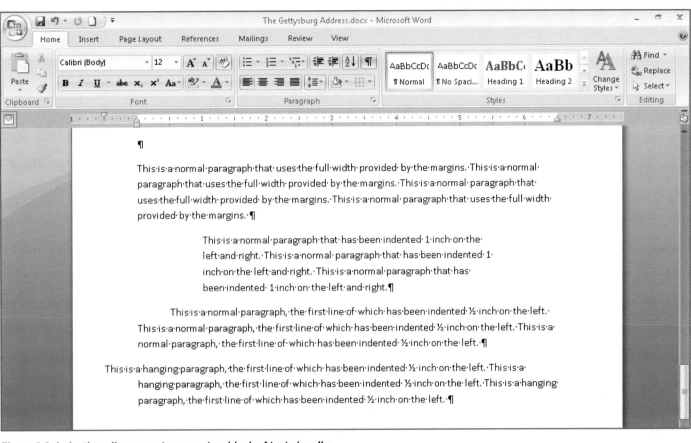

*Figure 3-9: **Indenting allows you to separate a block of text visually.***

REMOVE A LEFT INDENT

To move the left edge of an entire paragraph back to the left:

1. Click in the paragraph to select it.

2. In the Home tab Paragraph group, click **Decrease Indent** one or more times to un-indent the left edge a half-inch each time.

   –Or–

   Press **CTRL+SHIFT+M** one or more times to un-indent the left edge a half-inch each time.

   –Or–

In the Home tab Paragraph group, click the **Paragraph Dialog Box Launcher** to open the Paragraph dialog box. In the Indents And Spacing tab, under Indentation, click the Left spinner's down arrow until you get the amount of indentation you want, and then click **OK**.

CHANGE THE RIGHT INDENT

To move the right edge of an entire paragraph to the left:

1. Click in the paragraph to select it.

2. In the Page Layout tab, Paragraph group, click the **Right Indent** spinner.

   –Or–

   In the Home tab Paragraph group, click the **Paragraph Dialog Box Launcher** to open the Paragraph dialog box. In the Indents And Spacing tab, under Indentation, click the **Right** spinner's up arrow until you get the amount of indentation you want, and then click **OK**.

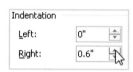

INDENT THE FIRST LINE

To move the right edge of an entire paragraph to the left:

1. Click in the paragraph to select it.

2. In the Home tab Paragraph group, click the **Paragraph Dialog Box Launcher** to open the Paragraph dialog box. In the Indents And Spacing tab, under Indentation, click the **Special** down arrow, and click **First Line**. Then click the **By** spinner to set the amount of indentation you want, and click **OK**.

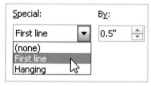

MAKE A HANGING INDENT

To indent all of a paragraph except the first line:

1. Click in the paragraph to select it.

2. Press **CTRL+T** one or more times to indent the left edge of all but the first line a half-inch each time.

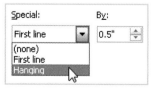

   –Or–

   In the Home tab Paragraph group, click the **Paragraph Dialog Box Launcher** to open the Paragraph dialog box. In the Indents And Spacing tab, under Indentation, click the **Special** down arrow, and select Hanging. Enter the amount of the indent, and click **OK**.

TIP

You can reset all paragraph formatting, including indents and hanging indents, to their default settings by pressing **CTRL+Q**.

UICKSTEPS

USING THE RULER FOR INDENTS

You can use the horizontal ruler to set tabs and indents.

DISPLAY THE RULER

To display the ruler:

1. Click the **View** tab.

2. In the Show/Hide group, click **Ruler**. Vertical and horizontal rulers will be displayed on the top and left sides of the document window.

    –Or–

    Click **View Rulers** at the top of the vertical scroll bar.

SET A PARAGRAPH INDENT ON THE LEFT

To move the paragraph to the left:

1. Click or select the paragraph to be indented.

2. Drag the left indent tab to where you want the paragraph moved.

SET A PARAGRAPH INDENT ON THE RIGHT

To move the right side of the paragraph to the left:

1. Click or select the paragraph to be indented.

2. Drag the right indent tab on the right of the ruler to where you want the paragraph moved.

Continued . . .

REMOVE A HANGING INDENT

To un-indent all but the first line of a paragraph:

1. Click in the paragraph to select it.

2. Press **CTRL+SHIFT+T** one or more times to un-indent the left edge of all but the first line a half-inch each time.

   –Or–

   In the Home tab Paragraph group, click the **Paragraph Dialog Box Launcher** to open the Paragraph dialog box. In the Indents And Spacing tab, under Indentation, click the **Special** down arrow, and click **None**. Click **OK**.

Determine Line and Paragraph Spacing

The vertical spacing of text is determined by the amount of space between lines, the amount of space added before and after a paragraph, and where you break lines and pages.

SET LINE SPACING

The amount of space between lines is most often set in terms of the line height, with *single-spacing* being one times the current line height, *double-spacing* being twice the current line height, and so on. You can also specify line spacing in points, as you do the size of type. Single-spacing is just under 14 points for 12-point type. To set line spacing for an entire paragraph:

1. Click in the paragraph for which you want to set the line spacing.

2. In the Home tab Paragraph group, click the **Line Spacing** down arrow, and then click the line spacing, in terms of lines, that you want to use.

   –Or–

   Press **CTRL+1** for single line spacing, press **CTRL+5** for one-and-a-half line spacing, and press **CTRL+2** for double line spacing.

   –Or–

	¶ Normal	¶ N
1.0		
✓ 1.15		
1.5		
2.0		
2.5		
3.0		
Line Spacing Options...		
Add Space Before Paragraph		
Remove Space After Paragraph		

USING THE RULER FOR INDENTS

(Continued)

SET A FIRST-LINE OR HANGING INDENT

To indent the first line either to the right or left of the rest of the paragraph:

1. Click or select the paragraph to be indented.

2. Drag the first line indent on the left of the ruler to where you want the paragraph moved.

NOTE

In the Paragraph dialog box, you can specify the amount of space between lines in a format other than the number of lines. From the Line Spacing drop-down list, click **Exactly**, and then enter or select the number of points to use between lines. With 12-point type, single spacing is about 14 points, one-and-a-half line spacing (1.5) is about 21 points, and so on. With 11-point type, single spacing is about 12 points.

CAUTION

If you reduce the line spacing below the size of the type (below 12 points for 12 point type, for example), the lines will begin to overlap and become hard to read.

In the Home tab Paragraph group, click the **Paragraph Dialog Box Launcher** to open the Paragraph dialog box. In the Indents And Spacing tab, under Spacing, click the **Line Spacing** down arrow. From the menu that appears, select the line spacing you want to use, as shown in Figure 3-10. Click **OK**.

ADD SPACE BETWEEN PARAGRAPHS

In addition to specifying space between lines, you can add extra space at the beginning and end of paragraphs. With typewriters, many people would add an extra blank line between paragraphs. That has carried over to computers, but it does not always look good. If you are using single spacing, leaving a blank line will leave an extra 14 points (with 12-point type) between paragraphs. Common paragraph spacing is to leave 3 points before the

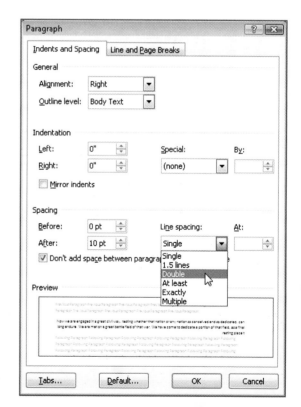

*Figure 3-10: **If a document is going to be edited on paper, it is a good idea to use double spacing to allow room for writing between the lines.***

paragraph and 6 points afterward, so if you have two of these paragraphs, one after the other, you would have a total of 9 points, in comparison to the 14 points from an extra blank line. To add extra space between paragraphs:

1. Click in the paragraph to which you want to add space.

2. In the Page Layout tab, Paragraph group, click the **Spacing** spinners to set the spacing before and after the paragraph.

–Or–

In the Home tab Paragraph group, click the **Paragraph Dialog Box Launcher** to open the Paragraph dialog box. In the Indents And Spacing tab, under Spacing, click the **Before** spinner or enter a number in points ("pt") for the space you want to add before the paragraph. If desired, do the same thing for the space after the paragraph. When you are ready, click **OK.**

SET LINE AND PAGE BREAKS

The vertical spacing of a document is also affected by how lines and pages are broken and how much of a paragraph you force to stay together or be with text either before or after it.

You can break a line and start a new one, thereby creating a new line, paragraph or page.

- **Create a new paragraph** by moving the insertion point to where you want to break the line and pressing **ENTER**.

- **Stay in the same paragraph** by moving the insertion point to where you want to break the line and pressing **SHIFT+ENTER**.

- **Break a page and start a new one** by pressing **CTRL+ENTER**.

  –Or–

  Click the **Insert** tab, and click **Page Break** in the Pages group.

  –Or–

  Click the **Page Layout** tab, and click **Breaks** in the Page Setup group. Click **Page** from the menu.

HANDLE SPLIT PAGES

When a paragraph is split over two pages, you have several ways to control how much of the paragraph is placed on which page.

1. Click in the paragraph you want to change.

2. Click the **Home** tab, click the **Paragraph Dialog Box Launcher**, and click the **Line And Page Breaks** tab.

3. Click the following options that are correct for your situation, and then click **OK**:

- **Widow/Orphan Control** adjusts the pagination to keep at least two lines on one or both pages. For example, if you have three lines, without selecting Widow/Orphan Control, one line is on the first page and two on the second. When you select this option, all three lines will be placed on the second page. Widow/Orphan Control is selected by default.

- **Keep Lines Together** forces all lines of a paragraph to be on the same page. This option can be used for a paragraph title where you want all of it on one page.

- **Keep With Next** forces the entire paragraph to stay on the same page with the next paragraph. This option is used with paragraph headings that you want to keep with the paragraph.

- **Page Break Before** forces a page break before the start of the paragraph. This option is used with major section headings or titles that you want to start on a new page.

Use Numbered and Bulleted Lists

Word provides the means to automatically number or add bullets to paragraphs and then format the paragraphs as hanging indents so that the numbers or bullets stick out to the left (see Figure 3-11).

CREATE A NUMBERED LIST USING AUTOCORRECT

You can create a numbered list as you type. Word will automatically format it according to your text. Word's numbered lists are particularly handy, because you can add

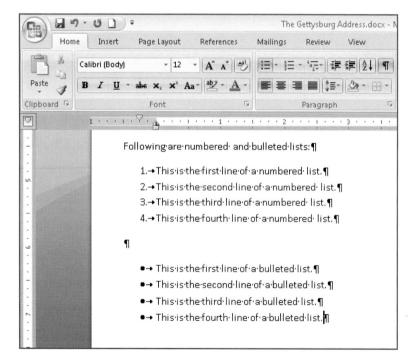

Figure 3-11: Bullets and numbering help organize thoughts into lists.

or delete paragraphs in the middle of the list and have the list automatically renumber itself. To start a numbered list:

1. Press **ENTER** to start a new paragraph.

2. Type 1, press either **SPACEBAR** or **TAB** two times, and then type the rest of what you want in the first item of the numbered list.

3. Press **ENTER**. The number "2" automatically appears, and both the first and the new lines are formatted as hanging indents. Also, the AutoCorrect lightning icon appears as you type the first line.

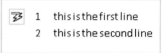

4. After typing the second item in your list, press **ENTER** once again. The number "3" automatically appears. Type the item and press **ENTER** to keep numbering the list.

5. When you are done, press **ENTER** twice. The numbering will stop and the hanging indent will be removed.

If you click the **AutoCorrect** icon, you may choose to undo the automatic numbering that has already been applied, stop the automatic creation of numbered lists, and control the use of AutoCorrect (see Chapter 4 for more information on AutoCorrect).

CREATE A NUMBERED OR BULLETED LIST BEFORE YOU TYPE TEXT

You can also create a numbered or bulleted list before you start typing the text it will contain.

1. Press **ENTER** to start a new paragraph.

2. In the Home tab Paragraph group, click **Numbering** to begin a numbered list, or click **Bullets** to start a bulleted list.

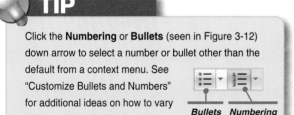

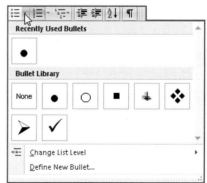

Figure 3-12: Clicking the Bullets down arrow displays a list of choices for formatting bullets. A similar menu is displayed when you click the Numbering down arrow.

NOTE

To apply bullets or numbering to a list that has already been typed, highlight the text, right-click it, and point to **Bullets** or **Numbering** on the context menu. Then click the format option you want. Or, on the Home tab Paragraph group, click **Numbering** to format the selected text as a numbered list, or click **Bullets** to format the text as a bulleted list.

☷	Bullets ▸
☷	Numbering ▸

3. Type the first item, and press **ENTER** to start the second numbered or bulleted item with the same style as the first. When you are done creating the list, press **ENTER** twice to stop the automatic list.

–Or–

Click **Numbering** or click **Bullets** in the Home tab Paragraph group to end the list.

CUSTOMIZE BULLETS AND NUMBERS

You saw in Figure 3-12 that Word offers seven different types of bullets. Word also offers eight different styles for numbering paragraphs. For those to whom eight choices is not enough, there is a Define New option for both bullets and numbering that includes the ability to select from hundreds of pictures and to import others to use as bullets. To use custom bullets or numbering:

1. Click the **Home** tab, and click the **Bullets** or **Numbering** down arrow to open the Bullets or Numbering context menu.

2. Depending on whether you are using bullets or numbering, you have these choices:

   ● For bullets, click **Define New Bullet**. The Define New Bullet dialog box appears (see Figure 3-13). Click **Font** and then select the font and other attributes in the dialog box for the character that you want to use. Alternatively, click **Symbol** to select a symbol, or click **Picture** to choose from a number of picture bullets that are included in Office's clip art catalog (see Figure 3-14). To use your own picture, click **Import** and select that picture. Click **OK** to close the Picture dialog box, select both the bullet and text position, click **OK** again, and use the new bullet.

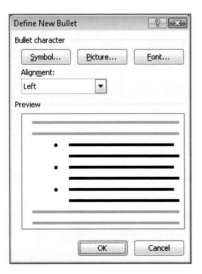

Figure 3-13: You can select any character in any font to use as a bullet.

Figure 3-14: Word provides a number of pictures that can be used as bullets.

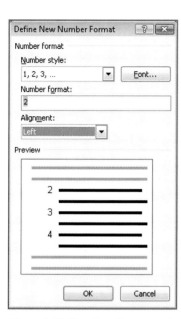

Figure 3-15: *Numbered paragraphs can use numbers, letters, or even uppercase or lowercase roman numerals.*

TIP

You can switch a numbered list to a bulleted one or vice versa by selecting the list and clicking the other icon in the Home tab Paragraph group.

- For numbering, click **Define New Number Format**. The Define New Number Format dialog box appears (see Figure 3-15). Click the **Number Style** down arrow to choose the style (numbers, capital letters, lowercase letters, roman numerals, and so on). Click **Font** to choose the numbers formatted with a particular font, and click **OK** to close the Font dialog box. Press **TAB** to select the number in the Number Format text box, and type a sample of the number you want (delete the period for a number without the period). Click the **Alignment** down arrow to choose between right alignment, left alignment, or centered. Click **OK** to apply the customized numbering.

REMOVE NUMBERING AND BULLETING

To remove the numbering or bulleting (both the numbers or bullets and the hanging indent):

1. Select the paragraphs from which you want to remove the numbering or bulleting.

2. In the Home tab Paragraph group, click **Numbering or Bullets**, as appropriate.

Add Borders and Shading

Borders and shading allow you to separate and call attention to text. You can place a border on any or all of the four sides of selected text, paragraphs, and pages; and you can add many varieties of shading to the space occupied by selected text, paragraphs, and pages—with or without a border around them (see Figure 3-16). You can create horizontal lines as you type, and you can add other borders from both the Home tab, Paragraph group and the Borders And Shading dialog box.

CREATE HORIZONTAL LINES AS YOU TYPE

Horizontal lines can be added on their own paragraph as you type.

1. Press **ENTER** to create a new paragraph.

2. Type --- (three hyphens) and press **ENTER**. A single, light horizontal line will be created between the left and right margins.

   –Or–

   Type === (three equal signs) and press **ENTER**. A double horizontal line will be created between the left and right margins.

   –Or–

   Type _ _ _ (three underscores) and press **ENTER**. A single, heavy horizontal line will be created between the left and right margins.

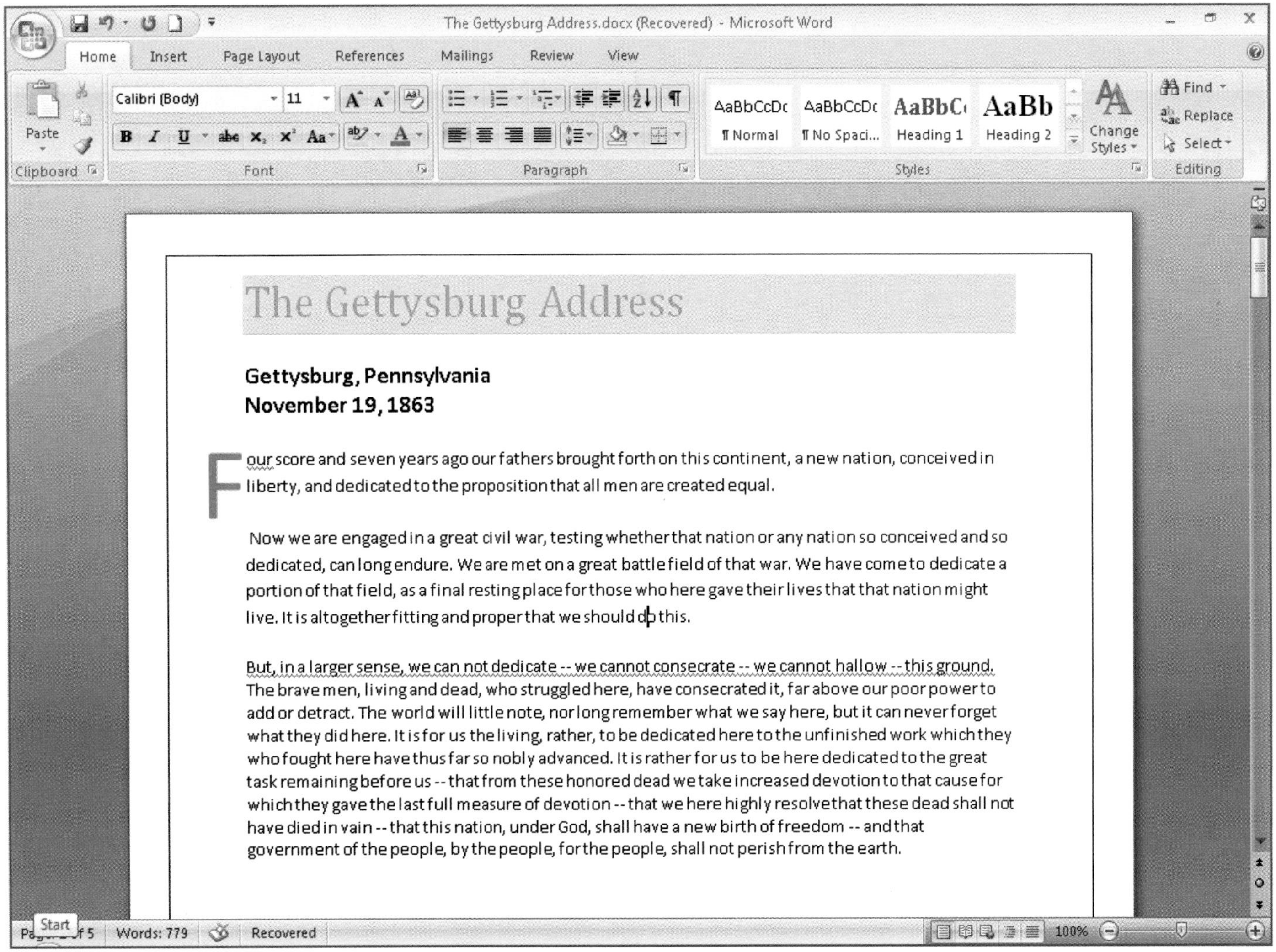

The Gettysburg Address.docx (Recovered) - Microsoft Word

The Gettysburg Address

Gettysburg, Pennsylvania
November 19, 1863

F our score and seven years ago our fathers brought forth on this continent, a new nation, conceived in liberty, and dedicated to the proposition that all men are created equal.

Now we are engaged in a great civil war, testing whether that nation or any nation so conceived and so dedicated, can long endure. We are met on a great battle field of that war. We have come to dedicate a portion of that field, as a final resting place for those who here gave their lives that that nation might live. It is altogether fitting and proper that we should do this.

But, in a larger sense, we can not dedicate -- we cannot consecrate -- we cannot hallow -- this ground. The brave men, living and dead, who struggled here, have consecrated it, far above our poor power to add or detract. The world will little note, nor long remember what we say here, but it can never forget what they did here. It is for us the living, rather, to be dedicated here to the unfinished work which they who fought here have thus far so nobly advanced. It is rather for us to be here dedicated to the great task remaining before us -- that from these honored dead we take increased devotion to that cause for which they gave the last full measure of devotion -- that we here highly resolve that these dead shall not have died in vain -- that this nation, under God, shall have a new birth of freedom -- and that government of the people, by the people, for the people, shall not perish from the earth.

Page   of 5 | Words: 779 | Recovered   100%

Figure 3-16: Borders and shading can be applied to text, blank paragraphs, phrases, characters, and words.

ADD BORDERS AND SHADING TO TEXT

Borders and shading can be added to any amount of text, from a single character to several pages.

1. Select the text for which you want to have a border or shading.

2. In the Home tab Paragraph group, click the **Borders** down arrow, and then select the type of border you want to apply. If you have selected less than a full paragraph, you can only select a four-sided box (you actually can select less, but you will get a full box).

–Or–

In the Home tab Paragraph group, click **Borders**, and click **Borders And Shading** on the context menu. The Borders And Shading dialog box will appear, as shown in Figure 3-17:

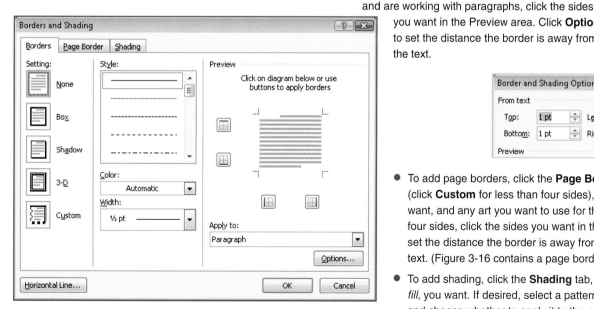

- To add text or paragraph borders, click the **Borders** tab, click the type of box (click **Custom** for less than four sides), the line style, color, and width you want. If you want less than four sides and are working with paragraphs, click the sides you want in the Preview area. Click **Options** to set the distance the border is away from the text.

- To add page borders, click the **Page Border** tab, click the type of box (click **Custom** for less than four sides), the line style, color, width you want, and any art you want to use for the border. If you want less than four sides, click the sides you want in the Preview area. Click **Options** to set the distance the border is away from either the edge of the page or the text. (Figure 3-16 contains a page border.)

- To add shading, click the **Shading** tab, and click the color of shading, or *fill*, you want. If desired, select a pattern (this is independent of the fill), and choose whether to apply it to the entire page, paragraph, or just to the selected text.

NOTE

Borders will be discussed further as they relate to tables in Chapter 6.

Figure 3-17: Borders can be created with many different types and widths of lines.

QUICKSTEPS

TURNING ON FORMATTING MARKS

To make any formatting and what is causing the spacing in a document easier to see, you can display some of the formatting marks. In the Home tab Paragraph group, click **Show/Hide Formatting Marks** ¶ to show all of the formatting marks—paragraph marks ¶ , tabs, and spaces, among other characters—as you can see in Figure 3-18.

You can fine-tune exactly which formatting marks to display by clicking the **Office Button**, clicking **Word Options**, and clicking the **Display** option. Under Always Show These Formatting Marks On The Screen, you can choose which marks to display.

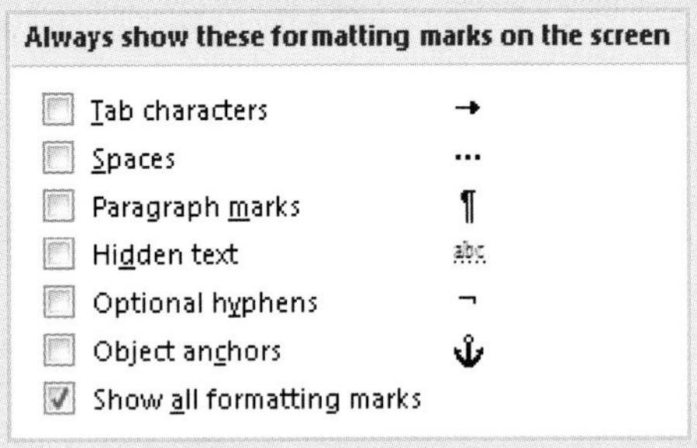

Always show these formatting marks on the screen	
☐ Tab characters	→
☐ Spaces	···
☐ Paragraph marks	¶
☐ Hidden text	a̲b̲c̲
☐ Optional hyphens	¬
☐ Object anchors	⚓
☑ Show all formatting marks	

CAUTION

Remember that page formatting changes the margins and other formatting for whole pages. If you select a part of the document to have special formatting, it will separate that section by pages. To change formatting for smaller sections of text, use indenting.

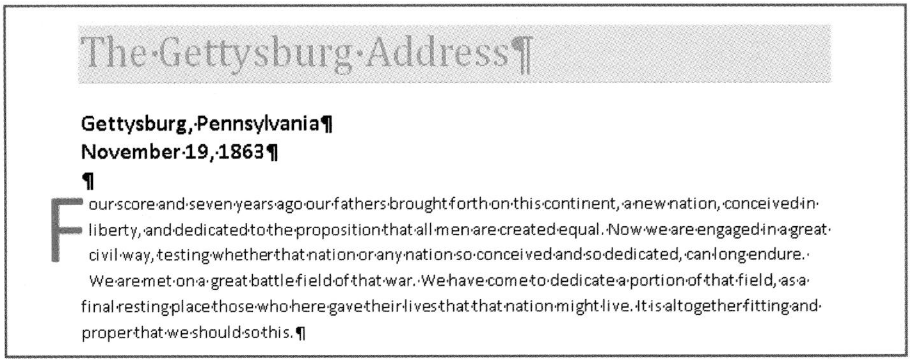

The·Gettysburg·Address¶

Gettysburg,·Pennsylvania¶
November·19,·1863¶
¶
Four·score·and·seven·years·ago·our·fathers·brought·forth·on·this·continent,·a·new·nation,·conceived·in· liberty,·and·dedicated·to·the·proposition·that·all·men·are·created·equal.·Now·we·are·engaged·in·a·great· civil·way,·testing·whether·that·nation·or·any·nation·so·conceived·and·so·dedicated,·can·long·endure.·· We·are·met·on·a·great·battlefield·of·that·war.·We·have·come·to·dedicate·a·portion·of·that·field,·as·a· final·resting·place·those·who·here·gave·their·lives·that·that·nation·might·live.·It·is·altogether·fitting·and· proper·that·we·should·so·this.¶

Figure 3-18: Turning on formatting marks helps you see what is making your document look the way it does.

- To add a graphic horizontal line, click **Horizontal Line**, click the line you want, and click **OK**.

- When you are done with the Borders And Shading dialog box, click **OK** to close it.

Format a Page

Page formatting has to do with the overall formatting of items, such as margins, orientation, size, and vertical alignment of a page. You can set options for page formatting either from the Page Layout tab or in a dialog box.

Set Margins

Margins are the space between the edge of the paper and the text. To set margins:

1. Open the document whose margins you want to set (see Chapter 2). If you want the margins to apply only to a selected part of a document, select that part now.

2. Click the **Page Layout** tab, and click **Margins** in the Page Setup group. A menu will open, as shown in Figure 3-19.

3. Click the option you want.

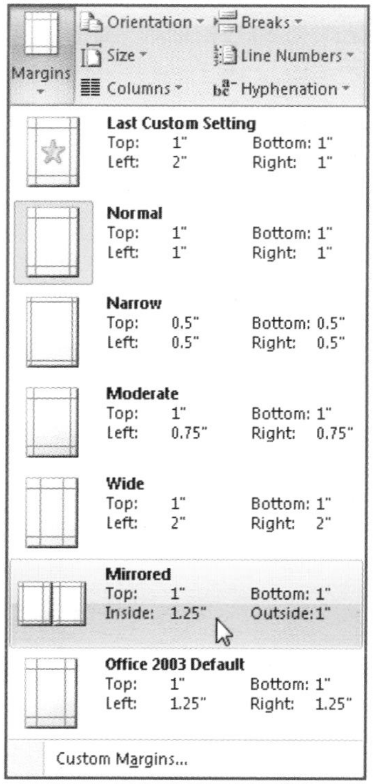

Figure 3-19: *You can select from a group of "canned" margins, according to the needs of your document, or you can create a custom margin.*

TIP

If you are going to bind the document and want to add an extra amount of space on one edge for the binding, enter that amount opposite Gutter, and select the side the gutter is on opposite Gutter Position.

Use a Dialog Box to Format a Page

You can do much of the page formatting using the Page Layout dialog box.

1. In the Page Layout tab, click the **Page Setup Dialog Box Launcher**. The Page Setup dialog box appears, as shown in Figure 3-20.

2. Click the **Margins** tab. You have these options:

   ● Under Margins, click the spinners or manually enter the desired distance in inches between the particular edge of the paper and the start or end of text.

   ● Under Orientation, click either **Portrait** or **Landscape**, depending on which you want.

   ● Under Pages, click the **Multiple Page** down arrow, and select an option: Click **Mirror Margins** when the inside gutter is larger (if you will be printing and binding the document, for example). Click **2 Pages Per Sheet** when a normal sheet of paper is divided into two pages, and click **Book Fold** when you are putting together a section of a book ("a signature") with four, eight, or more pages in the signature.

   ● If you want these changes to apply only to the selected part of a document, click **This Point Forward** under Preview Apply To.

3. When you are done setting margins, click **OK**.

Figure 3-20: *Many page-formatting tasks can be done in the Page Setup dialog box.*

Use Mirror Margins

Mirror margins allow you to have a larger "inside" margin, which would be the right margin on the left page and the left margin on the right page, or any other combination of margins that are mirrored between the left and right pages. To create mirror margins:

1. Open the document whose margins you want mirrored (see Chapter 2).

2. Click the **Page Layout** tab, and click **Margins** in the Page Setup group.

3. Click **Mirrored**, as shown earlier in Figure 3-19. When you do that, the left and right margins change to inside and outside margins.

Determine Page Orientation

Page orientation specifies whether a page is taller than it is wide ("portrait") or wider than it is tall ("landscape"). For 8½-inch by 11-inch letter size paper, if the 11-inch side is vertical (the left and right edges), which is the standard way of reading a letter, then it is portrait. If the 11-inch side is horizontal (the top and bottom edges), then it is landscape. Portrait is the default orientation in Word. To change it:

1. Open the document whose orientation you want to set (see Chapter 2). If you want the orientation to apply only to a selected part of a document, select that part now.

2. In the Page Layout tab, click **Orientation** in the Page Setup group.

3. On the menu, click the option you want.

Specify Paper Size

Specifying the paper size gives you the starting perimeter of the area within which you can set margins and enter text or pictures.

1. In the Page Layout tab, click the **Size** down arrow in the Page Setup group. A menu will open, shown in Figure 3-21.

2. Click the size of paper you want.

QUICKSTEPS

COPYING FORMATTING *(Continued)*

3. Drag across each piece of text or paragraph that you want to format.

4. When you are done, click the **Format Painter** button again or press **ESC**.

TIP

If you want to further differentiate between the left and right pages, you need to use sections (described in Chapter 4).

QUICKSTEPS

TRACKING INCONSISTENT FORMATTING

When you turned on the formatting marks (see the "Turning On Formatting Marks" QuickSteps earlier in the chapter), you might have felt a bit disappointed that they didn't tell you more. You can direct Word to track inconsistencies in your formatting as you type.

1. Click the **Office Button**, and click **Word Options**.

2. Click **Advanced** on the left pane.

3. Under Editing Options, click both **Keep Track Of Formatting** and **Mark Formatting Inconsistencies**.

> ☑ Keep track of formatting
> ☐ Mark formatting inconsistencies

Figure 3-21: **Choose the paper size from a selection of popular sizes in the Page Layout tab.**

Size	Line Numbers

Letter (8 ½ x 11 in)
8.5" x 11"

Legal (8 ½ x 14 in)
8.5" x 14"

Executive (7 ¼ x 10 ½ in)
7.25" x 10.5"

A4 (21 x 29.7 cm)
8.27" x 11.69"

A5 (14.8 x 21 cm)
5.83" x 8.27"

B5 (18.2 x 25.7 cm)
7.17" x 10.12"

Size 10 Envelope
4.12" x 9.5"

C3 Envelope
4.49" x 6.38"

DL Envelope
4.33" x 8.66"

More P<u>a</u>per Sizes...

Set Vertical Alignment

Just as you can right-align, center, left-align, and justify text between margins (see "Set Paragraph Alignment"), you can also specify vertical alignment so that text is aligned with the top, bottom, or center of the page or justified between the top and bottom.

1. In the Page Layout tab, click the **Page Setup Dialog Box Launcher**. The Page Setup dialog box appears.

2. In the Layout tab, under Page, click the **Vertical Alignment** down arrow, and click the vertical alignment that you want to use.

3. Click **OK** when you are done.

UNDERSTANDING THEMES, STYLES, AND TEMPLATES

Word 2007 has changed the way you apply formatting to documents. You can now quickly and easily make your documents look professional and consistent by using canned themes, styles, and templates. A *theme* changes the background, layout, color, fonts, and effects used in a document. Themes can be similar throughout most of the Office suite, so if you choose a theme in Word, you likely will be able to apply that theme to Excel or PowerPoint documents as well. Every document has a theme.

A *style* applies a specific set of formatting characteristics to individual characters or to entire paragraphs within the theme. For example, you can apply styles to headings, titles, lists, and other text components. Consequently, styles determine how the overall design comes together in its look and feel. Styles are beneficial to document creation, because they provide a consistent look and feel to all text selected for formatting. Every theme has a certain set of styles assigned to it. You can change styles within a theme and change themes within a document.

A *template* contains a theme, with its unique style of formatting, and is used to set up a document for the first time. You open a template file, save it as a document file, and then enter your own contents into it. In this way, you can standardize the look of all documents that are based on a given template.

Use Styles

Word 2007 provides a gallery of Quick Styles that provides you with sets of canned formatting choices, such as font, bold, color that you can apply to headings, titles, text, and lists. You use Quick Styles by identifying what kind of formatting a selected segment of text needs, such as for a header or title. Then you select the style of formatting you want to apply to the document. You can easily apply Quick Styles, change them, and create new ones.

Identify Text with a Style

To identify a segment of text within your document with a consistent style, such as for a heading, you apply a Quick Styles from the gallery.

1. Select the text to be formatted, for example, a title or heading.
2. Click the **Home** tab, and click the **Styles More** down arrow in the Styles group. The Quick Styles gallery is displayed, as shown in Figure 4-1.
3. Point at the thumbnails to see the effects of each style on your text, and the click the thumbnail of the style you want to apply.

Apply Style Sets to a Document

Before you begin entering text, or after you have identified the components in your document, you can apply a consistent set of color, styles, and fonts to your document using the Change Styles function.

1. Open the document that you want to contain a style set. It can be either a blank document or one that has already had the components identified, such as title, headings, and lists.
2. Click the **Home** tab, click **Change Styles** in the Styles group, and click **Style Set**. A menu is displayed.
3. Click the style you want. The document will be changed. However, if you have components that are not identified with the Quick Styles, such as headings, they will not receive the formatting properly.

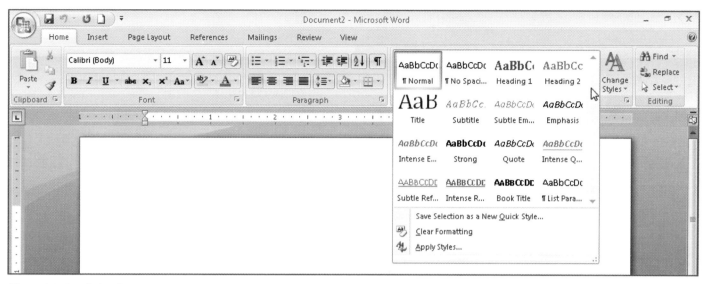

Figure 4-1: *The Quick Styles gallery shows you canned options for formatting headings, text, and paragraphs.*

TIP

If you do not find the style you want in the Quick Styles gallery for a segment of text, press **CTRL+SHIFT+S** to display the Apply Styles dialog box. Click the **Style Name** down arrow to find the style you want.

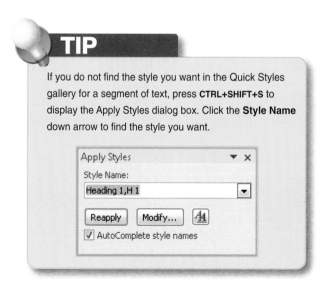

Save a New Quick Style

To create a new Quick Style option that will appear in the Quick Style gallery:

1. Format the text using the mini formatting toolbar or the commands in the Home tab Font group.

2. Right-click the selected text, click **Styles**, and click **Save Selection As A New Quick Style**. The Create New Style From Formatting dialog box appears.

3. Type the name you want for the style, and click **OK**. It will appear in the Quick Styles gallery.

Modify a Style

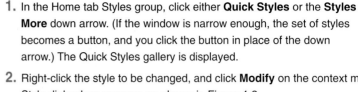

1. In the Home tab Styles group, click either **Quick Styles** or the **Styles More** down arrow. (If the window is narrow enough, the set of styles becomes a button, and you click the button in place of the down arrow.) The Quick Styles gallery is displayed.

2. Right-click the style to be changed, and click **Modify** on the context menu. The Modify Style dialog box appears, as shown in Figure 4-2.

–Or–

Click **Apply Styles** from the bottom of the gallery. The Apply Styles dialog box appears. Click the **Style Name** down arrow, and click the name of the style you wish to change. Click **Modify**, and the Modify Style dialog box appears.

Figure 4-2: You can change a style by modifying it in the Modify Style dialog box.

UICKSTEPS

DELETING A STYLE

You might choose to delete a style that you created for a one-time-use document and don't ever plan to use again. You can delete a style from the gallery or from the document being used.

DELETE/RESTORE A STYLE FROM THE GALLERY

To delete a style just from the gallery:

1. In the Home tab Styles group, click **Quick Styles** or the **Styles More** down arrow to display the Quick Styles gallery.

2. Right-click the style you want to delete, and click **Remove From Quick Style Gallery**.

The style will be removed from the Quick Style gallery. However, this does not mean that the style is gone; it is still in the list of styles.

Continued . . .

3. Change any formatting options you want.

4. To display more options, click **Format** in the lower-left area, and then click the attribute—for example, **Font** or **Numbering**—that you want to modify. Click **OK**.

5. Repeat step 4 for any additional attributes you want to change, clicking **OK** each time you are finished.

6. Type a new name for the style, if desired, unless you want to change existing formatted text.

7. Click **OK** to close the Modify Styles dialog box.

Automatically Update a Style

Sometimes, you may make changes to a style and want to have those changes automatically updated within a document.

1. Follow the steps in "Modify a Style" to display the Modify Style dialog box.

2. After making the changes you want, click the **Automatically Update** check box. Word will automatically redefine the style you selected whenever you apply manual formatting.

☑ Automatically update

Use Themes

One way that you can make a document look professional is by using themes. Themes combine coordinated colors, fonts (for body text and headings), and design effects (such as special effect uses for lines and fill effects) to produce a unique look. You can use the same themes with PowerPoint and Excel as well, thereby standardizing a look. All documents have themes; one is assigned to a new document by default.

ASSIGN A THEME TO YOUR DOCUMENT

To apply a theme to a document:

1. Click the **Page Layout** tab. Click **Themes** in the Themes group to display a gallery of themes, as seen in Figure 4-3.

2. Click the theme you want, and it will be applied to the current document.

DELETING A STYLE *(Continued)*

To restore the style to the gallery:

1. In the Home tab Styles group, click the **Styles Dialog Box Launcher**. The Styles task pane is displayed.

2. Right-click the style that you want to restore, and click **Add To Quick Style Gallery**.

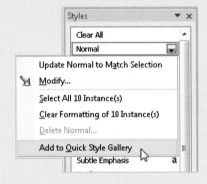

DELETE A STYLE FROM A DOCUMENT

To completely delete a style from a document:

1. In the Home tab Styles group, click the **Styles Dialog Box Launcher**. The Styles task pane is displayed.

2. Right-click the style to be deleted, and click **Delete** *stylename* from the context menu. A dialog box appears.

3. Click **Yes** to confirm that you want to delete the style.

Some styles cannot be deleted; the command to delete them will be unavailable or grayed out, such as with the Normal or Heading style. If you delete a style from the document, any text formatted with that style will be reformatted with the Normal style.

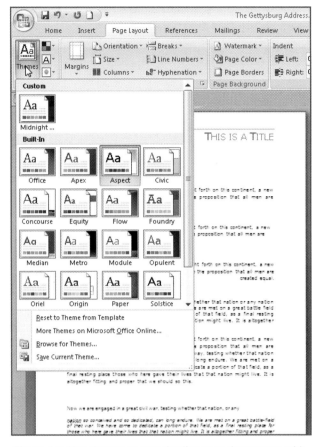

Figure 4-3: Use themes to standardize your documents with other Office products, such as PowerPoint and Excel.

Change a Theme

Themes can be changed to fit your own document requirements. You can then change a theme by altering the fonts, color, and design effects.

CHANGE THE COLOR OF A THEME

Each theme consists of a set of four colors for text and background, six colors for accents, and two colors for hyperlinks. You can change any single color element

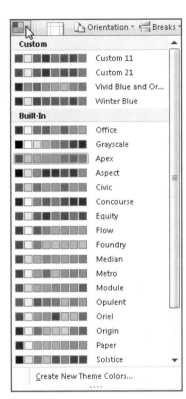

Figure 4-4: The menu of color combinations offers alternatives for your theme colors.

TIP

You may have to drag your text to the right or left to see the effects of the fonts as you pass your pointer over them.

or all of them. When you change the colors, the font styles and design elements remain the same.

1. With your document open, click the **Page Layout** tab.

2. Click **Theme Colors**. The menu of color combinations will be displayed, as seen in Figure 4-4.

3. Point at the rows of color combinations to see which ones appeal to you.

4. When you find the one you want, click it.

CHANGE THEME FONTS

Each theme includes two fonts: the *body* font is used for general text entry, and a *heading* font is used for headings. The default fonts used in Word for a new document are Calibri for body text and Cambria for headings. After you have assigned a theme to a document, the fonts may be different, and they can be changed.

1. In the Page Layout tab Themes group, click **Theme Fonts**. The drop-down list displays various theme fonts. The current theme font combination is highlighted in its place in the list.

2. Point to each font combination to see how the fonts will appear in your document.

3. Click the font name combination you decide upon. When you click a font name combination, the fonts will replace both the body and heading fonts in your document on one or selected pages.

CREATE A NEW THEME FONT SET

You may also decide that you want a unique set of fonts for your document. You can create a custom font set that is available in the list of fonts for your current and future documents.

1. In the Page Layout tab Themes group, click **Theme Fonts**.

2. Click **Create New Theme Fonts** at the bottom of the drop-down list.

3. In the Create New Theme Fonts dialog box (see Figure 4-5), click either or both the **Heading Font** and **Body Font** down arrows to select a new font combination. View the new combination in the Sample area.

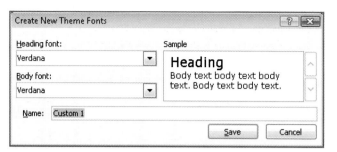

Figure 4-5: You can choose a heading or body font from the fonts available in your Office program.

4. Type a new name for the font combination you've selected, and click **Save**. Custom fonts are available for selection at the top of the Theme Fonts drop-down list.

CHANGE THEMED GRAPHIC EFFECTS

Shapes, illustrations, pictures, and charts include graphic effects that are controlled by themes. Themed graphics are modulated in terms of their lines (borders), fills, and effects (such as shadowed, raised, and shaded). For example, some themes simply change an inserted rectangle's fill color, while other themes affect the color, the weight of the border, and whether it has a 3-D appearance.

1. In the Page Layout tab Themes group, click **Theme Effects**. The drop-down list displays a gallery of effects combinations. The current effects combination is highlighted.

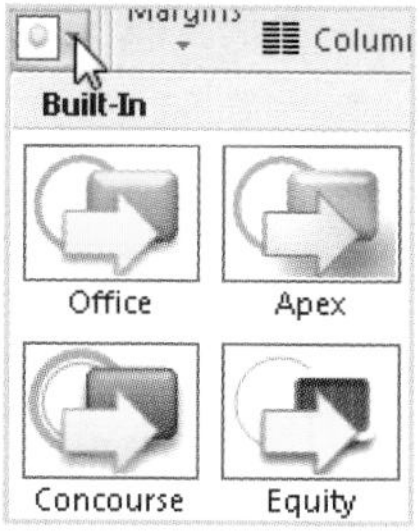

2. Point to each combination to see how the effects will appear in your document, assuming you have a graphic or chart inserted on the document page (see Chapters 7 and 8 for information on inserting tables, charts, graphics, and drawings).

3. Click the effects combination you want.

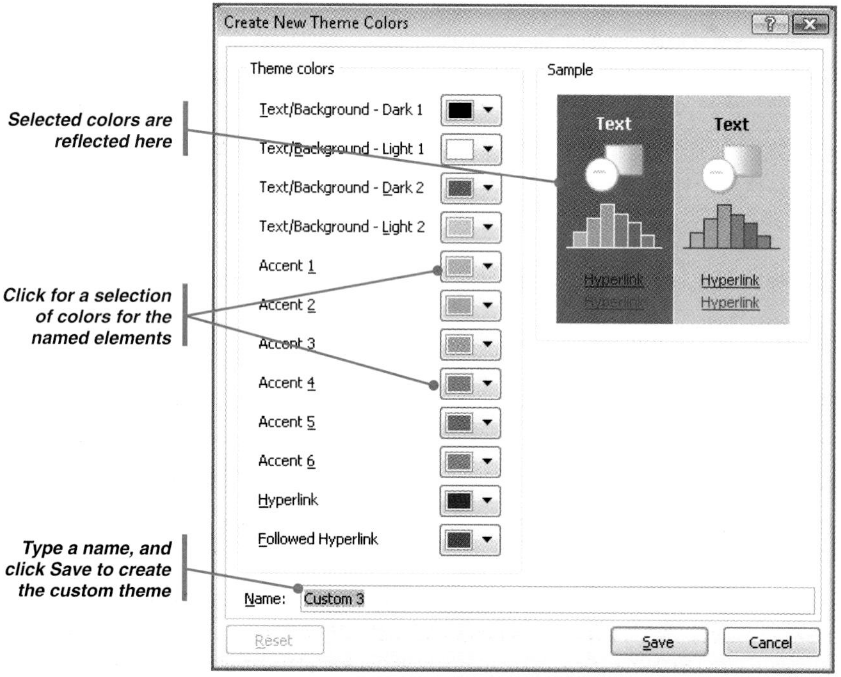

Create a Custom Theme

You can create a new theme, save it, and use it in your documents. You select a group of text, background, accent, and hyperlink colors, and then give them a collective name.

1. In the Page Layout tab Themes group, click **Theme Colors**.

2. At the bottom of the menu of colors, click the **Create New Theme Colors** link. The Create New Theme Colors dialog box appears, as shown in Figure 4-6.

Selected colors are reflected here

Click for a selection of colors for the named elements

Type a name, and click Save to create the custom theme

Figure 4-6: The Create New Theme Colors dialog box allows you to create a new theme to use with multiple documents.

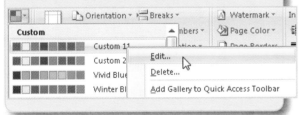

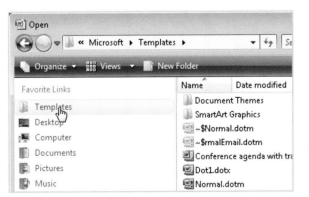

3. To select a color for one of the color groups, click the text/background/accent/ hyperlink down-arrow and click the color you want to test. It will be displayed in the Sample area.

4. Go through each set of colors that you want to change.

5. When you find a group of colors that you like, type a name in the **Name** text box, and click **Save**.

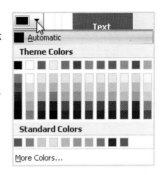

Use Templates

A *template* is a collection of styles, associated formatting and design features, and colors used to determine the overall appearance of a document. A Word 2007 template file has an extension of .dotx. Templates are used to create new document or to change the look of existing ones.

Create and Change Templates

Word 2007 comes with several templates that you can use to create letters, faxes, memos, and more. In addition, as you saw earlier, the Microsoft Office Web site has online templates that you can make use of. You can also create your own templates.

CHANGE THE DEFAULT NORMAL TEMPLATE

The *Normal* template is the default template used by Word unless you tell it otherwise. It, like all templates, includes default styles, AutoText, and other customizations that determine the general look of your document. You can customize the Normal template to include the styles you want to use on a regular basis. To change the default styles of the Normal template:

1. With a Word document open, click the **Office Button**, click **Open**, and then click **Templates** under Favorite Links.

2. If no templates are listed in the Open dialog box, click the **Files Of Type** down arrow (immediately above the Cancel button), and click **All Files (*.*)**. If you still do not see Normal.dotm (indicating a macro-enabled template), right-click **Computer**, click **Search**, type normal.dotm in the Search field, and click **Go**.

CAUTION

Keep in mind that any changes you make to the Normal template will be applied to any future documents you create, unless you specifically apply a different template.

NOTE

If the Normal.dotm template is renamed, damaged, or moved, Word automatically creates a new version (with the original default settings) the next time you start it. The new version will not include any changes or modifications you made to the version that you renamed or moved.

NOTE

You can also create a new template based on a previously created document.

TIP

If you want to create a template based on a different type of document—for example, a Web page or an e-mail message—select the relevant template instead of the Blank Document template in the Templates Or Microsoft Office Online list.

3. Click **Normal.dotm** and click **Open** to open it. Ensure that you're working in the template by verifying that that "Normal.dotm" appears in the Word title bar.

4. Change the template by changing the styles using the steps described in "Modify a Style" earlier in this chapter.

5. When you are finished making the changes that you want, click the **Office Button**, and click **Save** to resave Normal.dotm.

CREATE A TEMPLATE

1. With Word open, click the **Office Button**, and click **New**. The New Document dialog box appears, as shown in Figure 4-7.

2. Under Templates, click **Blank And Recent** to display a blank document template and the templates that you most recently used. Click the **Blank Document** thumbnail.

3. Click **Create**. A new document opens.

4. Save the document as a new template file and with a new name.

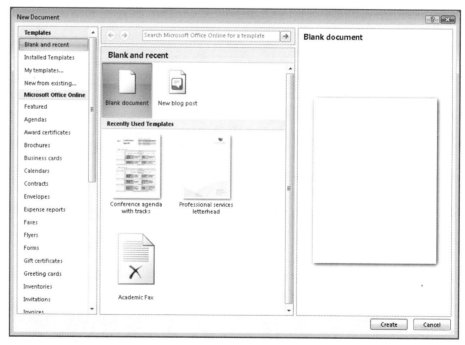

Figure 4-7: Word comes with several templates you can use to create letters, faxes, and more.

APPLY A TEMPLATE TO A NEW DOCUMENT

1. Click the **Office Button**, and click **New** to open the New Document task pane.

2. Under Templates, scroll down to review the list of templates that are installed on your computer and available online.

3. Click the template you want to use, and click **OK**.

Work with Documents

In addition to using styles and templates to format your documents, you can use section breaks, columns, tabs, headers and footers, tables of contents, and indexes to further refine your documents.

Create Section Breaks

A *section break* indicates the end of a section in a document. You can use section breaks to vary the layout of a document within a page or between pages. For example, you might choose to format the introduction of a magazine article in a single column and format the body of the article in two columns. You must separately format each section, but the section break allows them to be different. Section breaks allow you to change the number of columns, page headers and footers, page numbering, page borders, page margins, and other characteristics and formatting within a section.

INSERT A SECTION BREAK

1. Open the document and click where you want to insert a section break.

2. Click the **Page Layout** tab, and click **Breaks** in the Page Setup group. The Breaks context menu appears.

3. To create a new section, in the Section Break Types area, select what comes after the break. You have the following options:

- Click **Next Page** to begin a new section on the next page.

- Click **Continuous** to begin a new section on the same page.

- Click **Even Page** to start the new section on the next even-numbered page.

- Click **Odd Page** to start the new section on the next odd-numbered page.

··Section Break (Continuous)··

··Section Break (Even Page)··

4. When you click the option you want, the section break is inserted. If the Show/Hide Formatting feature is turned on (in the Home tab Paragraph group), you'll be able to see the section breaks in the text.

DELETE A SECTION BREAK

When a section break is inserted on a page, you will see a note to that effect if the Show/Hide Formatting feature is turned on. You can delete the break by selecting that note.

1. Click the section break that you want to delete.

2. Press **DELETE**.

Create and Use Columns

You can format your documents in a single column or in two or more columns, like text found in newspapers or magazines. You must first create either a continuous or a page break, not a column break, before you create the columns in order to prevent columns from forming in the previous section. To create columns in a document:

1. Place the insertion point at the place where you want the columns to begin. On the Page Layout tab, click **Breaks** in the Page Setup group and click **Continuous**.

2. Click the **Page Layout** tab, and click **Columns** in the Page Setup group to display a context menu.

3. Click the thumbnail option that corresponds to the number or type of columns you want.

   –Or–

   If you do not see what you want, click **More Columns** to display the Columns dialog box (see Figure 4-8):

   ● Click a thumbnail in the Presets area, or type a number in the Number Of Columns box to set the number of columns you want.

   ● Use the options in the Width And Spacing area to manually determine the dimensions of your columns and the amount of space between columns. To do this, you will have to clear the **Equal Column Width** check box. (You may have to click a thumbnail option to make it available first.)

Figure 4-8: *Use the Columns dialog box to create and format columns in your documents.*

TIP

The Preview area in the Columns dialog box displays the effects of your changes as you change the various column settings.

TIP

To see tabs, the ruler needs to appear on the screen. If you do not see the ruler, click the **View** tab, and click **Ruler** in the Show/Hide group.

- Click the **Line Between** check box if you want Word to insert a vertical line between columns.
- Use the **Apply To** list box to select the part of the document to which you want your selections to apply: Whole Document, This Section, or This Point Forward. Click **This Point Forward**, and then click the **Start New Column** check box if you want to insert a column break at an insertion point.

4. Click **OK** when finished.

Use Tabs

A *tab* is a type of formatting usually used to align text and create simple tables. By default, Word 2007 has *tab stops* (the horizontal positioning of the insertion point when you press TAB) every half-inch. Tabs are better than space characters in such instances, because tabs are set to specific measurements, while spaces may not always align the way you intend due to the size and spacing of individual characters in a given font. Word 2007 supports five kinds of tabs:

- **Left tab** left-aligns text at the tab stop.
- **Center tab** centers text at the tab stop.
- **Right tab** right-aligns text at the tab stop.
- **Decimal tab** aligns the decimal point of tabbed numbers at the tab stop.
- **Bar tab** left-aligns text with a vertical line that is displayed at the tab stop.

To align text with a tab, press the TAB key before the text you want aligned.

SET TABS USING THE RULER

To set tabs using the ruler at the top of a page:

1. Select the text, from one line to an entire document, in which you want to set one or more tab stops.

2. Click the **Left Tab** icon ⬜ located at the far left of the horizontal ruler until it changes to the type of tab you want: Left Tab, Center Tab ⬜, Right Tab ⬜, Decimal Tab ⬜, or Bar Tab ⬜.

3. Click the horizontal ruler where you want to set a tab stop.

4. Once you have the tabs set:

- Drag a tab off the ruler to get rid of it.
- Drag a tab to another spot on the ruler to change its position.
- Click the **First Line Indent** ![icon], and then click the top of the ruler line to insert the first line of the paragraph where you want it to start.
- Click the **Hanging Indent** ![icon], and then click the bottom of the ruler to insert a hanging indent for the rest of the lines in a paragraph.

SET TABS USING MEASUREMENTS

To set tabs according to specific measurements:

1. Double-click a tab, and the Tabs dialog box will appear, as shown in Figure 4-9.
2. Enter the measurements you want in the Tab Stop Position text box.
3. Click the tab alignment option you want. Click **Set**.
4. Repeat steps 2 and 3 for as many tabs as you want to set. Click **OK** to close the dialog box.

SET TABS WITH LEADERS

You can also set tabs with *tab leaders*—characters that fill the space otherwise left by a tab—for example, a solid, dotted, or dashed line.

1. Double-click any tab, and the Tabs dialog box appears, as shown in Figure 4-9.
2. In the Tab Stop Position text box, type the position for a new tab or select an existing tab stop to which you want to add a tab leader.
3. In the Alignment area, select the alignment for text typed at the tab stop.
4. In the Leader area, select the leader option you want, and then click **Set**.
5. Repeat steps 2–4 for additional tabs. When you are done, click **OK** to close the dialog box.

Add Headers and Footers

Headers and footers are parts of a document that contain information such as page numbers, revision dates, the document title, and so on. The header appears at the top of every page, and the footer appears at the bottom of every page. Figure 4-10 shows the buttons available on the Design tab of the Header And Footer Tools.

TIP

When working with tabs, it's a good idea to display text formatting so that you can distinguish tabs from spaces. To display formatting, click the **Show/Hide** button in the Home tab Paragraph group.

Figure 4-9: From the Tabs dialog box, you can format specific tab measurements and set tab leaders.

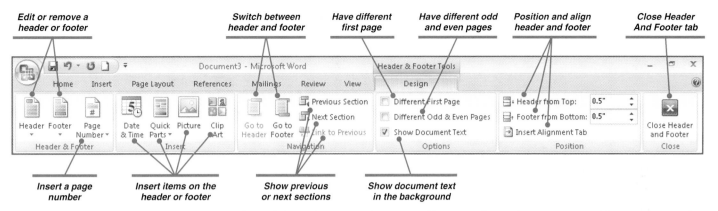

Edit or remove a header or footer

Switch between header and footer

Have different first page

Have different odd and even pages

Position and align header and footer

Close Header And Footer tab

Insert a page number

Insert items on the header or footer

Show previous or next sections

Show document text in the background

Figure 4-10: Headers and footers provide consistent information across the tops and bottoms of your document pages. These areas can also have unique tabs and other formatting.

CREATE A HEADER OR FOOTER

1. Open the document to which you want to add a header or footer (see Chapter 2).

2. Click the **Insert** tab, and click **Header** or **Footer** in the Header & Footer group. The header or footer area will be displayed along with the special contextual Header & Footer Design tab.

–Or–

Double-click in the top area of the document where a header would be, if it is visible. Or, first double-click the page break line, and then double-click the header or footer area. (If the page break and header area are hidden, you can't use the double-click method.)

3. Type the text you want displayed in the header:

- To switch between typing text in the header and typing it in the footer, click the **Go To Header** or **Go To Footer** buttons in the Navigation group, and type the text you want.

- Click **Date And Time** in the Insert group to insert a date or time.

- To insert a page number, click **Page Number** in the Header & Footer group, click a location in the drop-down menu, scroll down, choose a format, and then click **OK**.

NOTE

When you edit a header or footer, Word automatically changes the same header or footer throughout the document, unless the document contains different headers or footers in different sections. When you delete a header or footer, Word automatically deletes the same header or footer throughout the entire document. To delete a header or footer for part of a document, you must first divide the document into sections, and then create a different header or footer for part of a document. (See "Create Section Breaks" earlier in this chapter for more information.)

USING DIFFERENT LEFT AND RIGHT HEADERS

Different left and right pages use section breaks to allow different margins and tabs. Sometimes, you might want to create a document that has different left and right headers and/or footers. For example, you might have a brochure, pamphlet, or manuscript in which all odd-numbered pages have a title in the header and all even-numbered pages have the author's name or other information.

To create different left and right headers and/or footers:

1. Open the document to which you want to add a different left and right header or footer (see Chapter 2).

Continued . . .

- To enter a date that is left-aligned, a title that is centered, and a page number that is right-aligned, type the date, press **TAB**, type the title, press **TAB**, and type the page number.

- To go to the next or last section to enter a different header or footer, click **Previous Section** or **Next Section** in the Navigation group.

4. When finished, double-click in the document area or click the **Close Header And Footer** button.

EDIT A HEADER OR FOOTER

1. Open the document to which you want to add a header or footer (see Chapter 2).

2. Double-click the header or footer area, if it is visible. Or, first double-click the page break line, and then double-click the header or footer area to display the header and footer along with the Header And Footer Tools Design tab, as shown in Figure 4-10.

3. If necessary, click the **Previous Section** or **Next Section** button in the Navigation group to display the header or footer you want to edit.

4. Edit the header or footer. For example, you might revise text, change the font, apply bold formatting, or add a date or time.

5. When finished, double-click in the document area or click the **Close Header And Footer** button in the Close group.

DELETE A HEADER OR FOOTER

1. Open the document from which you want to delete a header or footer (see Chapter 2).

2. Double-click the header or footer area of the document, if it is visible. Or, first double-click the page break line, and then double-click the header or footer area. The header or footer area will be displayed along with the Header And Footer Tools Design tab.

3. If necessary, click **Previous Section** or **Next Section** in the Navigation group to move to the header or footer you want to delete.

4. Select the text or graphics you want to delete, and press **DELETE**.

–Or–

Click **Header** or **Footer** in the Header & Footer group, and click **Remove Header** or **Remove Footer**.

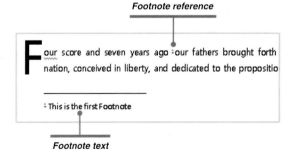

QUICKSTEPS

USING DIFFERENT LEFT AND RIGHT HEADERS *(Continued)*

2. Double-click in the header area, if it is visible. Or, first double-click the page break line, and then double-click the header or footer area; or click the **Insert** tab, click **Header**, and click **Edit Header**. The header area will be displayed, along with the special contextual Header & Footer Design tab.

3. In the Options group, click **Different First Page** to enter a separate title or no title for the first page. Create a different first page in the First Page Header area, create the normal header in the Header area of the second page, and so on.

4. Click the **Different Odd And Even Pages** check box to have a different heading on the odd- and even-numbered pages. For instance, perhaps your page number is on the left for even-numbered pages and on the right for odd-numbered pages. Create the header or footer for odd-numbered pages in the Odd Page Header or Odd Page Footer area, and create the header or footer for even-numbered pages in the Even Page Header or Even Page Footer area.

5. When finished, double-click in the document area or click the **Close Header And Footer** button in the Close group.

Add Footnotes and Endnotes

Footnotes and *endnotes* are types of annotations in a document usually used to provide citation information or to provide additional information for readers. The difference between the two is where they appear in a document. Footnotes appear either after the last line of text on the page or at the bottom of the page on which the annotated text appears. Endnotes appear either at the end of the section in which the annotated text appears or at the end of the document.

INSERT A FOOTNOTE OR ENDNOTE

1. To display the Print Layout view, click the **View** tab, and then click **Print Layout** in the Document View group.

2. In the Print Layout view, position the insertion point immediately after the text you want to annotate.

3. Click the **References** tab, and then click **Insert Footnote** or **Insert Endnote** in the Footnotes group. For a footnote, the insertion point will be positioned at the bottom of the page; for an endnote, it will be positioned at the end of the document.

4. Type the text of the endnote or footnote.

Footnote reference

F our score and seven years ago our fathers brought forth nation, conceived in liberty, and dedicated to the propositio

: This is the first Footnote

Footnote text

5. To return to the text where the footnote reference was placed, right-click the footnote and click **Go To Footnote** or **Go To Endnote**.

Figure 4-11: Footnotes and endnotes provide supplemental information to the body of your document. Use the dialog box to control location and formatting.

TIP

Sometimes it is easier to see a footnote or endnote than the text to which it refers. To quickly find the text in the document that a footnote or endnote refers to, right-click the footnote or endnote, and click **Go To Footnote** or **Go To Endnote**. The pointer will be positioned at that location in the text.

NOTE

When deleting an endnote or footnote, make sure to delete the number corresponding to the annotation and not the actual text in the note. If you delete the text but not the number, the placeholder for the annotation will remain.

CHANGE FOOTNOTES OR ENDNOTES

If you want to change the numbers or formatting of footnotes or endnotes, or if you want to add a symbol to the reference, use the Footnote And Endnote dialog box.

1. On the References tab, click the **Footnote & Endnote Dialog Box Launcher** in the Footnotes group. The Footnote And Endnote dialog box appears (see Figure 4-11).

2. You have these options:
   - In the Location box, click the **Footnotes** or **Endnotes** option, and click the down arrow to the right to choose where the footnote or endnote will be placed.
   - Click the **Number Format** down arrow, and select the type of numbering you want from the drop-down list.
   - To select a custom mark (a character that uniquely identifies a footnote or endnote), click the **Symbol** button, and select and insert the symbol you want. It will be displayed in the Custom Mark text box. You can also just type in a character into the text box.
   - Click the **Numbering** down arrow, and choose how the numbering is to start.
   - Click the **Apply Changes To** down arrow to select the part of the document that will contain the changes.

3. Click **Insert**. Word makes the changes as noted.

4. Type the note text.

5. When finished, return the insertion point to the body of your document, and continue typing.

DELETE A FOOTNOTE OR ENDNOTE

In the document, select the number of the note you want to delete, and then press **DELETE**. Word automatically deletes the footnote or endnote and renumbers the notes.

CONVERT FOOTNOTES TO ENDNOTES OR ENDNOTES TO FOOTNOTES

1. Select the reference number or symbol in the body of a document for the footnote or endnote.

2. Click the **References** tab, and click the **Footnotes Dialog Box Launcher**. The Footnote And Endnote dialog box appears.

3. Click **Convert**. The Convert Notes dialog box appears.

4. Select the option you want, and then click **OK**.

5. Click **Close**.

Create an Index

An *index* is an alphabetical list of words or phrases in a document and the corresponding page references. Indexes created using Word can include main entries and subentries as well as cross-references. When creating an index in Word, you first need to tag the index entries and then generate the index.

TAG INDEX ENTRIES

1. In the document in which you want to build an index, select the word or phrase that you want to use as an index entry. If you want an index entry to use text that you separately enter instead of using existing text in the document, place the insertion point in the document where you want your new index entry to reference.

2. Click the **References** tab, and click **Mark Entry** in the Index group (you can also press **ALT+SHIFT+X**). The Mark Index Entry dialog box appears (see Figure 4-12).

3. Type or edit the text in the Main Entry box. Customize the entry by creating a subentry or by creating a cross-reference to another entry, if desired.

4. Click the **Bold** or **Italic** check box in the Page Number Format area to determine how the page numbers will appear in the index.

5. Click **Mark**. To mark all occurrences of this text in the document, click **Mark All**.

6. Repeat steps 3–5 to mark additional index entries on the same page.

7. Click **Close** to close the dialog box when finished.

8. Repeat steps 1–7 for the remaining entries in the document.

GENERATE AN INDEX

1. Position the insertion point where you want to insert the finished index (this will normally be at the end of the document).

2. Click the **References** tab, and click **Insert Index** in the Index group. The Index dialog box appears (see Figure 4-13).

3. In the Index tab of the Index dialog box, set the formatting for the index. You have these options:

   - Click the **Type** option to indent subentries beneath and indented, or click **Run-In** to print subentries beside the upper-level category.

Figure 4-12: You need to tag index entries before you can generate an index.

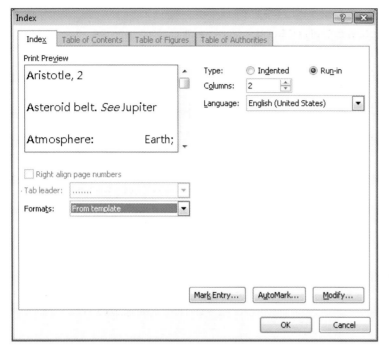

Figure 4-13: *Use the options and settings in the Index dialog box to determine how your index will look.*

- Click the **Columns** spinner to set the number of columns in the index page.
- Click the **Language** down arrow to set the language for the index.
- Click **Right Align Page Numbers** to right-align the numbers.
- Click **Tab Leader** to print a leader between the entry and the page number.
- Click the **Formats** down arrow to use an available design template, such as Classic or Fancy.

4. Click **OK** when finished. Word generates the index.

Create a Table of Contents

A *table of contents* is a list of the headings in the order in which they appear in the document. If you have formatted paragraphs with heading styles, you can automatically generate a table of contents based on those headings. If you have not used the heading styles, then, as with indexes, you must first tag table of contents (or TOC) entries and then generate the table of contents. (See "Use Styles" earlier in this chapter.)

TAG ENTRIES FOR THE TABLE OF CONTENTS

Use the Quick Style gallery to identify a segment of text within your document so that it can contain a consistent style for headings and other text that you want contained in a table of contents.

1. Select the text to be formatted, for example, a title or heading.
2. Click the **Home** tab, and click the **Styles More** down arrow in the Styles group.
3. Point at each thumbnail to determine which style it represents, and then click the thumbnail of the style you want to apply.

PLACE OTHER TEXT IN A TABLE OF CONTENTS

To add text other than identified headings in a table of contents:

1. Highlight the text or phrase to be shown in the table of contents.
2. Click the **References** tab, and click **Add Text** in the Table Of Contents group. A menu is displayed.

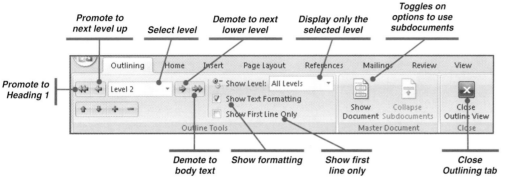

3. Click the option you want. You have these choices:

- **Do Not Show In Table Of Contents** removes the identification that something should be included in the TOC.

- **Level 1**, **Level 2**, or **Level 3** assigns selected text to a level similar to Heading 1 Heading 2, or Heading 3.

USE THE OUTLINING TAB FOR THE TABLE OF CONTENTS

The outlining tab contains an easy way to tag or identify entries for the table of contents.

Promote to next level up

Select level

Demote to next lower level

Display only the selected level

Toggles on options to use subdocuments

Promote to Heading 1

Demote to body text

Show formatting

Show first line only

Close Outlining tab

1. Click the **View** tab, and click **Outline** in the Document Views group. An Outlining tab will become available. Figure 4-14 shows the Outlining tab. Within the Outlining tab, Figure 4-15 shows the Master Document group from which you can insert and manipulate subdocuments.

2. Click the right or left arrows to promote or demote the levels, respectively.

Figure 4-14: Use the Outlining tab to mark entries for a table of contents. The Outlining toolbar provides a number of ways to work with outlines.

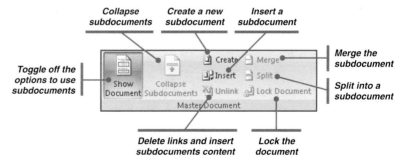

Collapse subdocuments

Create a new subdocument

Insert a subdocument

Toggle off the options to use subdocuments

Merge the subdocument

Split into a subdocument

Delete links and insert subdocuments content

Lock the document

Figure 4-15: The subdocument commands appear when Show Documents on the Outlining tab is clicked. These commands allows subdocuments to be inserted and manipulated.

TIP

You can also tag TOC entries by selecting the text that you want to include in your table of contents. Press **ALT+SHIFT+O**. The Mark Table Of Contents Entry dialog box appears. In the Level box, select the level and click **Mark**. If you have multiple tables of contents, you can identify to which TOC the current entry belongs by using the Table Identifier feature. To mark additional entries, select the text, click in the **Entry** box, and click **Mark**. When you have finished adding entries, close the dialog box.

TIP

It is a good idea to place a table of contents in its own section, where you can have separate formatting, margins, and page numbers. If you want to do this, create the section before creating the TOC. See "Create Section Breaks" earlier in this chapter.

GENERATE A TABLE OF CONTENTS

1. Place the insertion point where you want to insert the table of contents (normally at the beginning of the document).

2. Click the **References** tab, and click **Table Of Contents** in the Table Of Contents group. A menu is displayed.

3. Click **Insert Table Of Contents**. The Table of Contents dialog box, shown in Figure 4-16 is displayed.

4. The Print Preview and Web Preview features show how the TOC will appear based on the options selected. You have these options:

   - Clear the **Show Page Numbers** check box to suppress the display of page numbers.

   - Clear the **Right Align Page Numbers** check box to allow page numbers to follow the text immediately.

   - Clear the **Use Hyperlinks Instead Of Page Numbers** check box to use hyperlinks in place of page numbers.

   - Click the **Tab Leader** down arrow, and click **(None)** or another option for a leader between the text in the TOC and the page number.

   - Click the **Formats** down arrow to use one of the available designs.

   - Click the **Show Levels** down arrow, and click the lowest level of heading (or the highest number) you want to display in the TOC.

5. Click **OK** when finished.

Create and Use Outlines

An *outline* is a framework upon which a document is based. It is a hierarchical list of the headings in a document. You might use an outline to help you organize your ideas and thoughts when writing a speech, a term paper, a book, or a research project. The Outline tab in Word makes it easy to build and refine your outlines.

1. Open a new blank document (see Chapter 1). Click the **View** tab, and click **Outline** in the Document Views group. Word switches to the Outlining tab, displayed earlier in Figures 4-14 and 4-15.

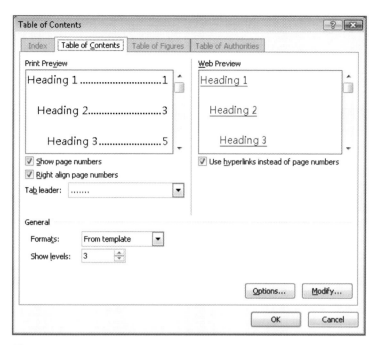

Figure 4-16: *Use the options and settings in the Table Of Contents dialog box to determine how your table of contents will look.*

USING VIEW BUTTONS

Word 2007 contains five views that you can use to display your document in different ways, as you can see in Figures 4-17 and 4-18:

- **Print Layout** is the default view in Word and shows text as you will see it when the document is printed.

Continued . . .

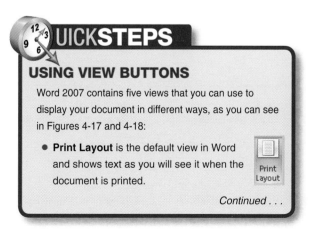

2. Type your heading text, and press **ENTER**. Word formats the headings using the built-in heading style Heading 1. Continue throughout the document. You have these ways of working with the levels:

- Assign a heading to a different level by selecting it from the Outline Level drop-down list box

  –Or–

  Place the insertion point in the heading, and then click the **Promote** or **Demote** button on the Outlining toolbar until the heading is at the level you want.

- To move a heading to a different location, place the insertion point in the heading, and then click the **Move Up** or **Move Down** button on the Outlining tab Outline Tools group until the heading is where you want it. (If a heading is collapsed, the subordinate text under the heading moves with it.)

3. When you're satisfied with the organization, click **Close Outline View**, which automatically switches to Print Layout view. (See the QuickSteps "Using View Buttons" for more information.)

Use Word Writing Aids

Word 2007 provides several aids that can assist you in not only creating your document, but also in making sure that it is as professional-looking as possible. These include AutoCorrect, AutoFormat, AutoText, AutoSummarize, an extensive equation-writing capability, character and word counts, highlighting, hyphenation, and a thesaurus.

Figure 4-17: *Click the View tab, and in the Documents Views group, click the view you want.*

USING VIEW BUTTONS *(Continued)*

- **Full Screen Reading** displays the document as a "book" with facing pages. You can "flip" through the pages rather than scroll through them. It uses the full screen in order to display as much of the document as possible. On the top is a restricted toolbar with limited options for using the document.

- **Web Layout view** displays a document in a larger font size and wraps to fit the window rather than the page margins.

- **Outline view** displays the document's framework as it has been laid out with headers identified, etc.

- **Draft** suppresses headings and footings and other design elements in order to display the text in draft form so that you can have an unobstructed view of the contents.

To display any of these views, click the **View** tab, and click the view you want in the Document Views group (Figure 4-17); or click the relevant button on the View toolbar on the right of the status bar (Figure 4-18).

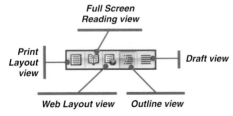

Figure 4-18: You can immediately switch to another view using the Views toolbar on the status bar.

Implement AutoCorrect

The AutoCorrect feature automatically corrects common typographical errors when you make them. While Word 2007 comes preconfigured with hundreds of AutoCorrect entries, you can also manually add entries.

CONFIGURE AUTOCORRECT

1. Click the **Office Button**, click **Word Options**, click **Proofing** in the left column, and click **AutoCorrect Options**. The AutoCorrect: *Language* dialog box appears.

2. Click the **AutoCorrect** tab (if it is not already displayed), and select from the following options, according to your preferences (see Figure 4-19):

   - **Show AutoCorrect Options buttons** displays a small blue button or bar beneath text that was automatically corrected. Click this button to see a menu, where you can undo the correction or set AutoCorrect options.

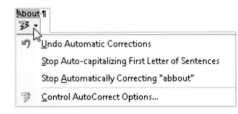

   - **Correct TWo INitial CApitals** changes the second letter in a pair of capital letters to lowercase.

   - **Capitalize First Letter Of Sentences** capitalizes the first letter following the end of a sentence.

   - **Capitalize First Letter Of Table Cells** capitalizes the first letter of a word in a table cell.

   - **Capitalize Names Of Days** capitalizes the names of the days of the week.

   - **Correct Accidental Usage Of cAPS LOCK Key** corrects capitalization errors that occur when you type with the **CAPS LOCK** key depressed and turns off this key.

   - **Replace Text As You Type** replaces typographical errors with the correct words as shown in the list beneath it.

   - **Automatically Use Suggestions From The Spelling Checker** tells Word to replace spelling errors with words from the dictionary as you type.

3. Click **OK** when finished.

ADD AN AUTOCORRECT ENTRY

1. Click the **Office Button**, click **Word Options**, click **Proofing** in the left column, and click **AutoCorrect Options**. The AutoCorrect: *Language* dialog box appears.

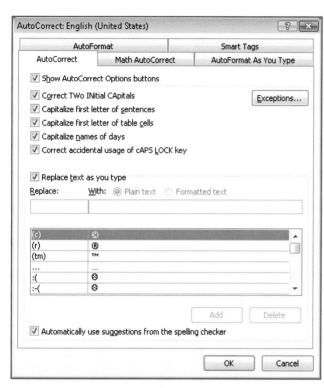

Figure 4-19: Use the AutoCorrect tab to determine what items Word will automatically correct for you as you type.

2. Click the **AutoCorrect** tab (if it is not already displayed).

3. Type the text that you want Word to automatically replace in the Replace box. Type the text that you want to replace it with in the With box.

4. Click **Add** and click **OK**.

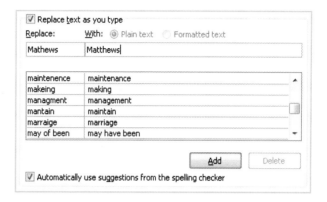

DELETE AN AUTOCORRECT ENTRY

1. Click the **Office Button**, click **Word Options**, click **Proofing** in the left column, and click **AutoCorrect Options**. The AutoCorrect: *Language* dialog box appears.

2. Click the **AutoCorrect** tab (if it is not already displayed).

3. Scroll through the list of AutoCorrect entries, and click the entry you want to delete.

4. Click **Delete** and click **OK**.

Use AutoFormat

AutoFormat automatically formats a document as you type it by applying the associated styles to text, depending on how it is used in the document. For example, Word will automatically format two dashes (--) into an em dash (—) or will automatically format Internet and e-mail addresses as hyperlinks.

To choose the formatting you want Word to apply as you type:

1. Click the **Office Button**, click **Word Options**, click **Proofing** in the left column, and click **AutoCorrect Options**. The AutoCorrect: *Language* dialog box appears. Click the **AutoFormat As You Type** tab.

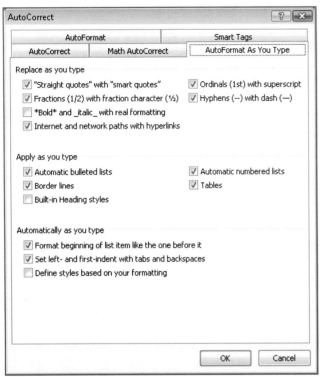

Figure 4-20: Use the AutoFormat As You Type tab to determine what items Word will automatically format for you as you type.

NOTE

The AutoFormat feature in Word 2003 that applied formatting to a document after it was written is not available in Word 2007. Also, the AutoFormat tab in the AutoCorrect dialog box does not do anything. The options have been replaced by the AutoFormat As You Type tab.

2. Select from among the following options, depending on your preferences (see Figure 4-20):

- **"Straight Quotes" With "Smart Quotes"** replaces plain quotation characters with curly quotation characters.

- **Ordinals (1st) With Superscript** formats ordinal numbers (numbers designating items in an ordered sequence) with a superscript. For example, 1st becomes 1st.

- **Fractions (1/2) With Fraction Character (½)** replaces fractions typed with numbers and slashes with fraction characters.

- **Hyphens (--) With Dash (—)** replaces a single hyphen with an en dash (–) and two hyphens with an em dash (—).

- ***Bold* And _Italic_ With Real Formatting** formats text enclosed within asterisks (*) as bold and text enclosed within underscores (_) as italic.

- **Internet And Network Paths With Hyperlinks** formats e-mail addresses and URLs (Uniform Resource Locator—the address of a Web page on the Internet or an intranet) as clickable hyperlink fields.

- **Automatic Bulleted Lists** applies bulleted list formatting to paragraphs beginning with *, o, or – followed by a space or tab character.

- **Automatic Numbered Lists** applies numbered list formatting to paragraphs beginning with a number or letter followed by a space or a tab character.

- **Border Lines** automatically applies paragraph border styles when you type three or more hyphens, underscores, or equal signs (=).

- **Tables** creates a table when you type a series of hyphens with plus signs to indicate column edges.

- **Built-In Heading Styles** applies heading styles to heading text.

- **Format Beginning Of List Item Like The One Before It** repeats character formatting that you apply to the beginning of a list item. For example, if you format the first word of a list item in bold, the first word of all subsequent list items are formatted in bold.

- **Set Left- And First-Indent With Tabs And Backspaces** sets left indentation on the tab ruler based on the tabs and backspaces you type.

- **Define Styles Based On Your Formatting** automatically creates or modifies styles based on manual formatting that you apply to your document.

3. Click **OK** when finished.

Use Building Blocks

Building blocks are blocks of text and formatting that you can use repeatedly, such as cover pages, a greeting, phrases, headings, or a closing. Word provides a number of these for you, but you can identify and save your own building blocks, and then use them in different documents.

CREATE A BUILDING BLOCK

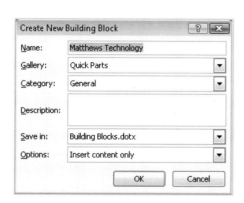

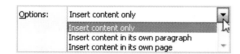

1. Select the text or graphic, along with its formatting, that you want to store as a building block. (Include the paragraph mark in the selection if you want to store paragraph formatting.)

2. Click the **Insert** tab, click **Quick Parts** [Quick Parts ▾] in the Text group, and then click **Save Selection To Quick Parts Gallery**.

3. The Create New Building Block dialog box appears. Accept the suggested name for the building block, or type a short abbreviation for a new one. For example, I changed this one to "mt" for Matthews Technology.

4. In most cases, you will accept the Quick Parts gallery, the General category, and the Building Blocks.dotx file name, since those provide for the easiest retrieval.

5. Click the **Options** down arrow, and, depending on what you are saving in your building block, click the option that is correct for you. If you want paragraph formatting, you must include the paragraph mark.

6. Click **OK**.

   –Or–

1. After selecting the text or graphic that you want as a building block, press **ALT+F3**. The Create New Building Block dialog box appears.

2. Follow steps 3–6 in the preceding procedure.

INSERT ONE OF YOUR BUILDING BLOCKS

1. Place the insertion point in the document where you want to insert the building block.

2. Click the **Insert** tab, click **Quick Parts** in the Text group, and then double-click the entry you want, as shown in Figure 4-21.

   –Or–

   At the point in the document where you want to insert the building block, type its name or the short abbreviation you entered in place of the name, and press **F3**. For example, if I type mt and press **F3**, "Matthews Technology" replaces "mt" in the text.

Figure 4-21: The Quick Parts feature provides direct access to your building block entries so that you can insert them in documents.

INSERT ONE OF WORD'S BUILDING BLOCKS

1. Place the insertion point in the document where you want to insert the building block.

2. Click the **Insert** tab, click **Quick Parts** in the Text group, and then click **Building Blocks Organizer**. The Building Blocks Organizer dialog box appears, as shown in Figure 4-22.

3. Scroll through the list of building blocks until you find the one that you want. Click the entry to see it previewed on the right. When you are ready, click **Insert**.

DELETE A BUILDING BLOCK

1. Click the **Insert** tab, click **Quick Parts** in the Text group, and then click **Building Blocks Organizer**. The Building Blocks Organizer dialog box appears.

2. Scroll through the list of building blocks until you find the one that you want. Click the entry to see it previewed on the right.

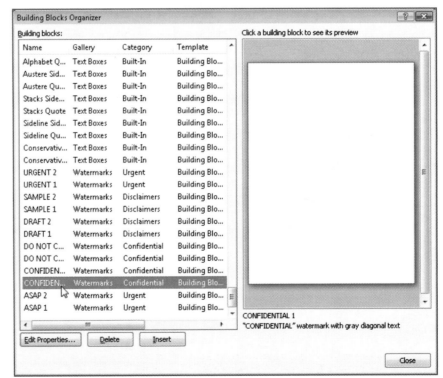

Figure 4-22: Word comes with a large number of building blocks that you can access.

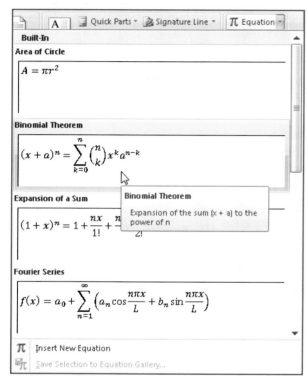

NOTE

You cannot undo the deletion of a building block. The only way to restore it is to re-create it.

3. When you are ready, click **Delete**, click **Yes** to confirm the deletion, and click **Close**.

4. When you are asked if you want to delete the selected building block, click **Yes**. The building block is deleted.

Enter an Equation

If you include mathematical equations in the documents you produce, Word has several helpful tools for producing them. These include ready-made equations, commonly used mathematical structures, a large standard symbol set, and many special mathematical symbols that can be generated with Math AutoCorrect. These tools allow you to create equations by modifying a ready-made equation, by using an equation text box with common mathematical structures and symbols, and by simply typing an equation as you would ordinary text.

MODIFY A READY-MADE EQUATION

1. Click at the location in the document where you want the equation.

2. Click the **Insert** tab, and click the **Equation** down arrow in the Symbols group. The list of built-in equations appears, as shown in Figure 4-23.

3. Click the equation you want to insert. An equation text box will appear, containing the equation, and the Equation Tools Design tab will display, as shown in Figure 4-24.

Figure 4-23: Word provides a number of ready-made equations for your use.

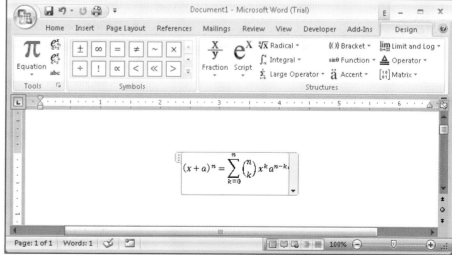

Figure 4-24: The equation text box automatically formats equations, which can be built with the structures and symbols in the Equation Tools Design tab.

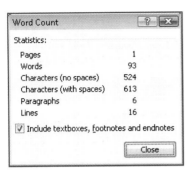

Figure 4-27: *The Word Count feature is a quick and easy way to view the specifics of your document.*

TIP

You can also apply highlighting by selecting the text first and then clicking **Highlight** in the Home tab Font group.

Highlighting·is·best·when·viewed·online.·When·it·is·printed,·the·highlighting·often·appears·gray·and·may·obscure·the·text·you·are·trying·to·call·attention·to.¶

Figure 4-28: *Highlighting is a great way to call attention to specific sections or phrases of your document.*

- Number of characters (including spaces)
- Number of paragraphs
- Number of lines

Use Highlighting

The Highlight feature is useful for marking important text in a document or text that you want to call a reader's attention to. Keep in mind, however, that highlighting parts of a document works best when the document is viewed online. When printed, the highlighting marks often appear gray and may even obscure the text you're trying to call attention to.

APPLY HIGHLIGHTING

1. In the Home tab Font group, click **Highlight** .
2. Select the text or graphic that you want to highlight. The highlighting is applied to your selection (see Figure 4-28.)
3. To turn off highlighting, click **Highlight** again or press **ESC**.

REMOVE HIGHLIGHTING

1. Select the text that you want to remove highlighting from, or press **CTRL+A** to select all of the text in the document.
2. In the Home tab Font group, click **Highlight**.

   –Or–

   In the Home tab Font group, click the **Highlight** drop-down arrow, and then click **No Color**.

CHANGE HIGHLIGHTING COLOR

In the Home tab Font group, click the **Highlight** drop-down arrow, and then click the color that you want to use.

FIND HIGHLIGHTED TEXT IN A DOCUMENT

1. In the Home tab, click **Find** in the Editing group.
2. If you don't see the Format button, click the **More** button.
3. Click the **Format** button, and then click **Highlight**.

4. Click **Find Next** and repeat this until you reach the end of the document.

5. Click **OK** when the message box is displayed indicating that Word has finished searching the document, and click **Close** in the Find And Replace dialog box.

Add Hyphenation

The Hyphenation feature automatically hyphenates words at the ends of lines based on standard hyphenation rules. You might use this feature if you want words to fit better on a line, or if you want to avoid uneven margins in right-aligned text or large gaps between words in justified text. (See Chapter 3 for information on text alignment.)

AUTOMATICALLY HYPHENATE A DOCUMENT

To automatically hyphenate a document:

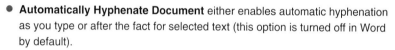

1. In the Page Layout tab, click **Hyphenation** in the Page Setup group. A drop-down menu appears.

2. Click **Hyphenation Options** to open the Hyphenation dialog box. Select the option you want (see Figure 4-29):

   - **Automatically Hyphenate Document** either enables automatic hyphenation as you type or after the fact for selected text (this option is turned off in Word by default).

   - **Hyphenate Words in CAPS** hyphenates words typed in all uppercase letters.

   - **Hyphenation Zone** sets the distance from the right margin within which you want to hyphenate the document (the lower the value, the more words are hyphenated).

   - **Limit Consecutive Hyphens** sets the maximum number of hyphens that can appear in consecutive lines.

3. Click **OK** when finished.

MANUALLY HYPHENATE TEXT

1. In the Page Layout tab, click **Hyphenation** in the Page Setup group. A drop-down menu appears.

2. Click **Manual**.

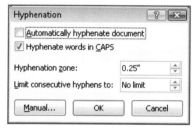

Figure 4-29: You can determine how Word will automatically hyphenate words.

TIP

You can also hyphenate existing text by selecting the text, clicking **Hyphenation** in the Page Layout tab, and clicking **Automatic** in the Page Setup group.

Print Documents

While printing documents may seem like a fairly basic function, there are several tasks associated with it that deserve attention, including setting up your printer, using Print Preview, and printing envelopes and labels.

Set Up Your Printer

Your printer will come with documentation that specifically tells you how to set it up, but there are two basic areas that you need to consider when setting up a printer: installing it on your computer and setting a default printer.

INSTALL A PRINTER

Follow the manufacturer's instructions to unpack, ready, and connect the printer to your computer or identify the network printer you want to use. If you install a Plug and Play printer, it will automatically install itself and you can ignore the following instructions. Otherwise, to install a printer:

1. From Windows Vista, click **Start**, click **Control Panel**, and then, under Hardware And Sound, click **Printer**. The Windows Explorer will open and display the Printers window.

2. In the Printers toolbar, click **Add A Printer**. The Add Printer Wizard starts.

3. Follow the instructions in the Add Printer Wizard, clicking **Next** as needed.

4. If you are using a local printer and you want to print a test page, make sure the printer is turned on and ready to print. When you are done, click **Finished**.

NOTE

If there is a check mark next to the Printer icon, that printer is already set as the default printer.

SET A DEFAULT PRINTER

1. From Windows Vista, click **Start**, click **Control Panel**, and then, under Hardware And Sound, click **Printer**.

2. Right-click the icon for the printer you want to use as the default printer, and then click **Set As Default Printer** from the context menu that appears. A check mark is displayed next to the icon you have selected.

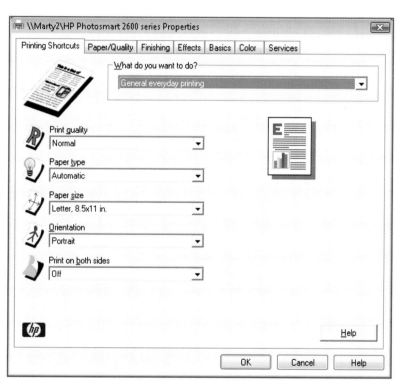

Figure 5-1: Use the Properties dialog box for your printer to define how your documents will be printed.

Define How a Document Is Printed

The Properties dialog box for your printer is where you define how your document will be printed. From here, you can set such things as orientation, number of copies to print, effects, and so on. An example of a Properties dialog box for an HP Photosmart 2600 printer is shown in Figure 5-1. Keep in mind that the Properties dialog box for your printer will probably have some different options, and can even be different for the same printer, depending on whether the printer is connected directly to the computer or is accessed over the network. Consult the documentation that came with your printer for specific instructions.

To open the Properties dialog box for your printer:

1. In Word, click the **Office Button**, and click **Print**. The Print dialog box appears.

2. Click **Properties**. The Properties dialog box for your printer appears. This particular printer model has seven tabs in its dialog box.

3. The Printing Shortcut tab for the HP Photosmart 2600 has the following options, as shown in Figure 5-1. Other printers will have different tabs and different options, but within the Properties dialog box, they will generally cover the same functions. Make your selections accordingly:

- **Print Quality** determines the quality of your print job. You can choose speed over quality or quality over speed.

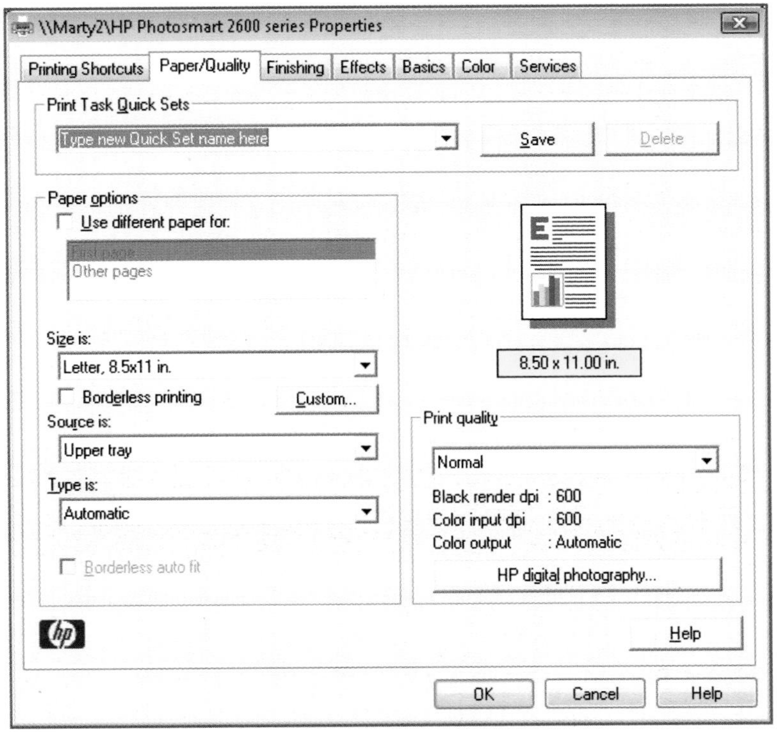

Figure 5-2: *The Properties dialog box for different printers will have different tabs, but similar types of printers—color inkjet, for example—will have similar options.*

NOTE

Print Layout view, set in the View tab Documents Views group, provides almost the exact same view as Print Preview view, and the View tab provides many of the same options.

- **Paper Type** determines the type of paper you are printing on, for example, plain or photo glossy.

- **Paper Size** determines the size of the paper you are printing on, for example, letter, legal, or postcard.

- **Orientation** determines how the document is aligned on the page and the order in which the pages will be printed.

- **Print On Both Sides** allows you to select from several options for two-sided printing.

3. Other tabs will have a variety of options, depending on your printer. Figure 5-2 shows the Paper/Quality tab for the HP Photosmart 2600. Some of the more common options are:

- **Copies** determines the number of copies to be printed.

- **Collate Copies** determines whether multiple copies of a document are printed one at a time. In other words, one copy is printed from start to finish and then the next copy is printed, and so on.

- **Source** determines which of several paper trays, if you have more than one, is used as the source of the paper.

- **Rotate** allows you to rotate the printing on the page by either a fixed or selectable number of degrees.

- **Pages Per Sheet** allows you to print two or more pages on a single sheet of paper, either directly (if the pages are sized accordingly) or by scaling.

4. When you have the settings the way you want them, click **OK** to close the dialog boxes.

Preview What You'll Print

You can use the Print Preview feature to view your document on the screen before you print it. Print Preview displays the page(s) of your document exactly as they will appear when printed. You can also set page breaks and margins using this feature.

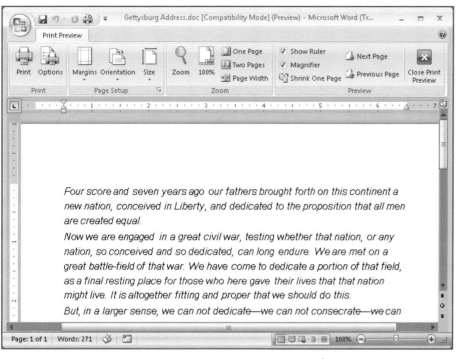

Figure 5-3: **By displaying your document in Print Preview, you can see how it will look when printed.**

To use Print Preview:

Click the **Office Button**, point at the **Print** arrow, and click **Print Preview**. Your document is displayed in Print Preview view, as shown in Figure 5-3.

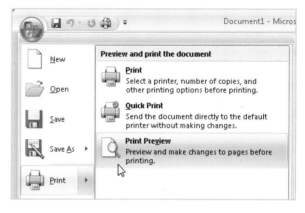

ZOOM IN AND OUT

1. Click **Zoom** on the Print Preview tab. The Zoom dialog box appears.

2. Click one of the preset percentages, directly enter a percent, or use the spinner to set the level of magnification you want.

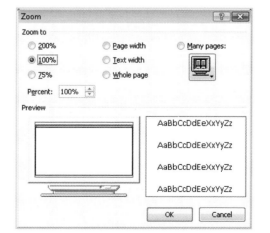

TIP

The Magnifier, which is turned on by default in the Preview group, allows you to quickly toggle between 100 percent and full-page views by simply clicking the page.

Figure 5-4: *You can either select preset margins from the Margin drop-down menu or enter the custom margins you want in the Page Setup dialog box.*

VIEW MULTIPLE PAGES

Depending on the size of your pages and the size of your Word window, you can display either one or two pages at a time.

In Print Preview, click **Two Pages** in the Zoom group to display a two-page view. Then, if and when you are ready, click **One Page** to return to the original one-page view.

CHANGE MARGINS

1. In the Print Preview tab, click **Show Ruler** in the Preview group. A ruler is displayed on the left and on the top of the document, as you saw in Figure 5-3. The margins are shown as the shaded areas on the ends of the rulers.

2. In the Page Setup group, click **Margins**. A drop-down menu of margin options will open.

3. Select the option that is correct for your document; or click **Custom Margins** at the bottom of the menu, and directly enter or select the individual margins you want to use (see Figure 5-4).

MOVE FROM PAGE TO PAGE

In the Print Preview tab, click **Previous Page** or **Next Page** in the Preview group to move forward or backward one page at a time.

REDUCE THE NUMBER OF PAGES

If, for example, you have a report that absolutely cannot be more than four pages and a line or two—or even several paragraphs—has caused the document to be five pages, click **Shrink One Page** in the Preview group on the Print Preview tab. Word reformats the document onto one less page by making slight adjustments to font size and paragraph spacing. You can keep doing this to reduce the number of pages one at a time. Obviously, after a while, the document is no longer attractive, if it is even readable.

EXIT PRINT PREVIEW

Click **Close Print Preview** on the right of the Print Preview tab.

VIEW YOUR DOCUMENT IN FULL-SCREEN MODE

A feature that was available in earlier versions of Print Preview in Word but that is not in Print Preview in Word 2007 is the ability to view a document in full-screen mode without the ribbon, status bar, or scroll bars present, as shown in Figure 5-5. This view, however, is available in Word 2007 from the View tab Document Views group. Click **Full Screen Reading** to see what is shown in Figure 5-5. When you are finished, click **Close** on the far right of the title bar to return to the regular Word window.

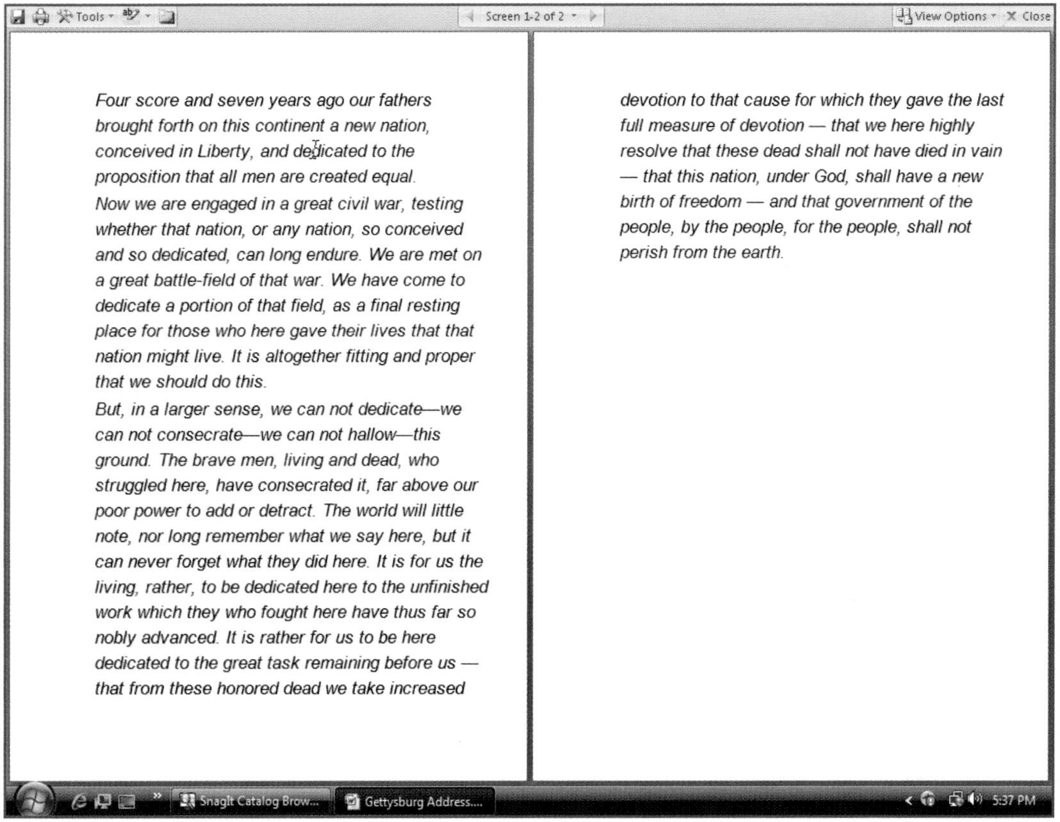

Figure 5-5: *Use Full-Screen Reading view to see your document without the ribbon, status bar, or scroll bars.*

Print a Document

If you're in a hurry, or if you don't care about changing margins, then printing a document can be as easy as clicking a **Print** icon on the Quick Access toolbar. By default, that icon isn't on that toolbar, but you can add it. To set specific options before printing your document, you need to use the Print dialog box.

ADD THE QUICK PRINT ICON

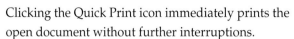

To add a single-click Print icon to the Quick Access toolbar:

1. Click **Customize** on the right of the Quick Access toolbar.

2. Click **Quick Print**. The Quick Print icon is added.

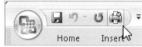

Clicking the Quick Print icon immediately prints the open document without further interruptions.

CUSTOMIZE A PRINT JOB

Customizing the print settings is done in the Print dialog box, shown in Figure 5-6.

1. Click the **Office Button**, and click **Print**. The Print dialog box appears.

2. If more than one printer is available to you, select the printer you want to use from the Name drop-down list. Usually, the default printer is displayed automatically in the Name list box.

3. Select an option in the Page Range area:

   - **All** prints all the pages in your document.

   - **Current Page** prints the currently selected page or the page in which the insertion point is active.

   - **Selection** prints only the content you have selected. Select text to print by dragging over it to highlight it.

   - **Pages** prints the range of pages you select. To print contiguous pages, use a hyphen (for example, 1-4); to print noncontiguous pages, use commas (for example, 1, 3, 5).

4. Select an option from the Print What drop-down list:

   - **Document** prints the document.

   - **Document Properties** prints the information about the document, such as the file name, the date the document was created, and when it was last saved.

   - **Document Showing Markup** prints the document with any revision marks present. (See Chapter 10 for more information on revision marks.)

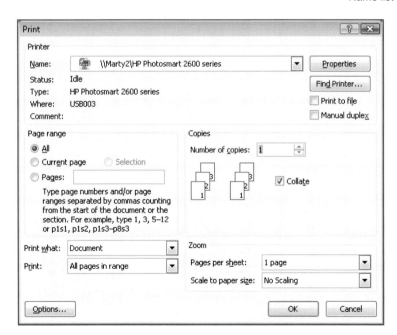

*Figure 5-6: **The Print dialog box provides many options for printing your document.***

- **List Of Markup** prints a list of the edits, insertions, and other markups or changes made to a document.

- **Styles** prints style information. (See Chapter 4 for more information on styles.)

- **Building Block Entries** prints a list of building block entries. (See Chapter 4 for more information on AutoText.)

- **Key Assignments** prints a list of shortcut keys defined by the user and available in Word. (See Chapter 8 for more information on shortcut keys.)

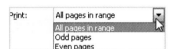

5. Select an option from the Print drop-down list:

- **All Pages In Range** prints all pages, either all the pages in the document or in the range you specify (see step 3).

- **Odd Pages** prints all the odd-numbered pages in the document or in the range you specify (see step 3).

- **Even Pages** prints all the even-numbered pages in the document or in the range you specify (see step 3).

6. Type or use the spinner to select the number of copies you want to print in the Number Of Copies box.

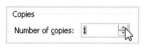

7. Click the **Pages Per Sheet** down arrow, and select a number if you want to print more than one page on a sheet of paper.

8. Click the **Scale To Paper Size** down arrow, and select a paper size to which your document needs to be scaled. For example, you might select Legal (8.5 x 14 in) if you are printing documents on legal-sized paper.

9. When you have selected all the options you want and are ready to print your document, click **OK**. Your document is printed.

Print an Envelope

You can print a mailing address on an envelope to give your correspondence a more professional look. If you have a business letter with an address in the normal location, Word will pick up that address and suggest it for the envelope. If you don't have a letter, you can still create and print an envelope.

1. In the Mailings tab Create group, click **Envelopes**. The Envelopes And Labels dialog box appears with the Envelope tab selected, as shown in Figure 5-7.

Figure 5-7: Printed envelopes give your correspondence a professional look.

2. In the Delivery Address box, if an address wasn't picked up from a letter, enter the mailing address.

3. In the Return Address box, accept the default return address, or enter or edit the return address. (If you are using preprinted envelopes, you can omit a return address by clicking the **Omit** check box.)

4. Click the **Add Electronic Postage** check box if you have separately installed electronic postage software and want to add it to your envelope.

5. To set options for the electronic postage programs that are installed on your computer, click **E-Postage Properties**.

6. To select an envelope size, the type of paper feed, and other options, click **Options**, select the options you want, and then click **OK**.

7. To print the envelope now, insert an envelope in the printer, as shown in the Feed box (see the accompanying Note), and then click **Print**.

8. To attach the envelope to a document you are currently working on and print it later, click **Add To Document**. The envelope is added to the document in a separate section.

Print Labels

You can print labels for a single letter or for a mass mailing, such as holiday cards, invitations, or for marketing purposes. See the section "Merge to Labels" later in this chapter for instructions on how to create labels for a mass mailing.

To print a single label:

1. In the Mailings tab Create group, click **Labels**. The Envelopes And Labels dialog box appears with the Labels tab displayed, as shown in Figure 5-8.

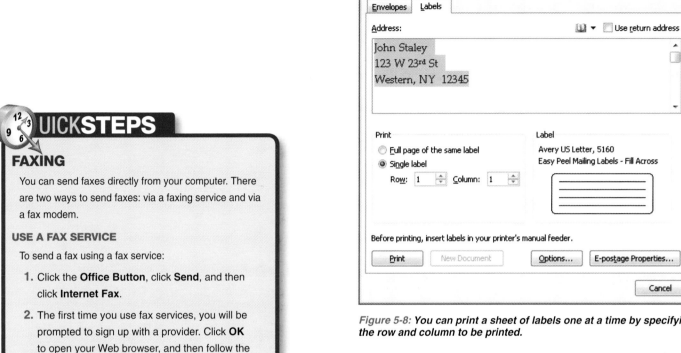

Figure 5-8: *You can print a sheet of labels one at a time by specifying the row and column to be printed.*

QUICKSTEPS

FAXING

You can send faxes directly from your computer. There are two ways to send faxes: via a faxing service and via a fax modem.

USE A FAX SERVICE

To send a fax using a fax service:

1. Click the **Office Button**, click **Send**, and then click **Internet Fax**.

2. The first time you use fax services, you will be prompted to sign up with a provider. Click **OK** to open your Web browser, and then follow the signup instructions on the Web site.

Microsoft Office

⚠ To use Fax Service to send your fax, you must first sign up with a fax service provider. Click OK to open a page in your Web browser where you can choose a provider.

OK   Cancel

3. When finished, close your Web browser, and then repeat step 1. An e-mail message will open in Outlook with your document attached as a .tif (image) file, or you can attach a file to the e-mail message.

4. Fill in the Fax Recipient, Fax Number, and Subject fields. Click **Send**.

Continued . . .

2. In the Address box, do one of the following:

- If you have a business letter open in Word with an address in the normal location, that address will appear in the Address box and can be edited.

- If you are creating a mailing label independent of a letter, enter or edit the address.

- If you want to use a return address, click the **Use Return Address** check box, and then edit the address if necessary.

- If you are creating another type of label, type the text you want.

3. In the Print area, do one of the following:

- Click the **Single Label** option to print a single label. Then type or select the row and column number on the label sheet for the label you want to print.

- Click **Full Page Of The Same Label** to print the same information on a sheet of labels.

QUICKSTEPS

FAXING *(Continued)*

USE A FAX MODEM

This procedure requires that your fax modem be set up as a printer on your system. To send a fax using a fax modem:

1. Click the **Office Button**, and click **Print**. The Print dialog box appears.

2. In the Printer Name drop-down list, click **Fax**, select the print range and other options, and click **OK**. The first time you do this, the Fax Setup window will open. After that, you'll go directly to the New Fax message form and you can jump to step 4.

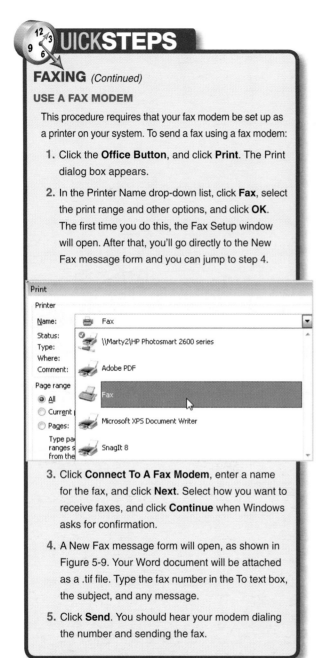

3. Click **Connect To A Fax Modem**, enter a name for the fax, and click **Next**. Select how you want to receive faxes, and click **Continue** when Windows asks for confirmation.

4. A New Fax message form will open, as shown in Figure 5-9. Your Word document will be attached as a .tif file. Type the fax number in the To text box, the subject, and any message.

5. Click **Send**. You should hear your modem dialing the number and sending the fax.

4. To select the label type, the type of paper feed, and other options, click **Options**, select the options you want, and then click **OK**. If the type of label you want to use is not listed in the Product Number box, you might be able to use one of the listed labels, or you can click **New Label** to create your own custom label.

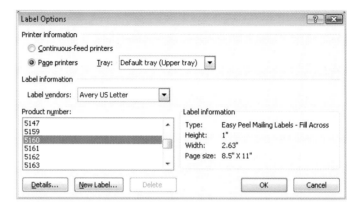

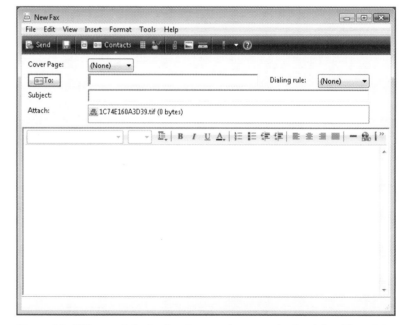

*Figure 5-9: **With e-mail, faxing has become less popular, but it is still useful.***

E-MAILING

You can e-mail documents that you create in Word as attachments to e-mail messages. To attach and send a document in an e-mail:

1. Click the **Office Button**, click **Send**, and then click **E-mail** to send your Word document as an attachment to your e-mail message.

   A new e-mail message is opened with your document title automatically filled in the Subject line and the document automatically attached to the e-mail.

2. Fill in the To and Cc fields (if you are sending the document to multiple recipients), add anything you want to the body of the message, and click **Send**. Your e-mail message with the document attached is sent.

NOTE

You can also send a Word document in the body of an e-mail message using copy and paste. While in Word, select as much of the document as you want to send, and use the Copy command or press **CTRL+C** to copy it. In your e-mail program, open a new message form; fill in the To, Cc, and Subject fields; click in the message field; and use the Paste command or press **CTRL+V** to paste the document in the message field. When ready, click **Send**.

5. To print one or more labels, insert a sheet of labels into the printer, and then click **Print**.

6. To save a sheet of labels for later editing or printing, click **New Document** and save the labels document.

Merge Lists with Letters and Envelopes

The *Mail Merge* feature allows you to combine a mailing list with a document to send the same thing to a number of people. You can merge a mailing list to

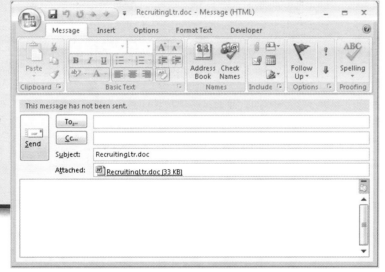

letters, e-mail messages, envelopes, and labels. A mail merge combines two kinds of documents: the *main document*, which is the text of the document—for example, the body of a letter, and the *data source*, which is the information that changes with each copy of the document—for example, the individual names and addresses of the people who will be receiving the letter.

The main document has two parts: static text and merge fields. *Static text* is text that does not change—for example, the body of a letter. *Merge fields* are placeholders that indicate where information from the list or data source goes. For example, in a form letter, "Dear" would be static text, while <<First Name>> <<Last Name>> are merge fields. When the main document and the data source are combined, the result is "Dear John Doe," "Dear Jane Smith," and so on.

TIP

You cannot use the Mail Merge feature unless a document is open, although it can be a blank document.

NOTE

Word also allows you to take a list other than a mailing list—a parts list, for example, and merge it with a document to create a catalog or directory.

The following sections will show you how to create a data source, create a main document, and then merge them together.

Begin a Mail Merge

You can compose the static text in a document first and then insert the merge fields, or you can compose the static text and insert the merge fields as you go. You cannot insert merge fields into a main document until you have created the data source and associated it with your main document.

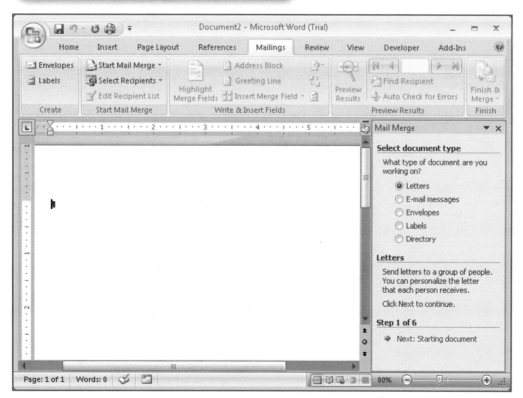

Figure 5-10: *The Mail Merge task pane is where you begin the merge process.*

To create a merge document:

1. In Word, open the document you want to use as your primary document, or open a new document (see Chapter 2).

2. Click the **Mailings** tab, click **Start Mail Merge** in the Start Mail Merge group, and click **Step By Step Mail Merge Wizard**. The Mail Merge task pane is displayed, as shown in Figure 5-10.

3. In the Select Document Type area, select one of the following options:

   • **Letters** are form letters designed to be sent to multiple people.

   • **E-mail Messages** are form letters designed to be sent to multiple people via e-mail.

   • **Envelopes** are envelopes addressed to multiple people.

   • **Labels** are labels addressed to multiple people.

   • **Directory** is a collection of information regarding multiple items, such as a mailing list or phone directory.

4. Click **Next: Starting Document** at the bottom of the task pane.

5. In the Select Starting Document area, select one of the following options:

- **Use The Current Document** uses the currently open document as the main document for the mail merge.

- **Start From A Template** uses a template you designate as the main document for the mail merge.

- **Start From Existing Document** uses an existing document you designate as the main document for the mail merge.

6. See the following section, "Set Up a Name and Address List," to create a data source.

Set Up a Name and Address List

A name and address list is a data source. A data source has two parts: fields and records. A *field* is a category of information. For example, in a mailing list, First Name, Last Name, and Street Address are examples of fields. A *record* is a set of fields for an individual. For example, in a mailing list, the record for John Doe would include all the relevant fields for this individual—his first and last name, street address, city, state, and ZIP code.

To set up a name and address list:

1. Follow steps 1-6 in the previous section, "Begin a Mail Merge."

2. Click **Next: Select Recipients** at the bottom of the task pane. In the Select Recipients area, click **Type A New List**.

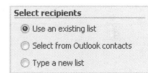

3. Click **Create** in the middle of the pane in the Type A New List area. The New Address List dialog box appears, as shown in Figure 5-11.

4. Enter the information for the first record in the fields you want to use. You may want to delete some of the columns or reorder them to facilitate entering data. Click **Customize Columns** to do that. Press **TAB** to move to the next field, or press **SHIFT+TAB** to move back to the previous field.

5. When you have completed all the fields you want for the first record, click **New Entry** and provide information for the second record.

*Figure 5-11: **Use the New Address List dialog box to create your mailing list.***

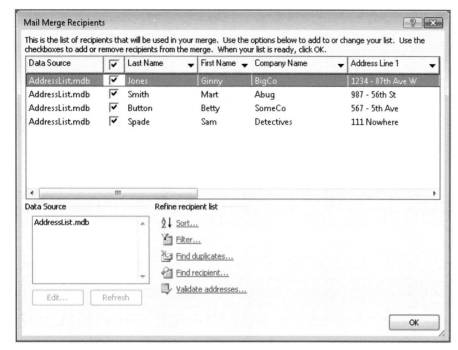

This is the list of recipients that will be used in your merge. Use the options below to add to or change your list. Use the checkboxes to add or remove recipients from the merge. When your list is ready, click OK.

Data Source	☑	Last Name ▼	First Name ▼	Company Name ▼	Address Line 1 ▼
AddressList.mdb	☑	Jones	Ginny	BigCo	1234 - 87th Ave W
AddressList.mdb	☑	Smith	Mart	Abug	987 - 56th St
AddressList.mdb	☑	Button	Betty	SomeCo	567 - 5th Ave
AddressList.mdb	☑	Spade	Sam	Detectives	111 Nowhere

Data Source

AddressList.mdb

Refine recipient list

↕ Sort...
Filter...
Find duplicates...
Find recipient...
Validate addresses...

Edit...   Refresh

OK

*Figure 5-12: **Use the Mail Merge Recipients dialog box to manage your mailing list prior to completing the merge.***

TIP

Sort the merge recipients by clicking the field name at the top of the list that will provide the sort order. For example, if you want the list ordered alphabetically by last name, click **Last Name.**

6. Repeat steps 4 and 5 until you have added all the records you want to your list. When you are done, click **OK**.

7. A Save Address List dialog box appears. Type a file name for the list, select the folder on your computer where you want to save it, and click **Save**.

8. The Mail Merge Recipients dialog box appears, as shown in Figure 5-12. Clear the check boxes next to the recipients you do not want to include in the list. To make further changes to the name list, select the file name in the Data Source list box, and click **Edit**.

9. Click **OK** when finished. See the following section, "Create a Merge Document."

Create a Merge Document

After creating the data source, you need to write the letter and insert the merge fields. This section will tell you how, after creating the main document, to insert merge fields in general; the example uses a letter; additional sections will show you how to use merge fields when creating envelopes and labels.

1. Follow the steps in the previous two sections, "Begin a Mail Merge" and "Set Up a Name and Address List."

2. Click **Next: Write Your Letter** at the bottom of the Mail Merge task pane. In the document pane, write the body of the letter—don't worry about the addressee and the greeting.

3. Place the cursor in the document where you want to insert a merge field, such as the addressee. Do one of the following:

   ● Select one of the three items in the top of the Mail Merge task pane if you want to insert a predefined block of merge fields, such as an address or a greeting. If you select anything other than More Items, a dialog box will appear and ask you to select options and formatting for that item (see Figure 5-13).

Write your letter

If you have not already done so, write your letter now.

To add recipient information to your letter, click a location in the document, and then click one of the items below.

Address block...

Greeting line...

Electronic postage...

More items...

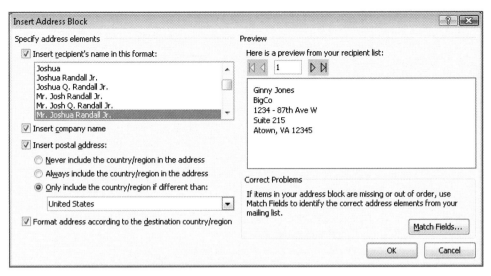

Figure 5-13: *You can customize the predefined field blocks to meet your mail-merge needs.*

- Click **More Items** (the fourth item in the list) to insert an individual merge field. The Insert Merge Field dialog box appears. Verify that **Database Fields** is selected, and then select the field that you want to insert (for example, First Name and Last Name). Click **Insert** to insert the merge field into your document. Click **Close** when you are done inserting all the fields you need.

4. Add commas, spaces, and other punctuation marks to the address as needed. Figure 5-14 shows an example of a letter with merge fields inserted. See the following section, "Preview a Merge."

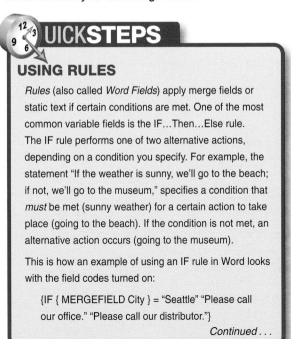

QUICKSTEPS

USING RULES

Rules (also called *Word Fields*) apply merge fields or static text if certain conditions are met. One of the most common variable fields is the IF...Then...Else rule. The IF rule performs one of two alternative actions, depending on a condition you specify. For example, the statement "If the weather is sunny, we'll go to the beach; if not, we'll go to the museum," specifies a condition that *must* be met (sunny weather) for a certain action to take place (going to the beach). If the condition is not met, an alternative action occurs (going to the museum).

This is how an example of using an IF rule in Word looks with the field codes turned on:

{IF { MERGEFIELD City } = "Seattle" "Please call our office." "Please call our distributor."}

Continued . . .

Preview a Merge

Prior to actually completing the merge, the Mail Merge task pane presents you with an opportunity to review what the merged document will look like. This way, you can go back and make any last-minute changes to fine-tune your merge.

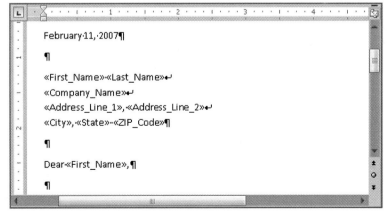

Figure 5-14: *Merge fields are a convenient way to create a form letter for multiple recipients.*

USING RULES *(Continued)*

This works as follows: If the current data record contains "Seattle" in the City field, then the first text ("Please call our office.") is printed in the merged document that results from that data record. If "Seattle" is not in the City field, then the second set of text ("Please call our distributor.") is printed. Using a rule is easy and doesn't require writing such a complex statement at all.

To insert a variable field into a merge document:

1. Position the insertion point where you want the rule.

2. In the Mailings tab, click **Rules** in the Write & Insert Fields group. A drop-down list appears.

3. Select the rule you want, for example, **If...Then...Else**.

4. The Insert Word Field dialog box appears. Fill in the text boxes with your criteria, and click **OK** when finished.

A̲sk...
F̲ill-in...
If...Then...Else...
Merge R̲ecord #
Merge Se̲quence #
N̲ext Record
Ne̲xt Record If...
Set B̲ookmark...
S̲kip Record If...

Insert Word Field: IF

IF

Field name: **City**
Comparison: **Equal to**
Compare to: **Seattle**

Insert this text:
Please call our office.

Otherwise insert this text:
Please call our distributor.

[OK] [Cancel]

To preview a merge:

1. Follow the steps in the previous three sections, "Begin a Mail Merge," "Set Up a Name and Address List," and "Create a Merge Document."

2. Click **Next: Preview Your Letters** at the bottom of the Mail Merge task pane.

3. Use the right and left arrow buttons under Preview Your Letters in the Mail Merge task pane to scroll through the recipient list.

4. If you want to exclude a particular recipient from the merge, click **Exclude This Recipient**.

   –Or–

   Click **Edit Recipient List** to edit a particular recipient's information. If you click this link, the Mail Merge Recipients dialog box appears again (see Figure 5-12). Click the file name under Data Source, click **Edit**, modify the information, and click **OK**. Click **OK** again to close the Mail Merge Recipients dialog box.

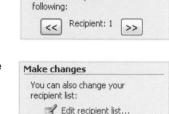

Preview your letters

One of the merged letters is previewed here. To preview another letter, click one of the following:

[<<] Recipient: 1 [>>]

Make changes

You can also change your recipient list:

📝 Edit recipient list...

[Exclude this recipient]

Complete a Merge

The last step in performing a mail merge is to complete the merge; that is, to accept the preview of how the merge will look and direct Word to perform the merge.

To complete a merge:

1. Follow the steps in the previous four sections, "Begin a Mail Merge," "Set Up a Name and Address List," "Create a Merge Document," and "Preview a Merge."

2. Click **Next: Complete The Merge** at the bottom of the Mail Merge task pane.

3. Click **Print** in the Merge area. The Merge To Printer dialog box appears.

Merge to Printer

Print records
- ⦿ A̲ll
- ○ Curr̲ent record
- ○ F̲rom: [   ] T̲o: [   ]

[OK] [Cancel]

4. Select one of the following options:

  - **All** prints all records in the data source that have been included in the merge.
  - **Current Record** prints only the record that is displayed in the document window.
  - **From/To** prints a range of records you specify. Enter the starting and ending numbers in the text boxes.

5. Click **OK** when finished. The Print dialog box appears.

6. Select the print options you want, and click **OK**. Your merged document is printed.

7. If you wish, save your merge document.

Merge to Envelopes

The process for merging to envelopes is similar to that for merging to letters.

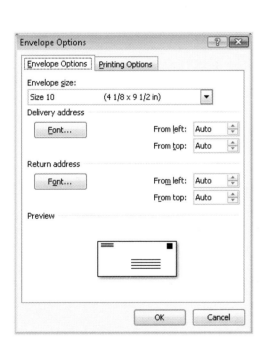

1. Follow steps 1–2 in the section "Begin a Mail Merge." In the Select Document Type area, click **Envelopes**.

2. Click **Next: Starting Document** at the bottom of the Mail Merge task pane. Select one of the following options:

  - **Change Document Layout** lets you modify the current document.
  - **Start From Existing Document** lets you use a different existing document.

3. If you selected Start From Existing Document, select the main document you want to use from the displayed list, and click **Open**. If you want to use a document that is not listed, click **Open**, and locate and select the document you want from the Open dialog box that appears.

   –Or–

   If you selected Change Document Layout, click **Envelope Options** in the middle of the Mail Merge task pane. The Envelope Options dialog box appears.

4. Select the options you want from the Envelope Options and Printing Options tabs. Click **OK** when finished.

5. An envelope will appear with your default return address in the upper-left corner and an indented paragraph mark where you will put the addressee. Type a return address, if needed, or make any changes you want to the return address and any other static text that you want. This will be printed on all envelopes.

6. Click **Next: Select Recipients** at the bottom of the Mail Merge task pane. Follow steps 2–9 in the section "Set Up a Name and Address List."

7. Click **Next: Arrange Your Envelope** at the bottom of the Mail Merge task pane. If the insertion point isn't already there, click where the address block goes in the middle of the envelope.

8. Select one of the first three options to insert a predefined block of merge fields, such as an address block or an e-postage.

–Or–

Click **More Items** to insert an individual mail merge field.

9. Repeat step 8 for each merge field that you want to insert.

10. Click **Next: Preview Your Envelopes** at the bottom of the Mail Merge task pane. Follow steps 3–4 in the section "Preview a Merge." Your envelope may look similar to that shown in Figure 5-15.

11. Click **Next: Complete The Merge** at the bottom of the Mail Merge task pane. Follow steps 3–7 in the section "Complete a Merge."

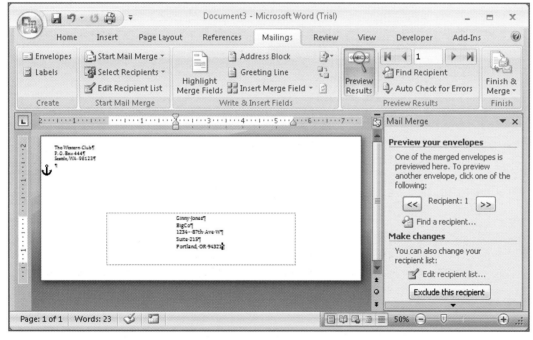

Figure 5-15: **You can see how your merged envelope will look when completed prior to printing.**

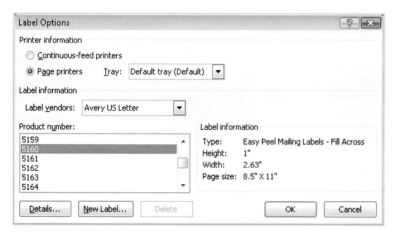

Merge to Labels

The process for merging to labels is similar to that for merging to letter and envelopes.

1. Follow steps 1–2 in the section "Begin a Mail Merge." In the Select Document Type area, click **Labels**.

2. Click **Next: Starting Document** at the bottom of the Mail Merge task pane. Select one of the following options:
   - **Change Document Layout** lets you modify the current document.
   - **Start From Existing Document** lets you use a different existing document.

3. If you selected Start From Existing Document, select the main document you want to use from the displayed list, and click **Open**. If you want to use a document that is not listed, click **Open**, and locate and select the document you want from the Open dialog box that appears.

4. If you selected Change Document Layout, click **Label Options** in the middle of the Mail Merge task pane. The Label Options dialog box appears.

5. Select the options you want. Click **OK** when finished. A page formatted for labels will appear in Word.

6. Click **Next: Select Recipients** at the bottom of the Mail Merge task pane. Follow steps 2–9 in the section "Set Up a Name and Address List." "Next Record" will appear in all but the first label.

7. Click **Next: Arrange Your Labels** at the bottom of the Mail Merge task pane.

8. Click in the blank space for the first label. Select one of the first three options to insert a predefined block of merge fields, such as an address block, for the first label. If you choose Address Block, the Insert Address Block dialog box will appear. Make any desired changes, and click **OK**.

   –Or–

   After clicking in the blank space for the first label, click **More Items** to insert an individual mail merge field into the first label.

9. Under Replicate Labels, click **Update All Labels** to copy the fields in the first label to all the labels, as shown in Figure 5-16.

QUICK**FACTS**

DISSECTING A TABLE

A table comes with an extensive vocabulary of terms that describe many of its elements, features, and how it's used, as shown in Figure 6-1.

Some of the ways that you can use tables are:

- Tabular data display, with or without cell borders
- Side-by-side columns of text
- Aligning labels and boxes for forms
- Text on one side, graphics on the other
- Placing borders around text or graphics
- Placing text on both sides of graphics or vice versa
- Adding color to backgrounds, to text, and to graphics

TIP

If you want to insert a table that is larger than the 8 rows by 10 columns shown in the Table drop-down menu, you can easily add rows or columns to an initial table that you create from the menu. See "Change the Table Size" later in this chapter.

Create a Table

When you create a table, you can specify the number of rows and columns in it. In addition, depending on how you created the table, you can select how the columns' width is determined and choose a table style. In all cases, you can easily modify the table attributes after the original table displays in your document. With the document open in Word, place the insertion point at the appropriate location in the document where you want a table.

INSERT A TABLE QUICKLY

The Insert tab Tables group offers a variety of methods for creating a table using the default settings. The quickest method is to use the Insert tab.

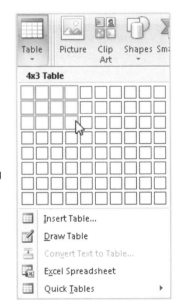

1. In the Insert tab Tables group, click the **Table** down arrow. In the drop-down menu that opens, click the lower-right cell needed to give you the number of rows and columns you want.

2. Type the information you want in the table, pressing **TAB** as needed to move from cell to cell (see the "Entering Information" QuickSteps later in this chapter).

INSERT A TABLE FROM A DIALOG BOX

The Insert Table dialog box provides several options when initially setting up a table.

1. In the Insert tab Tables group, click the **Table** down arrow. In the drop-down menu that opens, click **Insert Table**.

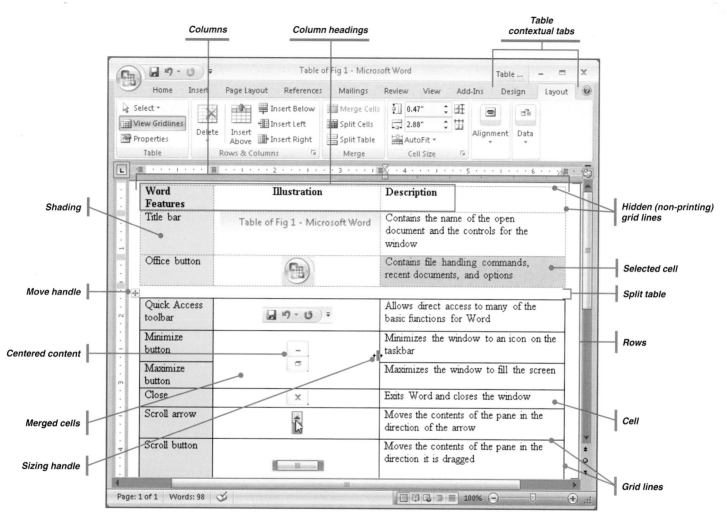

Figure 6-1: *Tables have a vocabulary all their own.*

Columns · **Column headings** · **Table contextual tabs**

Shading

Move handle

Centered content

Merged cells

Sizing handle

Hidden (non-printing) grid lines

Selected cell

Split table

Rows

Cell

Grid lines

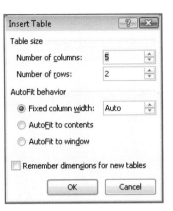

Figure 6-2: *You can determine several table attributes when creating a table using the Insert Table dialog box.*

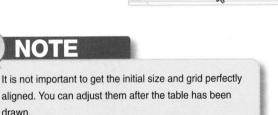

NOTE

It is not important to get the initial size and grid perfectly aligned. You can adjust them after the table has been drawn.

2. The Insert Table dialog box appears, as shown in Figure 6-2:

- Under Table Size, click the respective spinners, or enter a value, to determine the number of rows and columns in the table.

- Under AutoFit Behavior, choose a fixed column width by clicking the spinner or entering a value (*Auto*, the default, sizes the columns equally so that they fill the available width of the table), have Word set each column's width to fit the contents in each column, or have Word size the columns to fit the window the table is in. (See "Change Column Width and Row Height" later in the chapter for more ways to adjust column width after a table is created.)

2. If you want the size settings you choose to apply to future tables you create, select the **Remember Dimensions For New Tables** check box.

3. Click **OK** to display the table in your document.

DRAW A TABLE

The most hands-on way to create a table is to draw it.

1. With the document open in Word, scroll to the location where you want to draw a table.

2. In the Insert tab Tables group, click the **Table** down arrow. In the drop-down menu that opens, click **Draw Table**. The mouse pointer turns into a pencil.

3. Place the pencil-shaped pointer where you want the upper-left corner of the table, and drag it diagonally across and down the page, creating a table outline that is the height and width of the outer border of the table you want.

4. Place the pencil-shaped pointer on the top border at the location of the right edge of the leftmost column you want, and drag down to the bottom border. Repeat that for the other columns you want.

5. Place the pencil-shaped pointer on the left border at the location of the bottom of the topmost row you want, and drag to the right outer border. Repeat that for the other rows you want.

6. When you are done drawing, press **ESC** to return the pencil-shaped pointer to the I-beam pointer.

7. If you want to adjust the location of any of the outer borders or the row or column borders, point at the border you want to adjust. The mouse pointer will turn into a double-headed resize arrow. Drag the selected border to the location you want it.

8. Enter the information you want in the table, pressing **TAB** as needed to move from cell to cell.

Use Table Tools

Once you have created a table, you have two sets of tools with which to work with it: the table contextual tabs in the ribbon and the context menus that open when you right-click in a table.

USE THE TABLE'S CONTEXTUAL TABS

When you create a table in Word 2007, the ribbon automatically displays two new table-related tabs: Table Tools Design and Table Tools Layout. The Table Tools Design tab, shown in Figure 6-3, allows you to apply various styles to tables, as well as apply shading, customize the border, and draw and erase tables or their segments.

Figure 6-3: **The Table Tools Design tab is used to change the style of a table.**

The Table Tools Layout tab, shown in Figure 6-4, allows you to modify tables in many different ways, including selecting, deleting, and inserting various table elements, as well as working with cells and their contents.

Both contextual tabs are discussed at length later in this chapter.

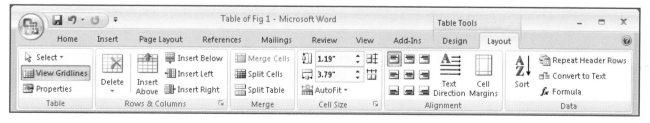

Figure 6-4: **The Table Tools Layout tab is used to modify tables.**

Figure 6-5: **The context menu allows you to format and modify tables.**

USE THE TABLE'S CONTEXT MENU

When you right-click a table or its contents, you see a context menu that, depending on what you clicked, will look similar to Figure 6-5. This context menu allows you to do many of the formatting tasks in the Home tab, as well as many of the table modification tasks in the Layout tab.

Change the Table Size

Rows, columns, and cells can be added to a table using the Layout tab Rows & Columns group or the context menus. You can also change a table's size by removing elements, splitting a table, or resizing the overall dimensions.

ADD CELLS

Cells can be added to a table above and to the left of existing cells.

1. Select the cells adjacent to where you want to add the new cells. (To add a single cell, select only the cell below or to the right of where you want the new cell. If adding more than one cell, you can select the number of cells you want added, and an equal number will be added above or to the left of your selection.) See the "Selecting Tables, Rows, Columns, or Cells" QuickSteps.

2. In the Layout tab Rows & Columns group, click the **Dialog Box Launcher**.

   –Or–

   Right-click the existing cell, click **Insert**, and click **Insert Cells**.

   In either case, the Insert Cells dialog box appears.

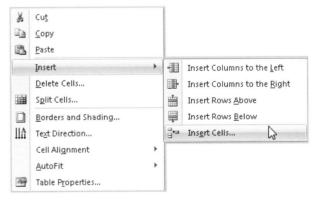

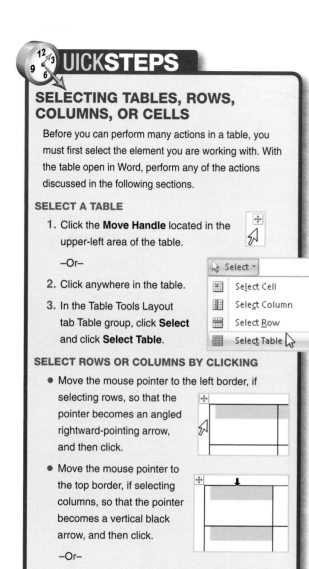
3. In the Insert Cells dialog box, click **Shift Cells Right** (existing cells are "pushed" to the right, inserting the new cell to the left of the existing cells).

   –Or–

   Click **Shift Cells Down** (existing cells are "pushed" down, inserting the new cells above the existing cells).

4. Click **OK**.

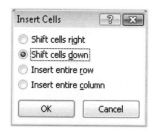

INSERT ROWS OR COLUMNS

You can quickly add rows or columns from either the Layout tab Rows & Columns group or the context menu.

1. Select the rows or columns in the table next to where you want to add rows or columns (the number of rows or columns added will equal the number of rows or columns selected).

2. In the Layout tab Rows & Columns group, click **Insert Above** or **Insert Below** (for new rows) or **Insert Left** or **Insert Right** (for new columns).

   –Or–

   Right-click an existing row or column, click **Insert**, and click **Insert Columns To The Left**, **Insert Columns To The Right**, **Insert Rows Above**, or **Insert Rows Below**.

RESIZE BY DRAGGING

1. In the View tab Document Views group, click **Print Layout** (the sizing handle doesn't display in other views).

2. Place your mouse over the table whose size you want to change, and drag the sizing handle that appears in the lower-right corner of the table to increase or decrease the table size. The rows and columns increase or decrease proportionately within the constraints of the cell contents.

ADD ROWS AT THE BOTTOM OF A TABLE

As you are entering information into a table and you reach the bottom rightmost cell, simply pressing TAB will add another row to the table.

QUICKSTEPS

SELECTING TABLES, ROWS, COLUMNS, OR CELLS *(Continued)*

SELECT ROWS OR COLUMNS BY DRAGGING

Move the mouse to the first cell of the row or column, and drag it to the last cell. You can easily select multiple rows and/or columns this way.

SELECT ROWS OR COLUMNS FROM THE RIBBON

1. Click any cell in the row or column you want to select.

2. In the Layout tab Table group, click **Select** and click either **Select Row** or **Select Column**.

SELECT A CELL BY CLICKING

1. Move the mouse pointer to the left border of the cell so that the pointer becomes an angled rightward-pointing black arrow.

2. Click the mouse to select the cell.

SELECT A CELL FROM THE RIBBON

Click your mouse pointer in the cell you want selected

In the Layout tab Table group, click **Select**, and click **Select Cell**.

SELECT CELLS BY DRAGGING

Place your mouse pointer in the upper-leftmost cell you want to select, and drag down and to the right across the remaining cells in the range you want selected, as shown in Figure 6-6. (If you are left-handed, you might find it easier to click in the upper-rightmost cell and then drag down and to the left).

REMOVE CELLS, ROWS, AND COLUMNS

1. Select the cells, rows, or columns you want to remove (see the QuickSteps "Selecting Tables, Rows, Columns, or Cells").

2. Right-click the selection.

3. Click **Delete Columns** to remove selected columns.

   –Or–

   Click **Delete Rows** to remove selected rows.

   –Or–

   Click **Delete Cells** to open the Delete Cells dialog box. Choose whether to fill the vacant area of the table by shifting cells to the left or up. Click **OK**.

SPLIT A TABLE

You can divide a table along any of its rows to split it into segments. Word will divide longer tables when it creates automatic page breaks, although you might find it handy to be able to control exactly where the break occurs in the table.

1. Click a cell in the row below where you want the split to occur.

2. In the Layout tab Merge Group, click **Split Table**. A blank paragraph is inserted between the two tables (see Figure 6-1).

Superior Office Supply	1st Qtr	2nd Qtr	3rd Qtr	4thQtr
Paper Supplies	$23,567	$35,938	$38,210	$39,876
Writing Instruments	5,482	5,836	5,923	6,082
Cards and Books	14,986	15,021	15,934	16,732
Forms	2,342	2,756	3,456	3,678
Labels	3,522	4,621	5,361	5,476
Equipment	45,328	47,934	51,830	55,638
Furniture	37,278	38,429	38,328	39,103

Click here and... ...drag... ...to here to select a range of cells

*Figure 6-6: **The fastest way to select contiguous cells is to drag across them.***

CAUTION

Removing cells also deletes any text or graphics contained within them.

NOTE

You can also remove parts of a table by erasing the elements you don't want. In the Design tab Draw Borders group, click **Eraser**. Drag a rectangle using the eraser pointer over the elements you want removed. The borders of the elements to be removed within the red rectangular selection are bolded. Release the mouse button to remove the selected elements (when cells are removed within the interior of the table, the "hole" that remains is one large merged cell). Press **ESC** to return to the standard pointer or click the **Eraser** button again.

Eraser

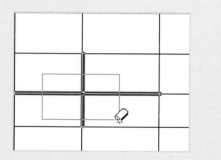

TIP

To see the dimensions of each column's width or each row's height, hold down **ALT** as you drag a column or row border. The horizontal ruler displays the column widths, and the vertical ruler displays the row heights.

⊞ ← 0.6" → ⊞ ⟡ ⊞ — 0.73" → ⊞ ← 0.54" → ⊞

Change Column Width and Row Height

By default, tables are created with equal column widths spanning the width of the table (margin-to-margin across the document) unless you manually draw them. You can change each column to a specific width you set or use AutoFit to adjust the width to fit the longest entry in the column. Row heights change vertically as needed to accommodate lines of text or larger font sizes (all cells in a row increase to match the highest cell in the row.

CHANGE COLUMN WIDTH AND ROW HEIGHT BY DRAGGING

1. Place the mouse pointer on the right border of the column whose width you want to change or on the bottom border of the row height you want to change. The mouse pointer changes to a resize pointer, showing the opposing directions in which you can drag.

2. Drag the border to increase or decrease the size.

CHANGE COLUMN WIDTH PRECISELY

1. Right-click the table that contains the columns whose width you want to change, and click **Table Properties** on the context menu.

2. In the Table Properties dialog box, click the **Column** tab, shown in Figure 6-7.

3. Use the **Previous Column** or **Next Column** button to select the initial column you want to set. (You may need to drag the dialog box to one side to see the table beneath it.)

4. Select the **Preferred Width** check box, and set a width in inches or as a percentage of the table width.

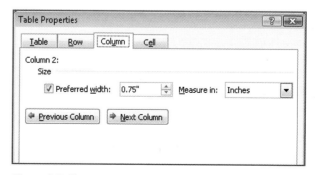

Figure 6-7: **You can set exact dimensions for each column's width or as a percentage of the table width.**

TIP

You can manually adjust column width and row heights to fit contents by selecting the columns or rows you want to adjust, pointing at the columns' rightmost border or the rows' lowermost border, and double-clicking when the pointer changes to a resizing icon.

TIP

Distributing columns or rows evenly is particularly useful when you draw a table manually.

QUICKSTEPS

ENTERING INFORMATION

Typing text in table cells is similar to typing text elsewhere in the document. You use familiar tools, such as bullets, tabs, and other options found on the Home, Insert, and Page Layout tabs. See Chapters 2 through 4 for basic techniques used when working with text.

TYPE TEXT ABOVE A TABLE

Place the insertion point in the upper-leftmost cell in the table (to the left of any text in the cell), and press **SHIFT+CTRL+ENTER**. A new paragraph is created above the table.

MOVE AROUND IN A TABLE

The most straightforward way to move between cells in a table is to simply click the cell where you want to add text or graphics. However, if you're adding a lot of data to a table, it's more efficient to keep your hands on the keyboard. See Table 6-1 for several keyboard shortcuts you can use.

Continued . . .

5. Repeat steps 3 and 4 to change the width of other columns.

6. Click **OK**.

CHANGE COLUMN WIDTH TO FIT CONTENTS

You can use AutoFit to dynamically adjust the column widths in a table to fit the longest single-line entry in that column.

Right-click the table whose columns you want to adjust to fit their content, click **AutoFit**, and click **AutoFit To Contents**. (To return to the default text-wrapping behavior, right-click the table, click **AutoFit**, and click **Fixed Column Width**. You will need to manually narrow any wide column widths to wrap text that has stretched the cell width.)

SPACE COLUMN WIDTHS OR ROW HEIGHTS EQUALLY

1. Select the columns or rows that you want to make the same size, and right-click that selection to open the context menu.

2. Click **Distribute Columns Evenly** to space selected column widths equally.

   –Or–

   Click **Distribute Rows Evenly** to space selected row heights equally.

TO...	PRESS...
Move to cells to the right and down at row end (with cell contents selected)	TAB
Move to cells to the left and up at row end (with cell contents selected)	SHIFT+TAB
First cell in a column	ALT+PAGE UP
Last cell in a column	ALT+PAGE DOWN
First cell in a row	ALT+HOME
Last cell in a row	ALT+END

*Table 6-1: **Keyboard Shortcuts to Move Around in a Table***

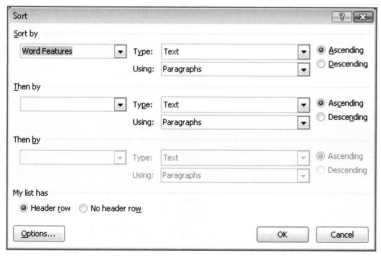

QUICKSTEPS

ENTERING INFORMATION (Continued)

MOVE CONTENT AROUND

You can cut and copy text and other content using the same techniques for basic text. Just select the content in the cells you want and, for example, press **CTRL+C** to copy the content. When pasting the content into other cells in the table, place the insertion point in the cell where you want the content to appear. Press **CTRL+V**. Any content in existing cells overlaid by the range of pasted cells will be overwritten with the new content.

Work with Tables

Tables can be set up for many purposes, and Word provides features to support many of them. You can use special shortcut key combinations to move through the cells in table, you can sort lists, and work with formulas. You can also move, copy, and delete tables.

Sort Data

You can sort information in ascending or descending order according to the values in one or more columns. You can sort an entire table or selected cells (all data in the table or range is realigned so that the data in each row remains the same, even though the row might be placed in a different order than it was originally) or just a column (data in columns outside the sorted column does not change order).

SORT A TABLE OR SELECTED CELLS

1. Place your insertion point in the table you want to sort, or select a range of cells to sort.

2. In the Layout tab Data group, click **Sort**. The Sort dialog box appears, as shown in Figure 6-8.

3. Click the **Sort By** down arrow, and click the column of primary importance in determining the sort order in the drop-down list (if the columns have headings, select one of the titles; if there are no headings, select a column based on numbers that start with the leftmost column).

4. Click the **Type** down arrow, and click the whether the column contains numbers, dates, and anything else (the Text option sorts everything). Click **Ascending** or **Descending**.

Figure 6-8: **You can reorganize information in a table by sorting by one or more columns in ascending or descending order.**

Sorting in Word is determined by a specified *sort order*. Each of the three types of information recognized by Word contains its own sort order. For example, Text entries beginning with punctuation characters are sorted first, followed by entries with numbers, and then entries starting with letters. When sorting is based on the Numbers type, all other characters are ignored. Dates are recognized by the separators used to define days, months, and years. Periods, hyphens (-), forward slashes (/), and commas are valid date separators.

You can sort by four columns, but you have to "trick" Word a bit by doing the sort in two steps. First, sort by the least specific column in the Sort dialog box, and click **OK**. Next, complete a second sort in the Sort dialog box as you normally would, from the most to the least specific column, using the three sorting sections. Click **OK** to close the Sort dialog box a second time.

MOVING AND COPYING TABLES, COLUMNS, AND ROWS

A table is easily moved or copied by dragging its move handle (the move handle is only displayed when viewing the document in Print Layout view). Columns and rows also can be dragged into new positions.

Continued . . .

5. Click the first **Then By** down arrow, and click the column in the drop-down list that you want to base the sort on that is secondary in importance. Select the type of information in the column, and click **Ascending** or **Descending**.

6. Repeat, if necessary, for the second Then By section to sort by a third column of information.

7. Under My List Has, click whether the table or selection has a heading row.

8. Click **OK** when finished. An example of a table sorted by two columns is shown in Figure 6-9.

SORT A SINGLE COLUMN

1. Select the column you want to sort (see the QuickSteps "Selecting Tables, Rows, Columns, or Cells").

2. In the Layout tab Data group, click **Sort**.

3. In the Sort dialog box, click **Options**.

4. In the Sort Options dialog box, click the **Sort Column Only** check box.

5. Click **OK** twice.

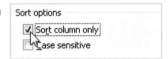

	Primary sort arranges list by publisher	Secondary sort arranges list by price within publisher

Title	Author	Publisher	Price	Category
Making of Microsoft	Ichbiah	1	12.30	Business
Hawaii: A Paradise Family Guid	Penisten	1	12.30	Travel
"Windows 3.1, Visual Learning"	Gardner	1	18.95	Computer
In The Shadow of the White Hou	Tidwell	1	18.95	Government
The Power of Windows and DOS	Matthews	1	23.70	Computer
2010	Clarke	3	3.95	Sci. Fic.
Spy Line	Deighton	3	5.95	Thriller
Me	Hepburn	3	5.99	Biography
Trevayne	Ludlum	4	5.95	Mystery
Nightfall	Asimov	4	5.99	Sci. Fic.
The Difference Engine	Gibson	4	5.99	Sci. Fic.

Figure 6-9: **Sort by multiple columns to arrange entries that have the same secondary sort value.**

MOVING AND COPYING TABLES, COLUMNS, AND ROWS *(Continued)*

MOVE A TABLE

1. Point at the upper-leftmost cell in the table you want to move to display its move handle.

Title
Making

2. Drag the table to the position you want.

COPY A TABLE

Hold **CTRL** and drag the table's move handle to position where you want the copy of the table.

–Or–

In the Layout tab Table group, click **Select** and click **Select Table**. Press **CTRL+C** to copy the table to the Clipboard. Place your insertion point where you want the new table, and press **CTRL+V**.

MOVE COLUMNS AND ROWS

1. Select the columns or rows you want to move (see the QuickSteps "Selecting Tables, Rows, Columns, or Cells" earlier in the chapter).

2. Drag the selection where you want the elements moved:

   - Selected columns display to the left of the column where you stop dragging.
   - Selected rows display above the row where you stop dragging.

COPY COLUMNS AND ROWS

Use the previous procedure for moving columns and rows, except hold **CTRL** while dragging to leave the selected elements in place while adding a copy of them to the new location.

Hawaii: A Paradise Family Guid
2010
Spy Line

SORT BY MORE THAN ONE FIELD IN A COLUMN

If you combine two or more fields of information in a single column, such as city, county, and state (for example, Everett, Snohomish, WA), instead of splitting them out into separate columns, you can sort your list by choosing which fields to sort by.

1. Place your insertion point in the table.

2. In the Layout tab Data group, click **Sort**.

3. In the Sort dialog box, click **Options**. In the Sort Options dialog box, under Separate Fields At, click the character used to separate the fields in a single column, or click **Other** and type the separator character. Click **OK** to close the Sort Options dialog box.

4. In the Sort dialog box, click the **Sort By** down arrow, and click the primary column that contains multiple fields. Click the **Type** down arrow, click an information type, and click **Ascending** or **Descending**. Click the **Using** down arrow, and click the record group, such as paragraphs.

5. Use the Then By sections if you want to sort by additional columns or fields.

6. Click **OK** when finished.

Calculate Values Using Formulas

You can use formulas in tables to perform arithmetic calculations and provide a result, either by putting together your own formulas or using an AutoSum feature.

ASSEMBLE YOUR OWN FORMULAS

1. Place your mouse pointer in the cell where you want the result displayed.

2. In the Layout tab Data group, click **Formula**. The Formula dialog box appears, as shown in Figure 6-10.

3. In the Formula text box, keep the Word-suggested formula, apply a number format, and click **OK** to display the result.

   –Or–

   Delete everything except the equal (=) sign.

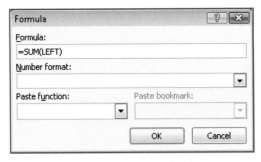

Figure 6-10: *The Formula dialog box provides tools to set up formulas for basic calculations.*

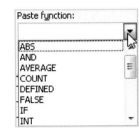

4. Click the **Paste Function** down arrow, and click the function you want to use.

5. In the Formula text box, type—between the parentheses following the function—the cell references or attribute the function applies to.

6. Click the **Number Format** down arrow, and click the style you want applied to the result.

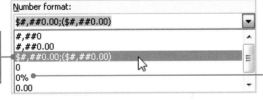

Format results with a currency symbol ($), thousands separator (,), and two digits (.00) for cents

Format results with a percent symbol and rounded to the nearest digit

7. Click **OK** to display the result.

Convert Tables to Text and Text to Tables

If you have information in text format, Word can convert it to a table and similarly convert information in a table to ordinary text.

QUICKSTEPS

WORKING WITH FORMULAS

Word provides a rudimentary spreadsheet capability with tables to perform calculations on numeric entries. Knowing a number of terms and concepts used when working with formulas will make using them in tables much easier. (Any number-crunching other than basic calculations using simple formulas should be relegated to Microsoft Excel, the Office product devoted to performing serious work with numbers. See *Microsoft Office Excel 2007 QuickSteps*, published by McGraw-Hill, for more information on working with formulas, functions, and worksheets.) Common terms and concepts are as follows:

- **Syntax** is the set of rules Word uses for you to communicate how to perform calculations with formulas. For instance, to identify to Word that a calculation is to be performed, you must precede the calculation with an equal sign.

- **Cell reference** is the scheme formulas use to provide a unique address for each cell, consisting of its column-and-row intersection. Columns are designated alphabetically, starting with the leftmost column as "A"; rows are sequentially numbered from top to bottom, with the topmost row as "1." For example, the third cell from the left in the second row would be identified as cell C2.

- **Cell reference operators** are the syntax used to identify multiple cells in a formula. For example, to add the values in cells A1, A2, B1, and B2, you use commas to list the cells the function is to sum: =SUM(A1,A2,B1,B2) or use a colon (:) operator to identify a *range* of contiguous cells: =SUM(A1:A3).

Continued . . .

CONVERT TEXT TO A TABLE

Converting text to a table requires that the text be appropriately formatted with tabs, commas, or another character between columns and a separate character, like a paragraph mark between rows.

1. Drag to select the text you want to convert to a table. In the Insert tab Tables group, click **Table** and click **Convert Text To Table**. The Convert Text To Table dialog box appears. Do not be concerned if the number of rows and columns do not yet match your expectations.

2. Under Separate Text At, click the character used to separate columns of text, or click **Other** and type the character. The number of columns and rows should now reflect how you formatted the text to be displayed in a table.

3. Under AutoFit Behavior, choose a fixed column width by clicking the spinner or entering a value (*Auto*, the default, sizes columns equally so that they fill the available width of the table), having Word set each column's width so that the contents fit in each column, or having Word size the columns to fit the window the table is in. (AutoFit To Window is primarily used when sizing tables in Web pages. See Chapter 9 for more information on saving Word documents as Web pages.)

4. Click **OK** when finished. Figure 6-11 shows both the original text data, as well as the resulting table that was created from it. (Under normal circumstances, the table replaces the data. Here a copy was converted to show both states.)

Superior·Office·Supply	→	1st·Qtr	→	2nd·Qtr¶
Paper·Supplies	→	23,567	→	35,938¶
Writing·Instruments	→	5,482	→	5,836¶
Cards·and·Books	→	14,986	→	15,021¶

Superior·Office·Supply¤	1st·Qtr¤	2nd·Qtr¤	¤
Paper·Supplies¤	23,567¤	35,938¤	¤
Writing·Instruments¤	5,482¤	5,836¤	¤
Cards·and·Books¤	14,986¤	15,021¤	¤

Figure 6-11: **Text properly formatted with separators is easily converted to a table in Word.**

WORKING WITH FORMULAS *(Continued)*

- **Functions** are pre-written formulas that you can use to perform specific tasks. For example, some functions perform arithmetic calculations, such as SUM and AVERAGE; some apply Boolean logic, such as AND, TRUE, and NOT; others are used for unique purposes, such as to COUNT the number of values in a list.

- **Attributes** communicate instructions to a function to perform an action. For example, if you click the bottom cell in a column and open the Formula dialog box, Word suggests a formula: =SUM(ABOVE). The ABOVE attribute eliminates the need for you to reference each cell in the column above the selected cell. Another frequently used attribute is LEFT, as in =COUNT(LEFT) to count the numeric entries in the cells to the left of the selected cell.

CONVERT A TABLE TO TEXT

Converting a table to text converts the contents of each cell to normal text separated by a character you choose, with each row becoming a separate paragraph.

1. Select the table that you want to convert to text (see the QuickSteps "Selecting Tables, Rows, Columns, or Cells").

2. In the Layout tab Data group, click **Convert To Text**. The Convert Table To Text dialog box appears.

3. Under Separate Text With, click the formatting character you want to be used to separate text in columns, or click **Other** and type the character you want.

4. If you have a table within a table, click the **Convert Nested Tables** check box to convert the nested table(s) as well.

5. Click **OK** when finished.

Repeat Header Rows

Headers are the column identifiers placed in the first row of a table (see Figure 6-1) to distinguish different categories of information. In tables, you can repeat the heading rows at the top of each page so that they span multiple document pages. The reader then does not have to remember the column identifier or keep returning to the beginning of the table. (Repeated headers only apply to Word-generated page breaks, not those you create manually.)

1. In the View tab Document Views group, click **Print Layout**, if it isn't already selected, so that you can see the headers displayed.

2. Select the header rows (see the QuickSteps "Selecting Tables, Rows, Columns, or Cells").

3. In the Layout tab Data group, click **Repeat Header Rows**.

Remove a Table

Removing a table removes the rows and columns of the table along with any text or data.

1. Place the insertion point in the table you want to remove.
2. In the Layout tab Rows & Columns group, click **Delete** and click **Delete Table**.

   –Or–

   In the Design tab Draw Borders group, click **Eraser**. Drag a rectangle using the eraser pointer over the table border, and then release the mouse button. Press **ESC** to return to the standard pointer.

   –Or–

   Click the move handle in the upper-left corner, just outside the table, to select the table, and press **CTRL+X**, or in the Home tab Clipboard group, click **Cut**. The table is removed but is available to be pasted elsewhere. (See Chapter 2 for information on using the Office Clipboard to paste material in Word documents.)

Change a Table's Appearance

A table chock full of data is informative, but not necessarily appealing. Word offers special features to help with this, including text wrapping and orientation options. You can also change the look of the table's structure by merging and splitting cells; adjusting margins surrounding cells; aligning the table on the document page; and applying color, shading, and emphasis to backgrounds and borders.

Merge and Split Cells

Cells can be *merged* by combining two or more cells into one cell. Merged cells can be used to create a banner that spans the width of a table, as a placeholder for larger inserted graphics, and for other special effects. You can also accomplish the opposite effect by subdividing a cell into multiple columns and/or rows by splitting the cell.

NOTE

You can apply most of the formatting features to text within a table as you can to narrative text outside a table—for example, you can add numbered and bulleted lists and change the color of text. Use the Home, Page Layout, and Design tabs or the formatting context menu (opened by right-clicking selected text) to add spice to your table contents!

TIP

Check out the alignment, lists, and indent options on the Home, Page Layout, and Layout tabs after you click a cell whose text direction has changed. The option faces become oriented vertically as well!

FORMATTING CONTENT

Tables provide several formatting features specifically focused on working with content in cells.

ALIGN CONTENT WITHIN A CELL

By default, content is aligned with the upper-left corner of a cell. You can change this to several other configurations.

1. Select the cells whose content alignment you want to change.

2. Right-click the selected cells, click **Cell Alignment** on the context menu, and click one of the nine alignment options.

–Or–

In the Layout tab Alignment group, click one of the nine alignment options.

CHANGE TEXT WRAPPING IN A CELL

By default, text is wrapped in a cell to the next line when it extends to the right border of the cell. (You can override this behavior by using AutoFit to adjust column widths to the content. See "Change Column Width to Fit Contents" earlier in this chapter.) To remove text wrapping in cells:

1. Select the cells for which you do not want text to wrap.

2. Right-click the selected cells, click **Table Properties** on the context menu, and click the **Cell** tab, if it isn't already selected.

3. Click **Options** to open the Cell Options dialog box. Under Options, clear the **Wrap Text** check box. (Fit Text changes the font size to fit the cell size.)

Continued . . .

MERGE CELLS

1. Select the cells you want to combine into one cell (see the QuickSteps "Selecting Tables, Rows, Columns, or Cells").

Document pane		Displays the contents of the document being created or edited

2. Right-click the selection and click **Merge Cells**.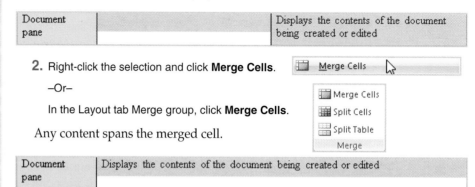

–Or–

In the Layout tab Merge group, click **Merge Cells**.

Any content spans the merged cell.

Document pane	Displays the contents of the document being created or edited

SPLIT CELLS

1. Select the cells you want to split into more columns or rows.

2. Right-click the cells and click **Split Cells**.

–Or–

In the Layout tab Merge group, click **Split Cells**.

In both cases, the Split Cells dialog box will appear.

3. Click the **Number Of Columns** spinner or enter a value to divide the selected cells vertically.

–And/Or–

Click the **Number Of Rows** spinner or enter a value to divide the selected cells horizontally. (Other cells in the rows of the cells being split increase their height to accommodate the increase.)

4. To split each selected cell into the number of rows or columns entered, clear the **Merge Cells Before Split** check box.

–Or–

To split the merged block of selected cells into the number of rows or columns entered, select the **Merge Cells Before Split** check box.

5. Click **OK**.

FORMATTING CONTENT *(Continued)*

4. Click **OK** twice to close the Cell Options and Table Properties dialog boxes.

Options
- ☐ Wrap text
- ☐ Fit text

ORIENT TEXT DIRECTION IN A CELL

For a special effect, you can change the typical horizontal text orientation to one of two vertical arrangements, as shown in Figure 6-12.

1. Select the cells whose text orientation you want to change.

2. Right-click the selected cells, and click **Text Direction** on the context menu. In the Text Direction –Table Cell dialog box, click an orientation and click **OK**.

–Or–

In the Layout tab Alignment group, click **Text Direction** to cycle through the one horizontal and two vertical orientation options.

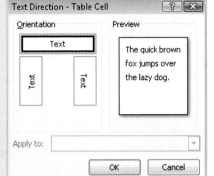

NOTE

Turning off the word-wrap option does not cause text to not word wrap unless the AutoFit option is selected. In other words, text continues to wrap onto the next line, regardless of the option, if the AutoFit option is not selected.

Wrap Text Around a Table

By default, tables are inserted *inline* with other text and objects in the document so that the other content is either above or below the table's position. You can choose to have adjacent text wrap on either side the table, as well as adjust how the table is positioned relative to the text.

1. Right-click the table you want to align, click **Table Properties** on the context menu, and click the **Table** tab (see Figure 6-13).

2. Under Text Wrapping, click the **Around** icon to wrap text around the sides of the table (the table's width must be less than the margin width for text to appear on the sides).

3. Click **Positioning** to open the Table Positioning dialog box, shown in Figure 6-14:

   ● Under Horizontal and Vertical, set values to position the table relative to other elements on the page.

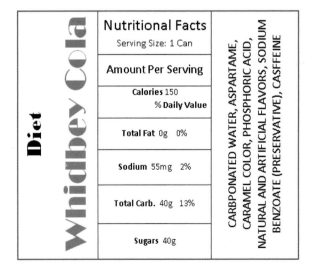

Figure 6-12: **Vertical text provides interesting opportunities for laying out logos and other information.**

QUICKSTEPS

CHANGING A TABLE'S ALIGNMENT

ALIGN A TABLE QUICKLY

1. Point just above the left-most column in the table you want to align, and drag to the right to select all the columns, *but not the final mark at the end of each row, just outside the right-most column.*

2. In the Home tab Paragraph group, click **Align Left**, **Center**, or **Align Right**. (See Chapter 3 for an explanation of the alignment buttons. Justify alignment doesn't work in paragraphs.)

ALIGN AND INDENT A TABLE

1. Right-click the table you want to align, click **Table Properties** on the context menu, and click the **Table** tab, as shown in Figure 6-13.

2. Click the **Left** alignment icon. Click the **Indent From Left** spinner or enter a value to shift the left edge of the table relative to the page margin (use negative values to shift the left edge to the left of the margin).

3. Click **OK**.

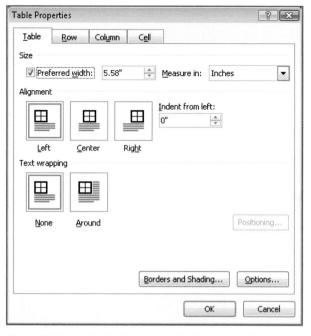

*Figure 6-13: **Use the Table tab of a table's properties dialog box to align and indent a table, as well as to size and determine text-wrapping options.***

- Under Distance From Surrounding Text, determine how much of a gap you want to exist between the table and surrounding text.

- Select the **Move With Text** check box if you want the table to move with text flow; clear it to keep the table in a fixed position, regardless of whether content is added or removed on the page.

- Select **Allow Overlap** to let text flow in front of the table.

4. Click **OK** twice.

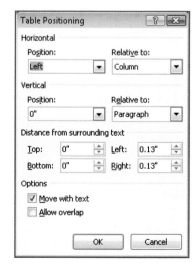

*Figure 6-14: **You can lock a table's position relative to a document's elements and set options for how text displays near the table.***

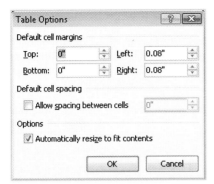

Change Cell Margins

You can change the distance between content and the cell borders, both for an entire table and for selected cells.

SET MARGINS FOR ALL CELLS IN A TABLE

1. Right-click the table whose default cell margins you want to change, and click **Table Properties** on the context menu.

2. On the Table tab, click **Options**. In the Table Options dialog box, under Default Cell Margins, change the **Top**, **Bottom**, **Left**, and **Right** values as needed by clicking their respective spinners or entering numbers.

3. Click **OK** twice.

SET MARGINS FOR SELECTED CELLS

1. Select the cells whose default cell margins you want to change, right-click them, and click **Table Properties** on the context menu.

2. Click the **Cell** tab, and click **Options**.

3. In the Cell Margins dialog box, clear the **Same As The Whole Table** check box, and change the **Top**, **Bottom**, **Left**, and **Right** values as needed by clicking their respective spinners or entering numbers.

4. Click **OK** twice.

Apply Shading and Border Effects

Tables and individual cells can be emphasized using Word's broad set of tools to apply shading and border outlines.

1. Select the table or cells to which you want to apply a shading or border effect.

2. Open the Borders And Shading dialog box, shown in Figure 6-15, by one of several means:

   - Right-click the selected element, and click **Borders And Shading** on the context menu.

TIP

Besides setting the margins for content within a cell, you can also create spacing between cells. In the Table Options dialog box (see "Set Margins for All Cells in a Table"), select the **Allow Spacing Between Cells** check box, and use the spinner or enter a value.

Superior Office Supply	1ˢᵗ Qtr	2ⁿᵈ Qtr
Paper Supplies	23,567	35,938
Writing Instruments	5,482	5,836
Cards and Books	14,986	15,021

1. In the Design tab Table Styles group, click **More** beneath the scroll arrows on the right of the style gallery.

2. Click **Modify Table Style** to change an existing style.

   –Or–

   Click **New Table Style** to create a new one.

3. In either dialog box:

   - Under Properties, enter a name for the style, click the **Style Based On** down arrow, and click a style to start with (the style appears in the preview area).

   - Under Formatting, click the **Apply Formatting To** down arrow, and click the part of the table to which you want the style to be applied. Use the formatting tools on the modified toolbars in the center of the dialog box. Or, you can click **Format** at the bottom of the dialog box to open a drop-down list of options that open additional dialog boxes with even more formatting choices.

   - Click **Only In This Document** if you want the formatting to apply only to your current document. Click **New Documents Based On This Template** if you want the style available to other documents.

4. Click **OK** to close all open dialog boxes when done.

DELETE A STYLE

1. In the Design tab Table Style group, scroll through the table styles gallery, and right-click the style you want to delete.

2. Click **Delete Table Style**, and click **Yes** to confirm the action. The style is removed from the gallery.

Chapter 7
Working with Graphics

Graphics is a term used to describe several forms of visual enhancements that can be added to a document. In this chapter you will learn how to insert, format, and manage graphic files (*pictures*), such as digital photos and clip art images. You will see how to create your own basic renderings (*drawings*) directly on a document and how to combine them with built-in drawings (*shapes*). In addition, you will see how to embed products of other programs (*objects*) alongside your text and how to produce organizational charts and other business-oriented *diagrams*.

Work with Pictures

Pictures can be manipulated in a number of ways once you have them within Word. You can organize your clip art collections, resize images, and move them into the exact positions that you want.

QUICK**FACTS**

LINKING PICTURE FILES

Pictures are *embedded* by default when inserted in a document. Embedding means that the picture files become part of the Word file and their file size is added to the size of the saved Word document. In a document with several high-resolution pictures, the document's size can quickly rise into several megabytes (the greater the number of pixels in a picture, the higher the resolution and the larger the file size). To dramatically reduce the size of a document that contains pictures, you can *link* to the picture files instead. In this case, the addresses of picture files are retained in the document file, not the pictures themselves. (Alternatively, you can reduce the resolution and compress embedded pictures, although the reduction in file size won't be as large as with linked files. See the "Reducing a Picture's File Size" QuickSteps later in the chapter.) Another characteristic of linked picture files is that any changes made and saved in the source file will be updated in the Word document. Linking does have the downside of requiring the picture files to remain in the same folder location they were in when the link was created. In addition, documents with linked files are not suitable for sharing outside your local network.

1. To link a picture file when you are inserting a picture into a document, click the **Insert** tab, and click **Picture** in the Illustrations group to open the Insert Picture dialog box.

2. Click the **Insert** down arrow in the lower-right corner, and click **Link To File**.

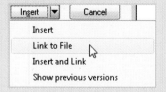

Add Pictures

You can browse for picture files, use the Clip Art task pane to assist you, drag them from other locations, or import them directly from a scanner or digital camera.

BROWSE FOR PICTURES

1. Place your insertion point in the paragraph or table where you want to insert the picture.

2. In the Insert tab, click **Picture** in the Illustrations group. The Insert Picture dialog box appears, as shown in Figure 7-1.

3. Browse to the picture you want, and select it. (If you do not see your pictures, click the **Views** down arrow on the dialog box toolbar, and click **Medium Icons** or a larger size.)

4. Click **Insert**. The picture is displayed in the document.

Figure 7-1: **The Insert Picture dialog box displays thumbnails of picture files accepted by Word.**

NOTE

Pictures are files that are produced by a device, such as a digital camera or scanner, or that are created in a painting or drawing program, such as Microsoft Paint or Adobe Illustrator. In either case, the files are saved in a graphic format, such as JPEG or GIF (popular formats used on the Internet) or TIF (used in higher-end printing applications). Table 7-1 lists the graphic file formats supported by Word. You might need to install filters from your Office CD or the Microsoft Office Web site before you can use some of these formats.

NOTE

Often, when you insert a picture, it is not the size that you want it to be. You can easily make a picture the size you want by dragging the corners of the picture to resize it.

FILE TYPE	EXTENSION
Computer Graphics Metafile	CGM
Encapsulated PostScript	EPS
Graphics Interchange Format	GIF, GFA
Joint Photographic Expert Graphics	JPG, JPEG, JFIF, JPE
Macintosh PICT/Compressed	PCT, PICT/PCZ
Portable Network Graphics	PNG
Tagged Image File Format	TIF, TIFF
Windows Bitmap	BMP, BMZ, RLE, DIB
Windows Enhanced Metafile/Compressed	EMF/EMZ
Windows Metafile/Compressed	WMF/WMZ
WordPerfect Graphics	WPG

Table 7-1: *Picture File Formats Accepted by Word*

ADD CLIP ART

1. Place your insertion point in the paragraph or table where you want to insert the picture.

2. In the Insert tab Illustrations group, click **Clip Art**. The Clip Art task pane opens.

3. In the Search For text box, type a keyword.

4. Click the **Search In** down arrow, and refine your search to specific collections. (The Web Collections category includes thousands of clips maintained at Office Online; therefore, it can take considerable time to find what you're looking for.)

5. Click the **Results Should Be** down arrow, and clear all file types other than clip art.

6. Click **Go**. In a few moments, thumbnails of the search results will appear, as shown in Figure 7-2.

7. Click the thumbnail to insert it in your document.

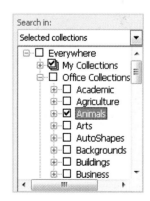

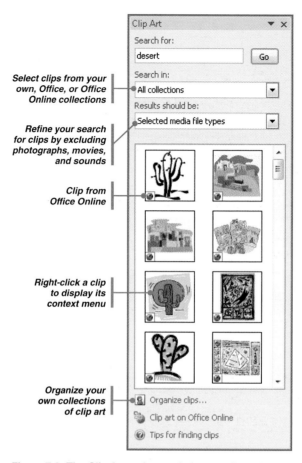

Figure 7-2: **The Clip Art task pane helps you find clips on your computer and on Office Online and then assists you in organizing them.**

Labels pointing to the Clip Art task pane:

Select clips from your own, Office, or Office Online collections

Refine your search for clips by excluding photographs, movies, and sounds

Clip from Office Online

Right-click a clip to display its context menu

Organize your own collections of clip art

TIP

Besides using the Insert Pictures command in Word to add pictures, you can drag picture files from the desktop or Windows Explorer into an open document. To best use Windows Explorer, close or minimize all windows other than Word and Windows Explorer. Right-click a blank area of the Windows taskbar, and click either **Show Windows Stacked** or **Show Windows Side By Side** on the context menu. Locate the picture file you want in the right pane of Windows Explorer, and drag it to the location in the document where you want it.

Context menu:

Toolbars	▶
Cascade Windows	
Show Windows Stacked	
Show Windows Side by Side	
Show the Desktop	
Task Manager	
Lock the Taskbar	
Properties	

ADD PICTURES DIRECTLY

In addition to adding pictures to Word from files on your computer or from clip art, you can directly bring pictures into Word from a camera plugged into your computer.

1. Place your insertion point in the paragraph or table where you want to insert the picture.

2. Make sure that the digital camera is connected to your computer and is turned on.

TIP

If you have plugged in and turned on your camera, and everything looks like it should be working but you can't find it, click **Start** and click **Control Panel**. In Control Panel Home, click **Hardware And Sound**, and click (double-click in Classic View) **Scanners And Cameras**. If your camera is not listed, click **Add Device** and click **Continue**. Click **Next**, select the manufacturer and model, click **Next**, enter a name for the device, click **Next**, and click **Finish**.

CAUTION

Material you copy from the Internet, books, magazines, and other sources is normally protected by copyright; therefore, before you put it on your Web site or use it for any commercial purpose, be sure to check the licensing agreement or contact the copyright owner.

3. In the Insert tab Illustrations group, click **Picture**. The Insert Picture dialog box appears.

4. Drag the Folders pane to the top of its area, and select the device that represents your camera. This may be called a "removable disk," as shown here:

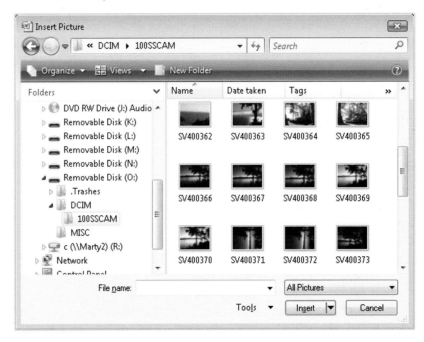

5. Double-click the picture you want to use. The picture will appear in Word.

6. On the Picture tools Format tab, you can adjust custom settings, such as adjusting brightness and contrast or choosing to display the image with various borders and effects, as you can see in Figure 7-3. (If the Format tab is not showing, click the picture to select it.)

Use the Clip Art Organizer

You can organize the clip art located on your hard disks into collections, either in a single or multiple folders, as you choose. Keywords are automatically added to the clips so that you can easily find them. Start by opening a document.

Figure 7-3: *After bringing a picture into Word, you can set several image properties.*

TIP

You can add clip art manually, either from a camera or scanner, or automatically at any time. In the Clip Organizer task pane, click **File**, click **Add Clips To Organizer**, and click the method of adding clips you want to use.

OPEN THE ORGANIZER

1. If necessary, display the task pane by clicking **Clip Art** in the Insert tab Illustrations group. The Clip Art task pane opens, as shown earlier in Figure 7-2.

2. Click **Organize Clips** near the bottom of the task pane. The Microsoft Clip Organizer dialog box appears. You can search for clip art, or you can pick collections and folders located either on your disks or online to be cataloged.

3. Open a collection and then open a folder of clips in the Collection List pane. The clips are displayed in the right pane, as shown in Figure 7-4.

FIND CLIP ART

1. Click **Search** on the Clip Organizer toolbar. A portion of the Clip Art task pane displays in the left pane of the window.

2. Type keywords in the Search For text box, and refine the search using the search options drop-down list boxes.

3. Click **Go**. Clips meeting your search criteria are displayed in the right pane.

MOVE AND COPY CLIPS IN A DIALOG BOX

1. Select a clip in the right pane of the Clip Organizer. To move and copy multiple clips, hold **CTRL** and click noncontiguous clips to select them, or hold **SHIFT** and click the first and last clip in a contiguous series. Click the down arrow of the clip or one of the selected clips, or click the **Edit** menu.

2. Click **Copy To Collection** or **Move To Collection**, depending on what you want to do (clips cannot be moved from online or Office collections).

   –Or–

   Click **Make Available Offline** if transferring an online clip.

11 Items

Figure 7-4: **The Clip Organizer searches your hard disk and creates collections of clips similar to your folder structure.**

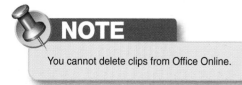

NOTE

You cannot delete clips from Office Online.

3. In the Copy Or Move To Collection dialog box, either browse to and select the collection where you want the clip, and click **OK**; or put the clip into a new collection by clicking **New**, naming the collection, browsing to and selecting where you want the new collection, and clicking **OK** twice.

4. Click the **Search** down arrow at the top of the task pane, and click **Collection List**.

MOVE AND COPY CLIPS BY DRAGGING

1. In the Collection List task pane, locate and open the folder from which you will copy or move the clips, and then locate the folder to which you want to copy or move the clips.

2. Click a clip in the right pane of the Clip Organizer. To move and copy multiple clips, hold **CTRL** and click noncontiguous clips to select them, or hold **SHIFT** and click the first and last clip in a contiguous series.

3. Copy the selected clips by dragging them from the right pane to the destination collection in the left pane.

–Or–

Move selected clips within your collection by holding down **SHIFT** while dragging them from the right pane to the destination collection in the left pane. Release the mouse before you release **SHIFT**.

DELETE CLIPS

1. In the Collection List task pane, locate and open the folder with the clips you want to delete.

2. Select a clip in the right pane of the Clip Organizer. To delete multiple clips, hold **CTRL** while clicking noncontiguous clips to select them, or hold **SHIFT** and click the first and last clip in a contiguous series. Click the down arrow of the clip or one of the selected clips, or click the **Edit** menu.

3. Click **Delete From** "*collection*" to remove the clips from the current collection.(If a clip was originally in My Collections, it is moved to the Unclassified Clips collection for future use; if the clip was added after My Collections was created, it's removed from all collections.)

–Or–

Click **Delete From Clip Organizer** to remove the clips from all collections.

EDIT KEYWORDS AND CAPTIONS

1. Select one or more clips in the right pane of the Clip Organizer. Click the down arrow in the last selected clip, and click **Edit Keywords**.

   –Or–

   After selecting one or more clips, click the **Edit** menu, and click **Keywords**.

2. In the Keywords dialog box, shown in Figure 7-5, click the **Clip By Clip** tab to address clips individually, or, if you have selected multiple clips, click the **All Clips At Once** tab to make changes to all selected clips.

3. In the Keyword text box at the top, type keywords separated by commas. Click **Add**. To delete a keyword, select it and click **Delete**.

4. Type a caption or select one from the drop-down list box. To delete a caption, select it and press **DELETE**.

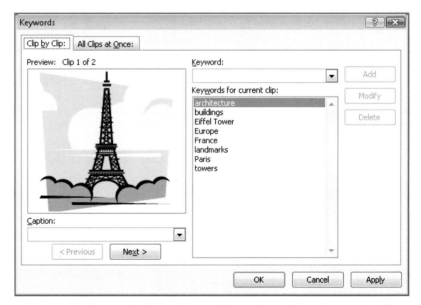

Figure 7-5: *Add keywords for easier searching and captions to better describe your clip art.*

Select a style

Align **Group**

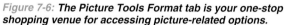

Figure 7-6: **The Picture Tools Format tab is your one-stop shopping venue for accessing picture-related options.**

Show all styles

Rotate

You can add a caption to inserted pictures to give a uniform appearance to your picture identifiers. Right-click a picture and click **Insert Caption**. In the Caption dialog box, choose a label (create your own labels by clicking **New Label**), where you want the caption, and a numbering format. You can also have Word use AutoCaption to automatically add a caption based on the type of picture or object inserted.

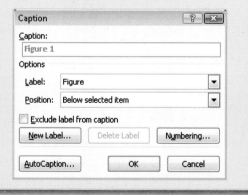

Remove Unwanted Areas

You can remove areas from a picture that you do not want by using the Crop tool on the Picture toolbar.

1. Open and select the picture you want to crop. See "Add Pictures" earlier in this chapter.

2. On the Picture Tools Format tab, click **Crop** in the Size group. The picture redisplays with eight sizing handles on the corners and sides, and the mouse pointer becomes a cropping icon when outside the picture, as shown in Figure 7-7.

3. Place the cropping tool over one of the eight sizing handles (it will morph into an angle or T icon), and drag the tool so that the area of the picture is cut away or cropped by what you have dragged over.

4. Release the mouse button. The area of the picture is cropped. Press **ESC** or click outside of the image to turn off the Crop tool.

Reduce a Picture's File Size

Pictures embedded in a document add to the document's file size. Just a few high-resolution pictures or several lower-resolution pictures can quickly increase a document's file size beyond the threshold established by many e-mail servers and network administrators. To mitigate against file size "bloat," you have a few options available to you. (An alternative method of reducing

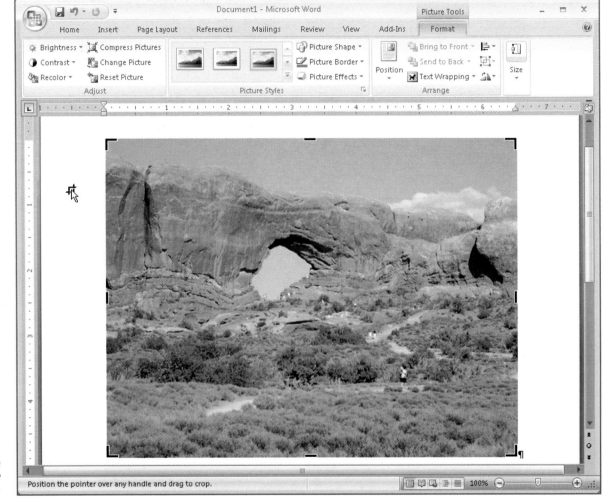

Figure 7-7: *Cropping removes the area of a picture outside the dashed area.*

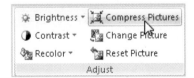

the impact of inserted pictures is to link the pictures to the document. See the QuickFacts "Linking Picture Files" earlier in this chapter for more information.)

1. Open and select the pictures whose file size you want to reduce.

2. In the Picture Tools Format tab Adjust group, and click **Compress Pictures**.

QUICKSTEPS

POSITIONING PICTURES

When you insert a picture, by default, the image is positioned in a paragraph similar to a character you enter from the keyboard; that is, the bottom of the image is aligned with the bottom of the text line at the insertion point. The paragraph will expand vertically the height of the picture and "push" any other text or objects down the page. The picture is "in line with text" and maintains its *relative* position to surrounding content as text and other objects are added to or removed from the page. (You can change this orientation, however. See "Position a Picture Independently of Text.")

ALIGN PICTURES

Use one of the following paragraph-formatting tools to align pictures with text (see Chapter 3 for details on how to format paragraphs):

- The paragraph alignment tools in the Home tab Paragraph group

- The Paragraph dialog box is opened from either the paragraph's context menu or the Home tab Paragraph group's Dialog Box Launcher

Continued . . .

3. Click **Apply To Selected Pictures Only** if that is what you want (versus applying it to all the pictures in the document), click **Options**, and select from the following options:

- Under Compression Options, choose whether to reduce the file size by software compression when you save the file (if not, the compression is not done at all) and/or whether to delete cropped areas of pictures, which removes any cropped areas not only from view, but totally from the document.

- Choose whether the target output should be printing the document, viewing it on the screen, or sending it via e-mail. For each option, the resolution of the resulting image is shown in pixels per inch (ppi). The greater the ppi, the higher the resolution.

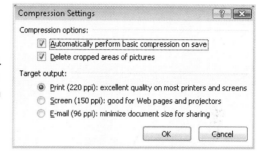

4. Click **OK** twice to close the Compression Settings and the Compress Pictures dialog boxes.

Position a Picture Independently of Text

Positioning a picture independently of the text on a page is called "absolute positioning" and offers three features that the default paragraph-positioning feature does not. You can:

- Place a picture in a document so that it keeps its position, even if other content shifts on the page

- Drag a picture to any location on a page, regardless of paragraph considerations

- Place the picture according to distances or positions relative to document areas

To position a picture absolutely:

1. Click the picture to select it. In the Picture Tools Format tab, click **Position** in the Arrange group.

2. Click any wrapping style, except In Line With Text. You can now drag the picture to anywhere in the document.

- Tabs and indents set in the horizontal ruler or the Tabs dialog box (opened from the Paragraph dialog box or by double-clicking a tab on the ruler)

MOVE PICTURES

1. Click the picture you want to move to select it.

2. Drag the picture to a new paragraph or table cell.

Create Drawings

Drawings may be comprised of pre-built shapes, text you add effects to, and renderings you put together using one or more drawing tools. You can manipulate drawings by altering their position, size, color, shape, and other characteristics using the Drawing Tools Format tab, shown in Figure 7-8. You can choose pre-made graphics or *shapes*; add styles, color, and effects; and position and size graphics using the tools available in the Drawing Tools Format tab.

Drawings are created within a drawing canvas, which is a rectangular area where you can move and size multiple drawings as one object. To start a new drawing:

Open a new drawing canvas. In the Insert tab Illustrations group, click **Shapes** and then, at the bottom of the drop-down menu, click **New Drawing Canvas**.

–Or–

Start with one of the many pre-built shapes on the Shapes drop-down menu, and a drawing canvas will be created for you.

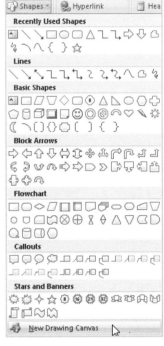

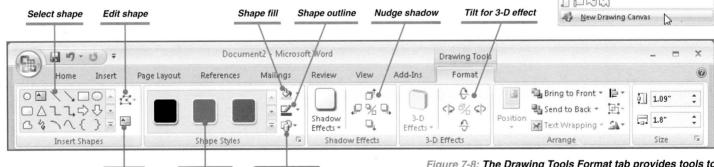

*Figure 7-8: **The Drawing Tools Format tab provides tools to create and insert drawings and to apply effects.***

TIP

The Align option in the Arrange group of the Drawing Tools Format tab has a number of options that help with the placement of several objects. These allow you to align a common edge of several objects or to evenly distribute them.

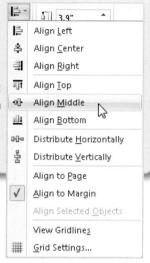

TIP

Several other shapes are available from clip art collections. Type <u>autoshapes</u> in the **Search For** text box in the Clip Art task pane. Choose to search in all collections, and click **Go** (see "Add Clip Art" earlier in the chapter).

TIP

If a curve doesn't have an edit point where you need one, right-click the curve, click **Edit Points**, and then, where you want a new point, click **Add Point** on the context menu.

Add Shapes

Shapes are small, pre-built drawings that you can select, or you can create your own by modifying existing shapes or drawing your own freeform shapes. The pre-built shapes and tools for creating your own are added either from the Insert tab Illustrations group or, with a drawing canvas open and selected, from the Drawing tools Format tab Insert Shapes group.

1. In the Insert tab Illustrations group, click **Shapes** to open the Shapes drop-down menu.
2. Choose a shape:

   Click a shape from one of the several categories.

   –Or–

   Click one of the lines or basic shapes to begin your own shape.
3. Drag the mouse crosshair pointer in the approximate location and size you want. In the case of freeform tools, see the QuickSteps "Working with Curves."

Add Special Effects to Text

Special text effects, as shown in Figure 7-9, can be easily added to text using WordArt to simulate a graphic artist's professional touch.

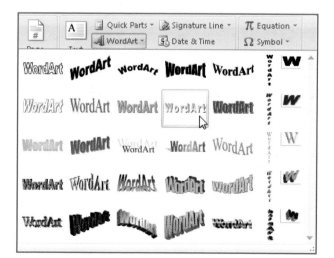

*Figure 7-9: **The WordArt Gallery provides 30 special effects that can be applied to text.***

QUICKSTEPS

WORKING WITH CURVES

Freeform tools, used to draw curved shapes, are available on the Insert tab Illustrations group, on the Shapes drop-down menu under Recently Used Shapes. (You will find that other shapes are displayed here after you have used them.)

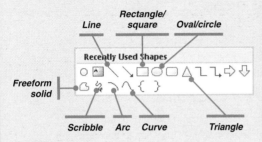

CREATE A CURVE

In the Insert tab Illustrations group, click **Shapes**. You can then perform any of the following actions:

- Click **Curve** and click the crosshair pointer to establish the curve's starting point. Move the pointer and click at each change in direction to continue creating other curvatures. Double-click to set the end point and complete the drawing.

- Click **Scribble** and drag the pencil icon to create the exact shape you want. Release the mouse button to complete the drawing.

- Click **Freeform** and use a combination of curve and scribble techniques. Click the crosshair pointer to establish curvature points, and/or drag the pencil pointer to create other designs. Double-click to set the end point and complete the drawing.

Continued . . .

APPLY A WORDART EFFECT

1. In the Insert tab Text group, click **WordArt** to display the WordArt gallery of text styles, shown in Figure 7-9.

2. Click a style that's close to what you want (you can "tweak" it later). The Edit WordArt Text dialog box appears.

3. Type the text you want styled, and click **OK**. The text is displayed with the effect you have selected.

WORK WITH WORDART

The WordArt Tools Format tab, shown in Figure 7-10, displays when you select text that has a WordArt effect applied to it. Use its options to edit, apply different styles, and change the contour of the effect:

- Click **Edit Text** to change the text and the font characteristics to which the effect is applied.

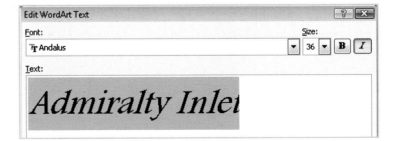

QUICKSTEPS

WORKING WITH CURVES *(Continued)*

ADJUST A CURVE

1. Right-click a handle or line of the curve, and click **Edit Points**. Black rectangles (*vertices*) appear at the curvature points.

2. Drag a vertex to reconfigure its shape.

3. Change any other vertex, and click outside the curve when finished.

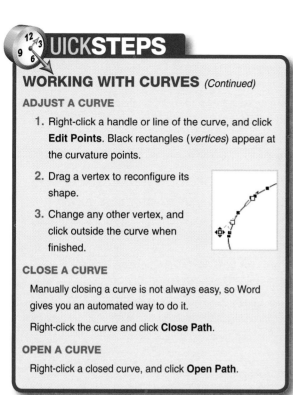

CLOSE A CURVE

Manually closing a curve is not always easy, so Word gives you an automated way to do it.

Right-click the curve and click **Close Path**.

OPEN A CURVE

Right-click a closed curve, and click **Open Path**.

- Click **Spacing** to choose from several character-spacing options.

- Click **Even Height** to make all the characters, both uppercase and lowercase, the same height.

- Click **WordArt Vertical Text** to stack the letters vertically from top to bottom.

- Click **Align Text** to choose from several alignment formats, including left, right, and center alignment.

- Point at a different WordArt style to see the effects on your text. Click the style to make it permanent.

- Click **Shape Fill** and then point at a color or other fill to see the effect on your text. Click the fill to make it permanent.

- Click **Shape Outline** and then point at a color or other outline format to see the effect on your text. Click the format to make it permanent.

- Click **Change WordArt Shape** to recontour the WordArt effect to one of 40 different shapes.

- Click **Shadow Effects** to change the location of the shadow on the lettering or to change its color.

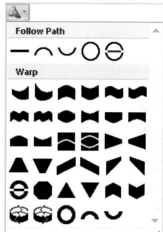

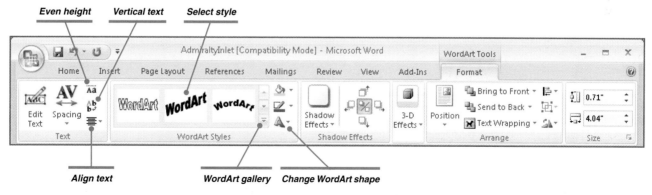

Figure 7-10: **The WordArt Tools Format tab provides everything you need to apply special effects to text.**

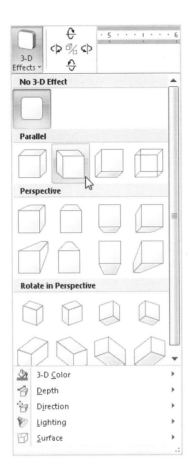

- Click one of the four **Nudge Shadow** buttons to move the shadow in that direction by a small increment.

- Click **3-D Effects** and then click it again in the drop-down list that opens to select one of the 3-D options or to change the settings.

Create a Diagram

You can quickly create and modify several different types of diagrams, some of which are easily interchangeable. One type, an organization or hierarchy chart, provides special tools and features that streamline the structuring of this popular form of charting.

1. In the Insert tab Illustrations group, click **SmartArt**. The Choose A SmartArt Graphic dialog box appears, as shown in Figure 7-11.

2. Click **Hierarchy** in the left column, and then double-click the upper-leftmost diagram to display the start of an organization chart and the SmartArt Tools Design tab, shown in Figure 7-12. Then personalize your chart by doing one or more of the following:

   - Click the highest level, or *manager* position, and in the SmartArt Tools Design tab, click **Layout** in the Create Graphic group to open a menu of hierarchical options. Click the structure that best matches your organization.

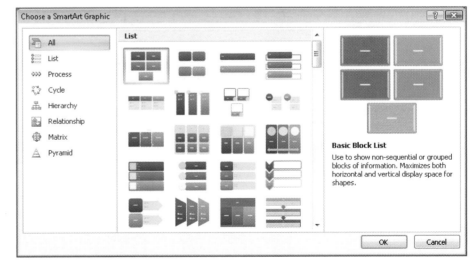

Figure 7-11: SmartArt allows you to easily create a number of diagram types, such as organizational charts.

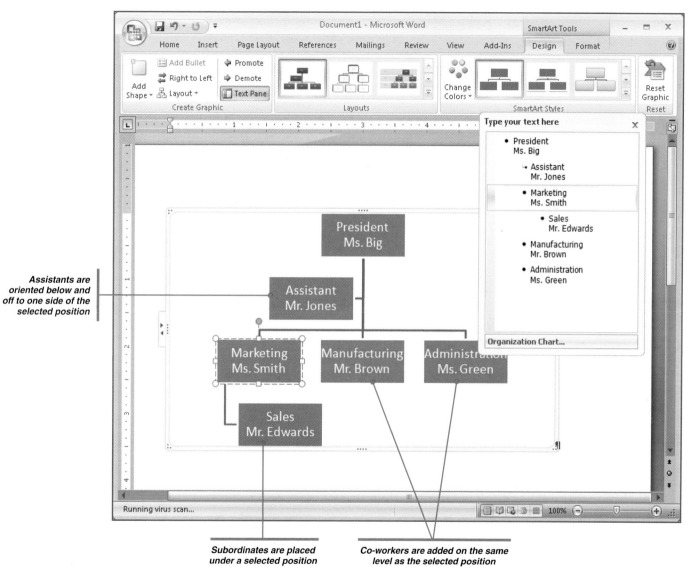

Assistants are oriented below and off to one side of the selected position

Subordinates are placed under a selected position

Co-workers are added on the same level as the selected position

Figure 7-12: *Organization charts are easily laid out and formatted using SmartArt in Word.*

- Click a current box on the chart, click **Add Shape**, and select the type of new position you want to add to the current structure. For a higher level, click **Add Shape Above**; for a subordinate level, click **Add Shape Below**; for a co-worker level, click either **Add Shape Before** or **Add Shape After**.

- To place text in a shape after adding a new shape, simply start typing. You can also click the insertion point in either the text pane ("Type Your Text Here") or the organization chart shape, and then add new or edit existing text. Type the name, title, or other identifier for the position. The font size will change to fit the text box. Press **SHIFT+ENTER** after each line for a subordinate line (like a name after a position), or press **ENTER** for a second but equal line. Format text in the shapes as you would standard text, using the Home tab and its associated options.

- Click **Right To Left** to flip the names and shapes on the right with the ones on the left.

- Click **Promote** or **Demote** in the Create Graphic group to move a shape and its text up or down in the organization chart.

- Click **Text Pane** in the Create Graphic group to turn the text pane on or off.

- Point at any of the layouts, colors, or SmartArt styles to see how your chart would look with that change. Click the layout, color, or style to make the change permanent.

- If you make a "permanent" change, as just described, you can return to the previous layout, color, or style by clicking **Reset Graphic** in the Reset Graphic group.

- To select a group of shapes and their text so that they can be acted upon all at once, hold down **CTRL** while clicking each shape (including the connecting lines). Or draw a selection area around the group of shapes by moving the mouse pointer to just outside the upper-left shape and then dragging the mouse to just outside the lower-right shape.

- Click the **SmartArt Tools Format** tab to display several options for changing the shape and its text, as shown in Figure 7-13.

NOTE

Diagrams are really just combinations of shapes that fit a specific need. As such, you can, for example, delete an element of a diagram by selecting it and pressing **DELETE**. Or you can delete the entire diagram by selecting its border and pressing **DELETE**. See "Modify Graphics" to learn how to format the overall diagram, as well as how to change various components of shapes.

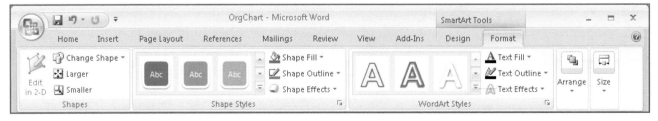

Figure 7-13: Quickly redesign the overall appearance of your organization chart.

ADDING OBJECTS FROM OTHER PROGRAMS

You might want to include the product of another program in a document as a graphic. The major difference between adding the graphic as an *object* (these are technically *OLE objects*, named for "object linking and embedding," which is the technology involved) and copying and pasting it is that the object maintains a link to the program that created it in case of OLE. This means that in addition to changing formatting and other graphics options, you can change the *content* using the menus, task panes, and other tools of the originating program while still in Word.

1. In the Insert tab Text group, click **Object**. If a context menu opens, click **Object** again. The Object dialog box appears.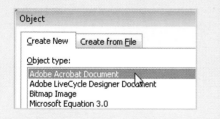

2. Choose whether to create a new object or use an existing one:

- Click the **Create New** tab, select an object type, and click **OK**.

   –Or–

- Click the **Create From File** tab, browse to an existing object, and click **OK**.

Continued . . .

Use Color Effects

Color can be added to interior fills, to borders, and to text in various shades, gradients, textures, and patterns. Click a drawing to select it, and in the Drawing Tools Format tab, click **Shape Fill** or **Shape Outline** in the Shape Styles group. A menu of coloring options opens. Depending on what attribute you want to format, you will see all or part of the following options.

SELECT A COLOR QUICKLY

Click one of 10 standard colors or one of the 60 theme colors in the color matrix on the drop-down menu.

–Or–

Click **More (*Fill* Or *Outline*) Colors** to have access to over 140 standard colors and many more custom colors.

SET GRADIENTS

1. Click **Gradient** on the Shape Fill drop-down menu to open the sub-menu of basic gradient options.

2. Click **More Gradients** to open the Fill Effects dialog box, shown in Figure 7-14.

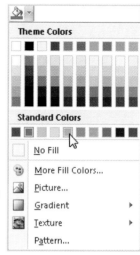

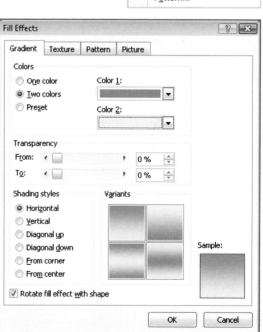

Figure 7-14: **You can blend colors to create gradient fills.**

ADDING OBJECTS FROM OTHER PROGRAMS *(Continued)*

Depending on the object, it opens in Word either in an image of what it is or in its original form, with the ribbon, toolbars, menus, and other tools taking on those of the object's originating program, as shown in Figure 7-15. If you see the image only, double-click the image to display it in its original form with its original tools.

3. With the originating program open in Word, add content and apply design and formatting changes using the original tools.

4. When you are ready to return to Word, click the page outside the object.

TIP

If you create an object from an existing file using the Create From File tab, you can create a *link* between the object in Word and the file. To create the link, click **Link To File** in the **Create From File** tab. See the QuickFacts "Linking Picture Files" for more information.

3. Select one of the following color options:

- **One Color** gives you a one-color gradient result.

- **Two Colors** gives you a gradient resulting from one color blending into another color.

- **Preset** allows you to select one of the gradient color schemes from the Preset Colors drop-down list box.

4. Select a transparency percentage to set the degree of transparency:

Click the **From** and **To** horizontal arrows to change the relative extent to which each extreme of the two colors will be transparent.

–Or–

Click the spinners to set the degree of transparency more precisely.

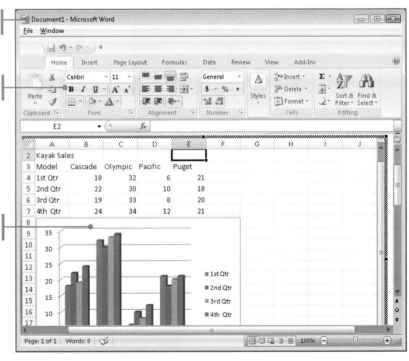

Word document

Excel ribbon

Excel object opened in Word

*Figure 7-15: **Many objects inserted in a document allow you to use their menus and toolbars within Word.***

5. Select a shading style to determine which direction the shading will fall across the drawing. To see the differences, click each option and view the results.

6. When you are done, click **OK**.

USE A PICTURE TO FILL YOUR DRAWING

1. Click **Picture** on the Shape Fill drop-down menu. The Select Picture dialog box appears.

2. Browse for the picture you want, select it, and click **Insert**. The picture will be inserted into the background of the drawing shape.

COLOR TEXT IN A TEXT BOX

1. Select the text to be colored by double-clicking or dragging. If you have trouble selecting the text you want, set your insertion point at the beginning or end of the selection, and press and hold **CTRL+SHIFT** while using the arrow keys to select the remaining characters.

2. On the mini toolbar (displayed when you select the text and place your pointer over the toolbar's vague outline), click the **Font Color** down arrow, and click the color you want from the color matrix. Your selected text is colored, and the Font Color button displays the selected color so that you can apply that same color to additional objects by just clicking the button.

REMOVE EFFECTS

- **To remove a fill**, select the drawing. In the Drawing Tools Format tab, click the **Shape Fill** down arrow in the Shape Styles group, and click **No Fill**.

- **To remove the outline border** around a drawing, select the drawing. In the Drawing Tools Format tab, click the **Shape Outline** down arrow in the Shape Styles group, and click **No Outline**.

- **To remove text coloring**, select the text, click the **Font Color** down arrow, and click **Automatic**. The text will turn black.

Modify Graphics

Pictures (those that use an absolute positioning layout) and drawings share a common Format dialog box, although many of the features and options are not available for every type of graphic you can add to a Word document. This section describes formatting and other modifications you can apply to graphics.

NOTE

Much like adding effects to fills, you can apply arrows to lines, change the thickness of a line, add shadows and 3-D effects to drawings, and introduce other enhancements. The tools work similarly—select the drawing by clicking it, and then click the tool whose effect you want.

CAUTION

Do not remove the line around a drawing unless you have first added a fill. Without the line and a fill, the drawing is invisible, except for the handles that display when it's selected.

TIP

Right-click a graphic and click **Format AutoShape** to open a dialog box that makes available only the options that pertain to that type of graphic. For example, if you right-click a rectangle you drew, the Arrows area of the Colors And Line tab is unavailable, as shown in Figure 7-16, because this is not an action you can do with this type of graphic.

NOTE

Pictures, such as photos and clip art, have more formatting options available to them and more closely behave like drawings when they are provided with an absolute positioning layout. To change the default paragraph-like formatting behavior of pictures to a more flexible layout, right-click the picture, click **Text Wrapping**, and click one of the wrapping styles in the sub-menu.

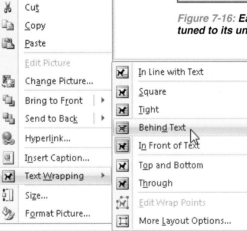

CAUTION

Enlarging an image beyond the ability of the pixels to span it can cause unwanted effects.

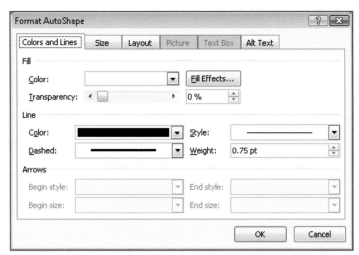

Figure 7-16: *Each type of graphic has a properties dialog box that's tuned to its unique characteristics.*

Resize and Rotate Graphics Precisely

You can change the size of graphics by setting exact dimensions and rotating them. (You can also drag handles to change them interactively. See "Use Handles and Borders to Position Graphics" later in this chapter for ways to resize and rotate graphics with a mouse.)

1. Click the graphic you want to resize to select it. In the Picture (or other graphic type) Tools Format tab, click the **Size Dialog Box Launcher** in the Size group. (For some graphics, such as an organization chart, the Size Dialog Box Launcher will not exist.)

2. Click the **Size** tab, shown in Figure 7-17, and, if it isn't already selected, click the **Lock Aspect Ratio** check box to size the graphic proportionally when entering either width or height values:

TIP

Display the Word rulers to help you draw, align, and arrange drawings more precisely. Click **View Ruler** at the top of the vertical scroll bar to display the horizontal ruler and, if it is turned on, the vertical ruler, or click the **View** tab in the Show/Hide group, and click **Ruler**. If the vertical ruler is not visible in Print Layout view, click the **Office Button**, click **Word Options**, and click **Advanced** in the left column. Under Display, click **Show Vertical Ruler In Print Layout View**. Click **OK**.

TIP

After you change a picture from its default style of being in-line with the text to a style that supports absolute positioning, it is difficult to return to the default style. It's easiest to just delete the picture and reinsert it.

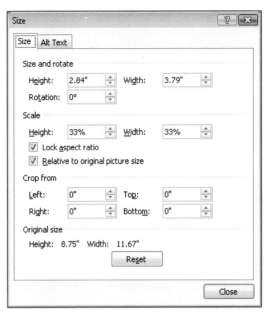

Figure 7-17: **You can size a graphic to exact dimensions in its Format dialog box.**

Under **Size And Rotate** (depending on the graphic, the option may be Height And Width), enter either the height or the width dimension, or use the spinners to increase or decrease one of the dimensions from its original size.

–Or–

Under **Scale**, enter a percentage for either the height or the width to increase or decrease it, or use the spinners to increase or decrease the percentage of the original picture size.

3. To rotate the graphic, under Size And Rotate, enter a positive (rotate clockwise) or negative (rotate counterclockwise) number of degrees of rotation you want.

4. Click **OK**. The picture will resize and/or rotate according to your values.

Position Graphics

Graphics (including pictures that use absolute positioning) can be positioned anywhere in the document by dragging or setting values. In either case, the

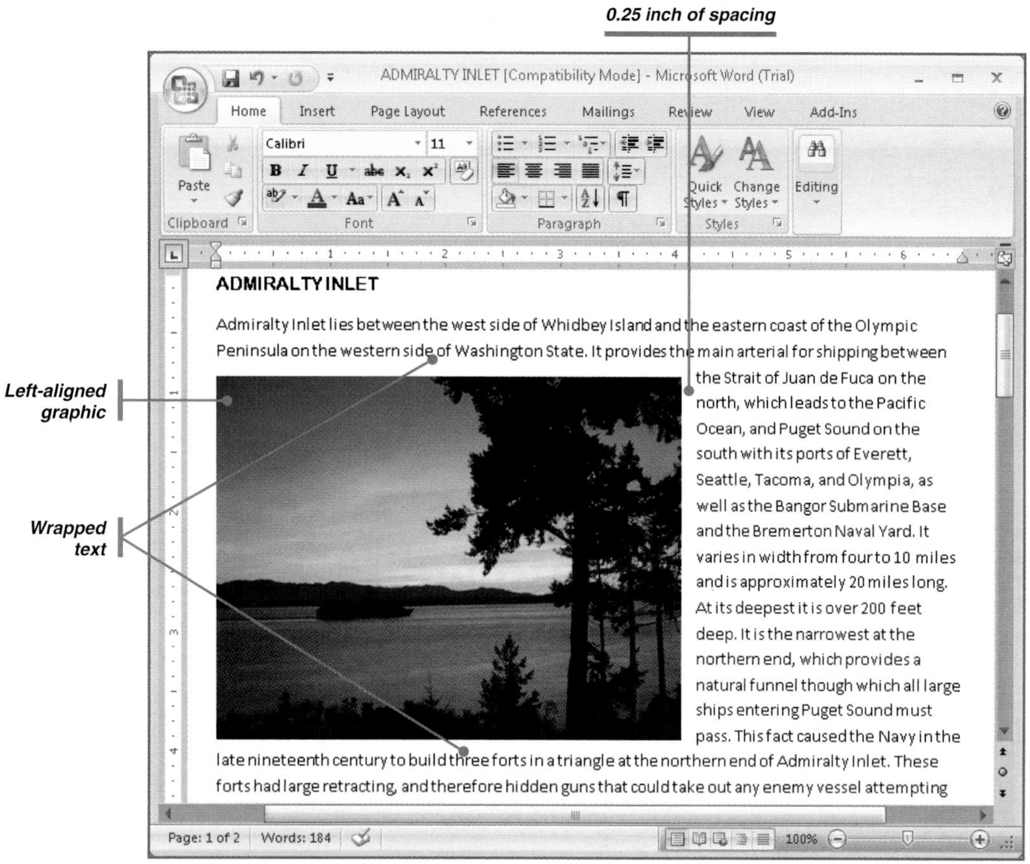
0.25 inch of spacing
Left-aligned graphic
Wrapped text
ADMIRALTY INLET [Compatibility Mode] - Microsoft Word (Trial)
Home
Insert
Page Layout
References
Mailings
Review
View
Add-Ins
Paste
Calibri
11
Quick Styles
Change Styles
Editing
Clipboard
Font
Paragraph
Styles
ADMIRALTY INLET
Admiralty Inlet lies between the west side of Whidbey Island and the eastern coast of the Olympic Peninsula on the western side of Washington State. It provides the main arterial for shipping between the Strait of Juan de Fuca on the north, which leads to the Pacific Ocean, and Puget Sound on the south with its ports of Everett, Seattle, Tacoma, and Olympia, as well as the Bangor Submarine Base and the Bremerton Naval Yard. It varies in width from four to 10 miles and is approximately 20 miles long. At its deepest it is over 200 feet deep. It is the narrowest at the northern end, which provides a natural funnel though which all large ships entering Puget Sound must pass. This fact caused the Navy in the late nineteenth century to build three forts in a triangle at the northern end of Admiralty Inlet. These forts had large retracting, and therefore hidden guns that could take out any enemy vessel attempting
Page: 1 of 2
Words: 184
100%

Figure 7-18: ***You can easily arrange text and graphics in several configurations using dialog box options.***

graphic retains its relative position within the document as text and other objects are added or removed. You can override this behavior by anchoring the graphic to a fixed location. You can also change how text and other objects "wrap" around the graphic. Figure 7-18 shows several of these features.

CHANGE HOW CONTENT DISPLAYS AROUND A GRAPHIC

By default, most graphics come into a document in-line with the text, like just another character. You don't have to worry about it—and you can't control how the text initially flows, or *wraps*, around the inserted graphic. You can change this behavior, however, to gain control of how the graphic and the text relate to each other.

1. Click the graphic that you want to wrap text around to select it. In the Picture Tools Format tab, click **Text Wrapping** in the Arrange group. A menu is displayed. You can click one of the options listed or continue with the following steps.
2. Click **More Layout Options** to open the Advanced Layout dialog box, shown in Figure 7-19. Click the **Text Wrapping** tab and, under Wrapping Style, click one of the styles to wrap as the icons indicate (if you select In Line With Text, the graphic will lose its absolute-positioning ability and can only be positioned using paragraph-like options—tabs, text, and spaces on the left).
3. Click where you want text to wrap, and under Distance From Text, click the relevant spinners to enter the distances you want between the text and the graphic.
4. Click **OK** to accept the wrapping style and other settings and to close the dialog box.

NOTE

The default wrapping option (In Line With Text) is the only style that provides paragraph-like formatting to position pictures. If you change to any of the other wrapping styles, you can position the picture absolutely, that is, by dragging it into position or by selecting positions relative to document areas, such as margins or paragraphs.

UNDERSTANDING GRAPHIC POSITIONING

When you position a graphic (picture, clip art, drawing, or shape) on the page, the position can be *inline*, or *relative*, to the text and other objects on the page, where the graphic moves as the text moves, like a character in a word. The alternative is *absolute* positioning, where the graphic stays anchored in one place, regardless of what the text does. If the graphic uses absolute positioning, you can then specify how text will wrap around the graphic, which can be on either or both sides or along the top and bottom of the graphic. Also, for special effects, the text can be either on top of the graphic or underneath it.

If you find that the movement of the graphic is not as you intended, or if you want to change the way the graphic behaves as you add text, use the Advanced Layout dialog box. Click the graphic and, on the Format tab, click **Position** in the Arrange group, and then click **More Layout Positions**. On the Position tab, you'll see horizontal and vertical absolute position options. If you click the rightmost down arrow, you'll see what the graphic is absolutely positioned to: the margin, page, paragraph, or line. See "Position a Graphic Relative to Areas in a Document."

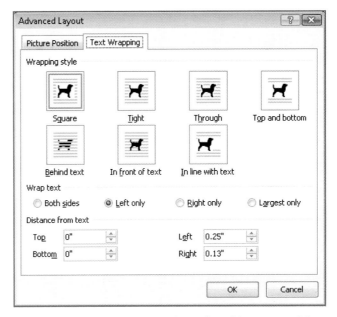

Figure 7-19: *Word allows you to determine with some precision how text and graphics interact.*

When a graphic uses absolute positioning, an anchor icon may be displayed. If the anchor is locked, a padlock icon may also be displayed. If you don't see the anchor icon and the graphic is using absolute positioning, click the **Office Button**, click **Word Options**, and click **Display** in the left column. Under **Always Show These Formatting Marks**, click the **Object Anchors** check box. Click **OK** to display anchor icons in the document.

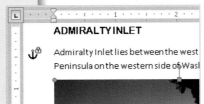

POSITION A GRAPHIC RELATIVE TO AREAS IN A DOCUMENT

Besides dragging a graphic into position, you can select or enter values that determine where the graphic is placed in relation to document areas.

1. Click the graphic that you want to position to select it. In the Picture Tools Format tab, click **Text Wrapping** in the Arrange group. A menu is displayed.

2. Click **More Layout Options** to open the Advanced Layout dialog box.

3. Click the **Picture Position** tab. Select or enter the horizontal- and vertical-positioning entries by selecting them from the drop-down menus, entering the values, or using the spinners to increase or decrease distances, as shown in Figure 7-20.

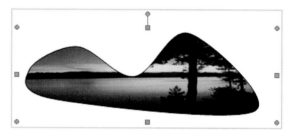

*Figure 7-20: **Using absolute positioning, you can choose where to place a graphic relative to other objects in the document.***

4. To anchor a graphic in place, regardless of whether other content is added or removed—for example, a graphic you want in the upper-left corner of a specific page—click the **Lock Anchor** check box and clear all other options.

5. Click **OK** to close the Advanced Layout dialog box.

Use Handles and Borders to Position Graphics

Graphics are easily manipulated using their sizing handles and borders.

SELECT A GRAPHIC

You select a graphic by clicking it. Handles appear around the graphic and allow you to perform interactive changes. Two exceptions include text boxes and text in text boxes:

- Click in a text box. A dotted border appears around the perimeter of the text box.

- Place the mouse pointer in the text in a text box; it will become an I-beam pointer. Click it to place an insertion point, or drag across the text to select it. The mini toolbar will dimly appear. Move the mouse pointer over the toolbar for it to fully appear, and then make a selection to change the formatting.

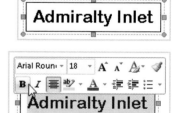

RESIZE A GRAPHIC

Drag one of the square or round (if using absolute positioning) sizing handles surrounding the graphic—or at either end of it, in the case of a line—in the direction you want to enlarge or reduce the graphic. Hold **SHIFT** when dragging a corner sizing handle to change the height and length proportionately (if you

WORKING WITH GRAPHICS

While graphics can be positioned absolutely by simply dragging them or choosing placement relative to other objects in a document, Word also provides a number of other techniques that help you adjust where a graphic is in relation to other graphics.

MOVE GRAPHICS INCREMENTALLY

Select the graphic or group of graphics (see "Combine Graphics by Grouping"), hold **CTRL**, and press one of the arrow keys in the direction you want to move the graphic by very small increments (approximately .01 inch).

REPOSITION THE ORDER OF STACKED GRAPHICS

You can stack graphics by simply dragging one on top of another. Figure 7-21 shows an example of a three-graphic stack. To reposition the order of the stack, right-click the graphic you want to change, click **Order** on the context menu, and then click one of the following:

- **Bring To Front** moves the graphic to the top of the stack.

- **Send To Back** moves the graphic to the bottom of the stack.

- **Bring Forward** moves the graphic up one level (same as Bring To Front if there are only two graphics in the stack).

- **Send Backward** moves the graphic down one level (same as Send To Back if there are only two graphics in the stack).

- **Bring In Front Of Text** moves the graphic on top of overlapping text.

- **Send Behind Text** moves the graphic behind overlapping text.

Continued . . .

have Lock Aspect Ratio selected in the Size tab of Format Pictures, the picture will remain proportionally sized without pressing **SHIFT**).

ROTATE A GRAPHIC

Drag the green dot in the direction you want to rotate the graphic. Hold **SHIFT** when dragging to rotate in 15-degree increments.

CHANGE A GRAPHIC'S PERSPECTIVE

If the graphic supports interactive adjustment, a yellow diamond adjustment handle is displayed. Drag the yellow diamond toward or away from the graphic to get the look you want.

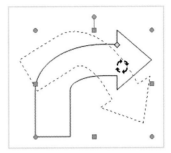

Middle graphic

Top graphic

Bottom graphic

Figure 7-21: *You can change the order of stacked graphics to achieve the look you want.*

can use to create professional-looking forms and allow someone using Word 2007 to interactively fill out the form. Using these same tools, Microsoft has built in, and included on Microsoft Office Online, a number of form templates for various purposes. You can use these templates as is, you can modify them, and you can create your own forms from scratch.

Use Microsoft Form Templates

You can use the Microsoft Office Online forms templates directly from Word, or you can download and store them on your computer, where they are available from My Templates.

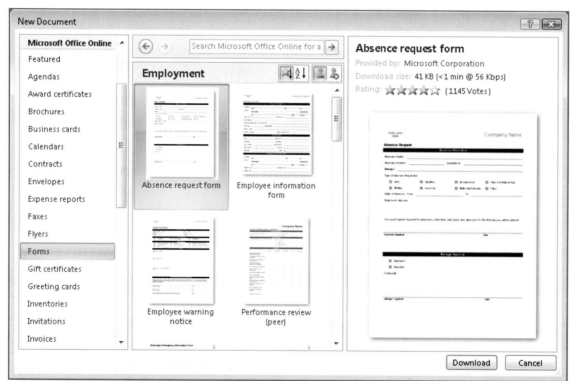

If you want to just use the Microsoft-provided templates, you can do so directly from Word.

1. Click the **Office Button**, click **New**, and click **Forms**. Microsoft Office Online is searched, and a list of forms is presented.

2. Click the category of form that you want. For example, click **Employment**.

3. Scroll down, reviewing the forms that are available to you, and click the form that you want to use. For example, click **Absence Request**, as shown in Figure 8-1.

Figure 8-1: *Microsoft Office Online provides a number of form templates for your use.*

4. Click **Download**. Click **Continue** to validate your software (Microsoft checks to make sure you have a legitimate copy of the software before letting you download the template). The form is opened in Word.

5. Click the **Office Button**, and click the **Save As** arrow.

If you want to use the form only once, click **Word Document**.

–Or–

If you want to use the form a number of times or modify it, click **Word Template**.

6. In either case, select a folder in which to store the form, enter a file name, and click **Save**. See the "Using A Form" QuickSteps in this chapter.

DOWNLOAD TEMPLATES TO YOUR COMPUTER

While you can save the templates obtained in the previous section as template files (instead of document files), another way is to download Microsoft Office Online templates using your browser and save them as template files.

1. Click **Start** and click **Internet**. In the address line, type office.microsoft.com/templates, and press **ENTER**.

2. Scroll down the page. Under Browse Templates, click **Forms**, scroll down, and click the category that is correct for you. For example, click **Employment**.

3. Scroll down and click the form that you want to use. For example, click **Absence Request Form**. Scroll down to see a large image of the form. If this is what you want to use, click **Download Now**.

4. The form is then opened in Word (see Figure 8-2). When you save the form, by default, Word will try to save it as a .doc or .docx in your Documents folder. If you want it to be a template, you must specify this (.dot or .dotx).

5. Click the **Office Button**, and click **Save As**. When the Save As dialog box appears, click **Save**. By default, the files are saved as templates in the Templates folder, which you can access at the top of the Favorite Links list on the left of the Save As dialog box, or in
C:\Users*user name*\AppData\Roaming\Microsoft\Templates.

Absence request form
Version: Word 7 or later
Downloads: 151635
Rating: ★★★★☆ (1145 votes)

CAUTION

In obtaining a form online, you'll see that Microsoft Office Online form templates are created for several different programs. Make sure that the one you choose has been created for Word.

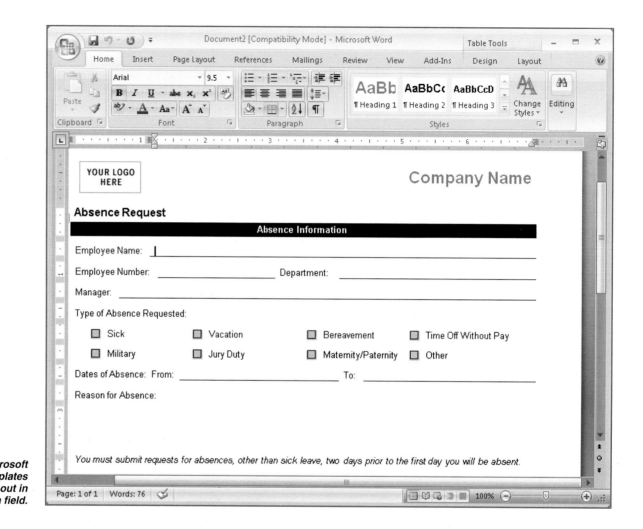

Figure 8-2: *The Microsoft Office Online form templates are ready to be filled out in Word—just click in a field.*

Modify a Template

The fields that you can fill out or select on a Microsoft forms template are created or modified using the content controls on the Developer tab in Word.

1. Click the **Office Button**, click **Word Options**, click **Popular** in the left column, click **Show Developer Tab In The Ribbon**, and click **OK**.

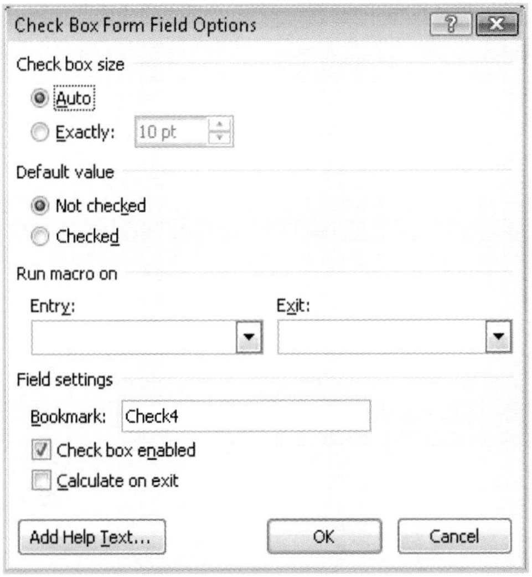

2. Open a Microsoft form template, and save it as a template, as explained in "Use Microsoft Form Templates" earlier in this chapter.

3. In the Developer tab Controls group, click **Design Mode** and take a minute to explore the form. Select a section of the form, right-click it, click **Borders And Shading**, click **All**, and click **OK**. You will see that most forms are based on a table, as you can see in Figure 8-3.

4. Click in the fields, and see how you can easily change the existing text or label simply by selecting it and typing new text. Depending on the type of field, field properties are available that you can work with. For example, if you double-click a check box, you'll see the dialog box to the left.

5. You can delete fields by selecting the table row and deleting it. You can also split and merge table cells to create fewer or more cells to hold fields. (See Chapter 6 for information on how to work with tables.)

6. You can add various kinds of fields, as described in the next section "Create a Form."

7. When you have the form template the way you want it, click the **Office Button**, click the **Save As** arrow, click **Word Template**, click the **Save As Type** down arrow, click either **Word Template (*.dotx)** to create a template for use with Word 2007 or **Word 97-2003 Template (*.dot)** to create a template that can be used with previous versions of Word.

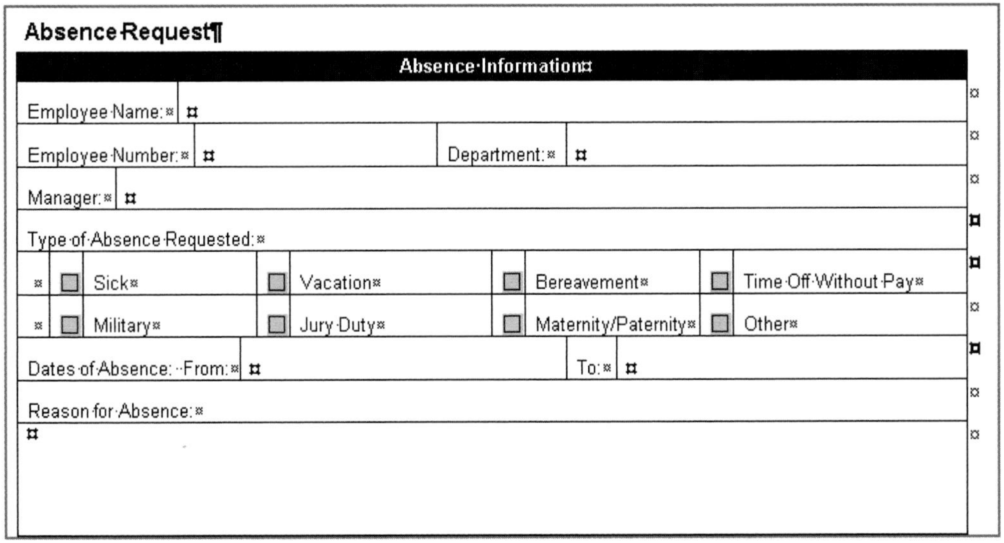

Create a Form

Your first step in creating a form is to decide how the form is to be used. Is it going to be printed and filled out by hand; is it going to be filled out using Word, and if so, what is the oldest version of Word that will be used; or will it be filled out in a browser over either an intranet or the Internet?

Secondly, are you going to use an existing layout in one of Microsoft's templates or design your own layout, perhaps using a table to provide the overall structure?

Figure 8-3: **A table is used as the organizing structure on most forms.**

You then need to add fields (Microsoft calls them "controls") to the form, but you determine which set of controls to use.

LAY OUT A FORM

Laying out a form is one way of visualizing how the information you want to collect will appear. That is why it is so helpful to at least look at, if not start with a form that is already completed. If you don't use an existing form, start by listing all of the fields you want on the screen. Then assign a type of control to each field:

- **Labels** are typed like any other text.
- **Text fields** allow the entry of text onto the form.
- **Check boxes** allow the selection of several options in a group.
- **Option buttons** allow the selection of one option in a group.
- **Spinners** allow the selection of a number in a series.
- **Combo boxes** (or drop-down lists) allow the selection of one item in a list, the first item of which is displayed.
- **List boxes** allow the selection of one item in a list where all items are displayed.
- **Command buttons** perform an action when clicked, such as saving or resetting the form.
- **Picture** (or image) allows the attachment of a picture or image when the form is filled out.

Next, sketch out the form so that you have a rough idea what will go where, and then create a table that has the general layout of the form (see Chapter 6 for information on creating tables). You can split and merge fields to make the final form layout.

SELECT CONTROLS

In the Developer tab Controls group, you have a choice of three different sets of form field controls: those that can be used only in Word 2007 forms, those that can be used in Word 2003 and later forms, and those that can be used in forms created in Word 97 and later. These are grouped into:

Form fields for use only in Word 2007

Form fields for use in versions of Word prior to 2003

Form fields for use in Word 2003

- Controls that must be saved in a .dotx file and accessed and used in Word 2007 are available in the upper-left area of the Developer tab Controls group.

- Active X controls that can be saved either in a .dot or .dotx file and accessed and used in Word 2003 or Word 2007 are available in the lower part of the Legacy Tools flyout menu. (Legacy Tools is at the bottom-right corner in the Developer tab Controls group.)

- Legacy forms controls that can be saved either in a .dot or .dotx file and accessed and used in Word 97 through Word 2007 are available in the upper part of the Legacy Tools flyout menu.

Choosing the type of controls to use depends a lot on how the form will be used. If you are going to print the form and have it manually filled out, then any of the controls will work. If the form will be filled out using Word, then you need to decide which versions of Word the form will support. Similarly, if the form will be filled out using a browser, you will need to decide which browsers you will support. The latest controls for use with Word 2007 only work with the latest browsers. The Active X controls for use with Word 2003 work with more browsers, but far from all of them.

The simple answer, of course, is to use the oldest set of controls. The problem is that these controls are the most limited and, therefore, restrict what you can do on the form. You need to determine which solution best meets your needs.

NOTE

Active X controls require knowledge of Visual Basic for Applications (VBA) to fully use their capabilities. Use of VBA is beyond the scope of this book.

INSERT FIELDS

The actual inserting of a field is anticlimactic:

1. Click in the table cell where you want a label for a field, and type the label.

2. Click in the table cell next to the label. In the Developer tab Controls group, click the control you want to use in that particular field.

3. Repeat steps 1 and 2 for each field in the form (see Figure 8-4).

Information Request

First Name		Last Name			
Street		Suite / Other			
City		State	WA	ZIP Code	
Phone		E-Mail			
Model		Number			
Type of Information Requested: ☐ Catalog ☐ Spec Sheet ☐ Web Site ☐ Have Representative Call
Comments

*Figure 8-4: **A simple form in design mode created using legacy controls.***

USING A FORM

Once you have created a form and saved it as a template, it can be used on any computer with a version of Word that is appropriate for the type of fields used on the form.

1. In Word, click the **Office Button**, and click **New**. In the left column, under Templates, click **My Templates** and double-click your template. The form will open as a document.

2. Click in the first field, and enter the information requested. Press **TAB** to move to the next field.

3. Repeat step 2 until all fields are filled in. Figure 8-5 shows the form in Figure 8-4 after it is filled out.

4. Click the **Office Button**, point at the **Save As** arrow, click either **Word Document** for a Word 2007 file or **Word 97-2003 Document** for earlier versions, select a folder in which to save the filled-out form, enter a file name, and click **Save.**

SET FIELD PROPERTIES AND SAVE A TEMPLATE

Once you have added the controls that you want in each field, you need to set the properties for those controls. The following steps are based on using the upper level of the Legacy Tools flyout menu. You'll find that the choices you have for the Properties dialog boxes differ, depending on which controls you use.

1. Right-click the control and click **Properties**. The properties dialog box for the control will open.

2. Select or enter the information needed for that control. For example, the illustration to the right shows the properties dialog box for a drop-down list box that will allow the selection of a state.

3. When the form is the way you want it, click the **Office Button**, point at the **Save As** arrow, and click **Word Template**. In the Save As dialog box, opposite Save As Type, select **Word Template (*.dotx)** if your template will be used with Word 2007; otherwise, select **Word 97-2003 Template (*.dot)** for earlier versions of Word.

4. Locate and open the Templates folder (called "My Templates" when you open a new document based on the template), which, by default, is in C:\ Users*username*\AppData\Roaming\ Microsoft\Templates.

5. Enter a file name, and click **Save**.

Information Request					
First Name	Guy	**Last Name**	Aguy		
Street	1234 – 96th Ave	**Suite / Other**	#205		
City	Atown	**State**	WA	**ZIP Code**	98000
Phone	206-555-1234	**E-Mail**	aguy@some.com		
Model	A Model	**Number**	123-45-678		
Type of Information Requested: ☒ Catalog ☐ Spec Sheet ☐ Web Site ☒ Have Representative Call					
Comments	Some comments				

Figure 8-5: **When you design a form, consider how easy it will be to gather information from it. Here the data is four points larger than the labels.**

Translate Text

You can translate words, or even entire documents, into several languages using the translation services offered by Word (and other Office products).

Translate a Word or Phrase

The Translate feature is presented in a task pane and allows you to choose the original and translated languages and whether you want to translate the whole document or only a selected part.

1. Open the document with Word in which you want translation help. Select the word or phrase you want translated.

2. In the Review tab Proofing group, click **Translate**.

    –Or–

    Right-click the selected word or phrase you want translated, click **Translate**, and click **Translate…**.

    In either case, the Research task pane appears on the right side of the Word window with the Translation option selected.

3. Under Translation, click the **From** and **To** down arrows, and click the language the text is in (From) and the language you want it translated into (To). The results are displayed in the Translation section of the Research task pane, as shown in Figure 8-6.

4. To translate another word or phrase, select the word or phrase and, in the Review tab Proofing group, click **Translate**.

    –Or–

    Type the word or phrase in the Search For text box, and click the green arrow button.

Translate an Entire Document

To translate a complete document for a fee, you can send the document over the Internet to a machine translation service.

1. Open the document with Word in which you want translation help, and click **Translate** in one of the ways described in the last section.

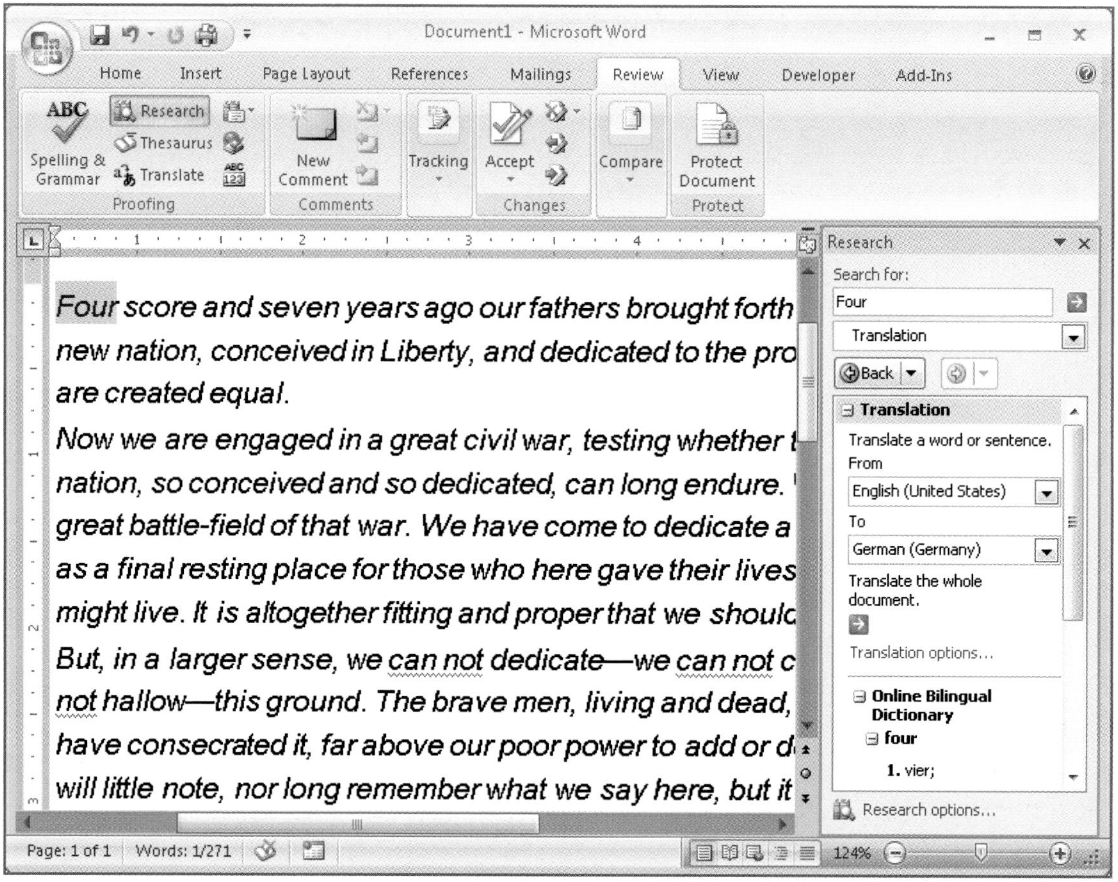

Document1 - Microsoft Word

Home | Insert | Page Layout | References | Mailings | Review | View | Developer | Add-Ins

ABC — Spelling & Grammar | Research | Thesaurus | Translate | Proofing | New Comment | Comments | Tracking | Accept | Changes | Compare | Protect Document | Protect

Four score and seven years ago our fathers brought forth
new nation, conceived in Liberty, and dedicated to the pro
are created equal.

Now we are engaged in a great civil war, testing whether t
nation, so conceived and so dedicated, can long endure.
great battle-field of that war. We have come to dedicate a
as a final resting place for those who here gave their lives
might live. It is altogether fitting and proper that we should
But, in a larger sense, we can not dedicate—we can not c
not hallow—this ground. The brave men, living and dead,
have consecrated it, far above our poor power to add or d
will little note, nor long remember what we say here, but it

Research ▾ ✕

Search for:
| Four | ⇒ |

| Translation | ▾ |

⊙ Back ▾ | ⊙ ▾

⊟ **Translation**
Translate a word or sentence.
From
| English (United States) | ▾ |
To
| German (Germany) | ▾ |
Translate the whole document.
⇒
Translation options...

⊟ **Online Bilingual Dictionary**
⊟ **four**
   1. vier;

Research options...

Page: 1 of 1 | Words: 1/271 | 124% ⊖ ⊕

*Figure 8-6: **Word provides the ability to translate a number of languages using both bilingual dictionaries and machine translation.***

NOTE

Machine translation is free, but it is, of course, less than perfect due to the rigid rules a machine must follow. If you want a more accurate translation you can get a human translation for a price.

2. In the Research task pane Translation option, click the **From** and **To** down arrows, and click the languages the text is in (From) and the language you want it translated into (To).

3. Below the From/To drop-down boxes, click the **Translate The Whole Document** green arrow. Click **Yes** to send the document unencrypted over the Internet. Your browser opens to a WorldLingo Web page with the document translated using machine translation, similar to that shown in Figure 8-7. You can then copy and paste the text into your Word document.

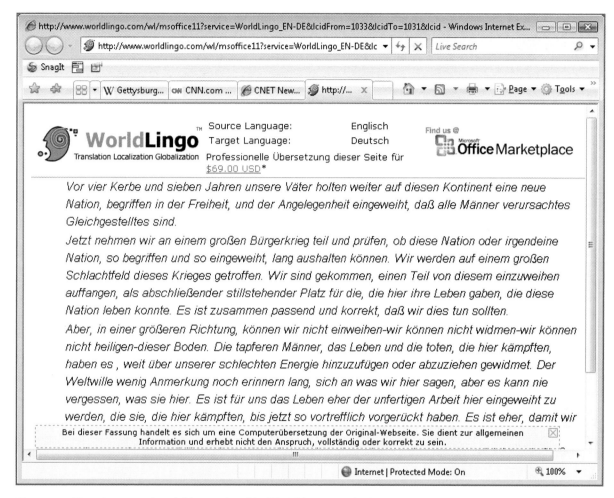

Figure 8-7: *Your document is quickly translated by WorldLingo machine translation. The price for human translation is displayed.*

Work with Charts

Word 2007 uses Excel 2007's extensive chart-building capability to embed a chart in a Word document. You have the full functionality of the chart program available to you, as shown in Figure 8-8. After the chart is created, you can change how your data is displayed—for example, you can switch from column representation to a line chart. In addition, you can add or remove chart items, such as titles, axes, legends, and gridlines, as well as format text and several of the chart items with color and other attributes.

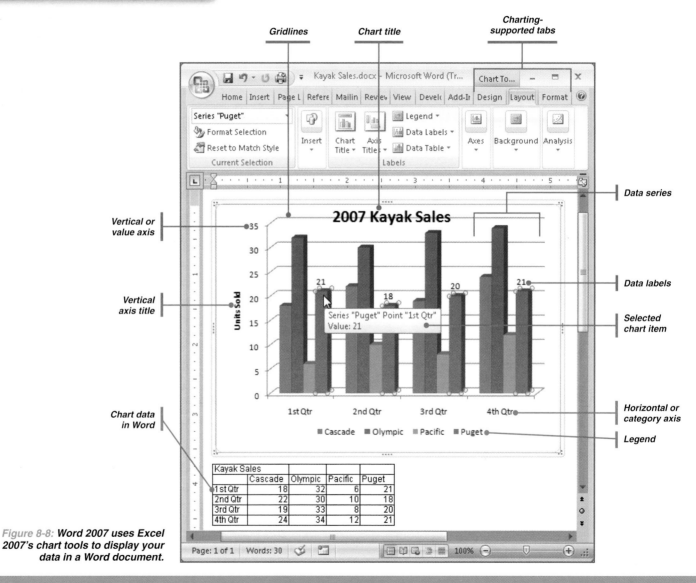

Figure 8-8: Word 2007 uses Excel 2007's chart tools to display your data in a Word document.

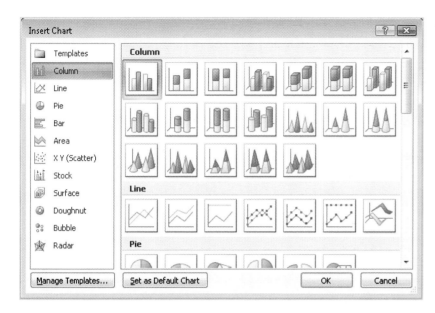

Create a Chart

Charts are created by initially opening the charting capability in Excel and using a sample table there to embed and display a chart of that data in Word. This chart can be easily formatted and reconfigured to meet your needs. You can then replace the sample data with the real data you want displayed, either by typing the data or by cutting and pasting it.

1. In Word, open the document and click the insertion point where you want the chart displayed.

2. In the Insert tab Illustrations group, click **Chart**. The Insert Chart dialog box appears.

3. In the Insert Chart dialog box, first click the type of chart you want in the left column, and then double-click the variation of that type on the right. Excel displays a table of sample data and in Word, a chart of the type you specified displays the sample data graphically. The two programs split the screen, as you can see in Figure 8-9.

4. You can replace the data in the Excel window by typing over it or by copying data from another table, perhaps in Word, to the Excel table. To directly replace the data in the Excel window, type your data over the sample data. To copy another table's data with one that exists in Word, select the Word table, copy it, click the upper-left cell in the Excel table, and paste the Word table there:

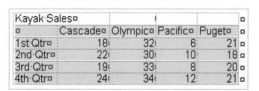

Word data transferred to Excel

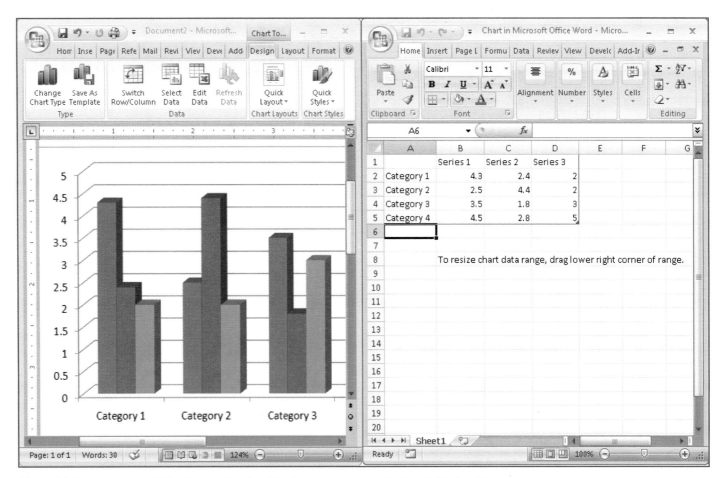

Figure 8-9: **To create a chart, Word opens Excel and the two programs are displayed side-by-side.**

Determine the Chart Type

In Excel, there are 11 standard chart types available to display your data. Each chart type has two or more variations you can choose. In addition, you can create a custom chart type based on changes you've made to a chart. Table 8-1 describes the different chart types.

CHART TYPE	FUNCTION
Column, Bar, Line	Compares trends in multiple data series in various configurations, such as vertical and horizontal, and in several shapes, such as cylinder, cone, and pyramid.
Pie and Doughnut	Displays one data series (pie) or compares multiple data series (doughnut), either as part of a whole or 100 percent.
XY (Scatter)	Displays pairs of data to establish concentrations.
Area	Shows the magnitude of change over time; useful when summing multiple values to see the contribution of each.
Radar	Connects changes in a data series from a starting or center point with lines, markers, or a colored fill.
Surface	Compares trends in multiple data series in a continuous curve; similar to line chart with a 3-D visual effect.
Bubble	Displays sets of three values; similar to an XY chart, with the third value being the size of the bubble.
Stock	Displays three sets of values, such as a high, low, and closing stock price.

*Table 8-1: **Chart Types***

CHANGE THE CHART TYPE

1. Click in the chart to select it.

2. Click the **Chart Tools Design** tab, and in the Type group, click **Change Chart Type**.

3. In the Change Chart Type dialog box, double-click a different chart type.

4. Repeat steps 1 and 2 as many times as needed to find the correct chart type for your data.

CREATE A CHART TEMPLATE

After you have applied formatting and added or removed chart items, your chart may not resemble any of the standard chart types provided by Excel. To save your work as a template so that you can build a similar chart at another time:

1. Create and customize the chart in Word, as described elsewhere in this chapter.

2. Select the chart (the sizing border and the Chart Tools tabs should appear), and in the Chart Tools Design tab Type group, click **Save As Template**.

3. In the Save Chart Template dialog box that appears, select the folder where you want the template stored. The default and recommended location (because it will automatically be found there) is: C:\Users*username*\AppData\Roaming\Microsoft\Templates\Charts.

4. Enter a chart name, and click **Save**.

USE A CHART TEMPLATE

You can use a chart template, either when creating a new chart or by making an existing chart look like the template.

1. Create and save a chart as a template, as described in the previous section.

2. In a new document, either:

Click in the document at the location where you want the chart. In the Insert tab Illustrations group, click **Chart**.

–Or–

SELECTING CHART ITEMS

You can select items on a chart using the Chart Tools Layout tab, the Chart Tools Format tab, the keyboard, or by clicking the item with the mouse. When selected, items will display small, rectangular handles (for some items, these are sizing handles; for others, they just show that they have been selected).

SELECT CHART ITEMS FROM THE LAYOUT TAB

1. Click the chart you are working on.

2. In the Chart Tools Layout tab, click the major item in the Labels, Axes, and Background groups that you want to select (such as Chart Title or Data Labels). A context menu is displayed. Click the specific variation you want.

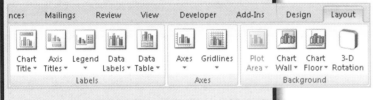

SELECT CHART ITEMS FROM THE CURRENT SELECTION GROUP

1. Click the chart you are working on.

2. In either the Chart Tools Layout or Format tab Current Selection group, click the down arrow, and then click the chart item you want.

SELECT CHART ITEMS USING THE KEYBOARD

Click the chart. Use the arrow keys on your keyboard to cycle through the chart items. A set of selection handles will appear around the selected item.

Chart Title

Back Wall
Chart Area
Chart Title
Floor
Horizontal (Category) Axis
Legend
Plot Area
Side Wall
Vertical (Value) Axis
Vertical (Value) Axis Major Gridlines
Vertical (Value) Axis Title
Walls
Series "1st Qtr"
Series "2nd Qtr"
Series "3rd Qtr"
Series "4th Qtr"
Series "4th Qtr" Data Labels

Continued . . .

Select the chart in the document that you want to change, and in the Chart Tools Design tab Type group, click **Change Chart Type**.

In either case, the chart type selection dialog box will appear (labeled either "Change Chart Type" or "Insert Chart").

3. Click **Templates** at the top of the left column, and then click the template you want to use on the right.

DELETE A CHART TEMPLATE

If you don't want a chart template you can delete the chart template from your folder of templates.

1. In any document open in Word, in the Insert tab Illustrations group, click **Chart**.

2. Click **Manage Templates** at the top of the left column, find and right-click the template you want to remove, and click **Delete** on the context menu.

Work with Chart Items

You can add or modify items on a chart to help clarify and emphasize the data it represents.

1. In an open Word document, click to select the chart you want to work on.

2. In the Chart Tools Layout tab or directly on the chart, select the chart item you want to work on, as described in the "Selecting Chart Items" QuickSteps.

ADD A CHART TITLE

1. With the chart selected, in the Chart Tools Layout tab, click **Chart Title** in the Labels group.

2. Click either **Centered Overlay Title** or **Above Chart**. The words "Chart Title" appear in a selected text box at the top of the chart.

3. Type your own title.

QUICKSTEPS

SELECTING CHART ITEMS *(Continued)*

SELECT CHART ITEMS BY CLICKING

Point your mouse at the item you want selected, and click. Again, a set of selection handles will appear around the selected item.

TIP

The chart item displayed at the top of the Current Selection group in the Chart Tools Format or Layout tab changes as you select an element on the chart. For example, when you select a column in a column chart, the option will be "Series *name*"; when you select an axis, the option will be "*named* Axis"; when you select a legend, the option will be "Legend."

ADD AN AXIS TITLE

1. With the chart selected, in the Chart Tools Layout tab, click **Axis Title** in the Labels group.

2. Click either **Primary Horizontal Axis Title** or **Primary Vertical Axis Title**. Then click the variant of the axis title you want to use. The words "Axis Title" appear in a selected text box either to the left of the vertical axis or below the horizontal axis.

3. Type your own title.

MOVE THE LEGEND

1. With the chart selected, in the Chart Tools Layout tab, click **Legend** in the Labels group.

2. Click where and how you want to display the legend. The legend will be moved accordingly.

SHOW DATA LABELS

Data labels are the actual numbers that generate the elements on a chart. For example, if you have a bar on a bar chart that represents 21 units sold, the data label, which you can optionally add to the chart, would be "21."

1. With the chart selected, click one of your data series (a column, bar, or line), and in the Chart Tools Layout tab, click **Data Labels** in the Labels group.

2. Click **Show**. The numbers appear next to the selected element.

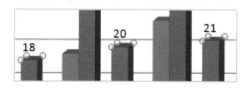

Format Chart Items

Each chart item has a number of attributes that can be formatted, such as the color, the fill, the line style, and the alignment. These attributes are set in the Format dialog box for that item, as shown in Figure 8-10. Table 8-2 shows the formatting options that are available in the Format dialog box for each item.

FORMATTING OPTIONS	DESCRIPTION	APPLIES TO
Fill	Provides options for gradient, picture, or texture fill, as well as color choices, degrees of transparency, and gradient options	Axis, chart area, data labels/series, legend, plot area, titles, walls/floors
Line	Offers solid or gradient lines, as well as color choices, degrees of transparency, and gradient options	Axis, chart area, data labels/series, error bars, gridlines, legend, plot area, titles, trend lines, walls/floors
Line Style	Provides options for width, dashed, and compound (multiple) lines, as well as styles for line ends and line joins	Axis, chart area, data labels/series, error bars, gridlines, legend, plot area, titles, trend lines, walls/floors
Shadow	Provides preset shadow styles and controls for color, transparency, size, blur, angle, and distance	Axis, chart area, data labels/series, legend, plot area, titles, trend lines, walls/floors
3-D Format	Adds a 3-D effect to shapes; provides top, bottom, material, and lighting presets and controls for depth contours and color	Axis, chart area, data labels/series, legend, plot area, titles, walls/floors
3-D Rotation	Provides angular rotation and perspective adjustments, as well as positioning and scaling controls	Walls/floors
Number	Provides the same number formats as the Format Cells Number tab, such as currency, accounting, date, and time	Axis, data labels
Alignment	Vertically aligns, rotates, and stacks text	Axis, data labels, titles, legends

Table 8-2: *Formatting Options Available to Chart Items*

NOTE

The options on the Format *elements* dialog box will vary, depending on the type of chart. For instance, a pie chart will have different options than a bar chart. In addition, the attributes within an option will be different. For example, the fill attributes for a pie chart are different from those for a bar chart.

To open the Format dialog box for a chart item:

● Select the item (see the "Selecting Chart Items" QuickSteps), and click **Format Selection** in the Current Selection group, either in the Chart Tools Format tab or the Chart Tools Layout tab.

–Or–

● In the Chart Tools Layout tab, click a chart item in the Labels, Axes, or Background groups. If needed, click a variation of that item, and then click **More *(item name)***.

–Or–

● Right-click the item on the chart, and click **Format *(item name)***.

Format Text

You may have noticed that there is no capability to format text in the various chart item dialog boxes. To format text:

Select a chart item (see the "Selecting Chart Items" QuickSteps), and in the Home tab Font group use the formatting options or click the **Dialog Box Launcher** to open the Font dialog box.

–Or–

Right-click a chart item, and either use the mini font toolbar that appears, or click **Font** to open the Font dialog box.

*Figure 8-10: **A typical Format dialog box, tailored to a chart item.***

QUICKSTEPS

WORKING WITH THE DATA TABLE

In addition to the chart data in Excel and possibly the original data in Word, you can display a *data table* as part of a chart with the same data. Data tables are for display only and simply reflect the data in Excel. The values in a data table cannot be changed on the chart without changing them in Excel. Figure 8-11 shows a chart with a data table that includes a legend.

DISPLAY THE DATA TABLE

Click the chart in Word to select it. Then in the Chart Tools Layout tab Labels group, click **Data Table**. From the context menu, click **Show Data Table** or **Show Data Table With Legend Keys**. The chart and data are displayed in Word.

FORMAT A DATA TABLE

A data table can be formatted in the same way as any other chart element.

Right-click the data table, and click **Format Data Table**.

–Or–

With the data table selected (see the "Selecting Chart Items" QuickSteps), click **Format Selection** in the Chart Tools Layout or Format tab Current Selection group.

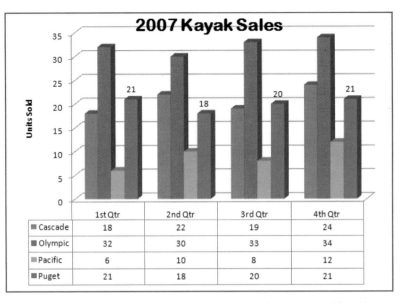

Figure 8-11: **Data tables add precision to the information presented in a chart.**

How to...

- Create a Web Page
- Save Word Documents as Web Pages
- Choosing Suitable Web File Formats
- Configure Web Options in Word
- Understanding HTML and How Word Uses It
- Understanding Hyperlinks
- Insert a Hyperlink
- Verify How a Page Will Look
- Remove Personal Information from the File Properties
- Remove Word-Specific Tags from a Document
- Using Word to Create HTML Elements

Chapter 9
Creating Web Pages

You can use Word 2007 to create and save documents as Web pages. These features enable you to put Word documents on a Web site or an intranet site (a Web site that is internal to an organization) in a format in which they can be viewed using a Web browser, such as Internet Explorer. Word also allows you to work with existing Web pages and provides a number of settings to control them.

Create and Save a Web Page in Word

Word provides the means to produce a moderate quantity of Web pages including the ability to save documents as Web pages, view a document as a Web page, and set a number of options unique to Web pages.

9

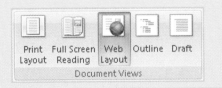

Create a Web Page

Creating a Web page in Word consists of creating a document page as you would for any other document, viewing it as a Web page, and then saving it as a Web page. Such a page can then be viewed with a browser, such as Microsoft Internet Explorer.

1. If Word is not already open, start it. Click the **Office Button**, and click **New**.

2. In the New Document dialog box, double-click **Blank Document**.

3. In the View tab Document Views group, click **Web Layout**.

4. Create content on the page by using standard Word techniques, as described in the earlier chapters of this book. For example:

   - To enter text, type it as usual.

   - To apply a style, select a style from the Quick Style gallery in the Home tab Styles group.

   - To apply direct formatting (for example, bold or italic), select the text to which you want to apply it, and then click the appropriate button in the Home tab font group.

   - To create tables and add pictures and other graphic elements, use Word's extensive table creation and graphics tools.

5. Save the document, as described in the section "Save Word Documents as Web Pages" next.

Save Word Documents as Web Pages

To save an existing Word document as a Web page:

1. Start Word, if it is not already running, or switch to it.

2. Click the **Office Button**, click **Open**, select the existing document you want to save as a Web page, and then click **Open**. The document opens.

3. Click the **Office Button**, point to **Save As**, and click **Other Formats**. The Save As dialog box appears.

4. Select the folder in which you want to save the Web page.

5. Click the **Save As Type** down arrow, and click the file format you want to use. (Your choices are Single File Web Page; Web Page; or Web Page, Filtered. See the "Choosing Suitable Web File Formats" QuickFacts for a discussion of the available formats).

CHOOSING SUITABLE WEB FILE FORMATS

Word offers three HTML formats to choose from; so before you save a file in HTML, you should understand how the formats differ from each other and which format is suitable for which purposes. Word offers the Single File Web Page format; the Web Page format; and the Web Page, Filtered format.

WEB PAGE FORMAT

The Web Page format creates an HTML file that contains the text contents of the document, together with a separate folder that contains the graphics for the document. This makes the Web page's HTML file itself smaller, but the page as a whole is a little clumsy to distribute, because you need to distribute the graphics folder as well. The folder is created automatically and assigned the Web page's name followed by *files*. For example, a Web page named Products.htm has a folder named Products_files.

Files in the Web Page format use the .htm and .html file extensions. These files also use Office-specific tags to preserve all of the information the file contains in an HTML format.

SINGLE FILE WEB PAGE FORMAT

The Single File Web Page format creates a Web archive file that contains all the information required for the Web page: all the text contents and all the graphics. Use the Single File Web Page format to create files that you can easily distribute.

Files in the Single File Web Page format use the .mht and .mhtml file extensions. These files use Office-specific tags that preserve all of the information the file contains in an HTML format.

Continued . . .

6. In the File Name text box, type the file name. If you want to use the .html extension instead of the .htm extension (for a file in either the Web Page format or the Web Page, Filtered format) or the .mhtml extension instead of the .mht extension (for a file in the Single File Web Page Format), type the extension as well.

7. To enter or change the page title (see Figure 9-1—the page title is what appears in the title bar of the browser), click **Change Title**, type the new title in the Set Page Title dialog box, and then click **OK**.

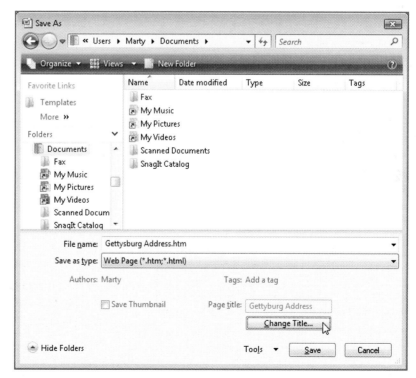

*Figure 9-1: **Word's Save As dialog box for saving Web pages includes the Page Title area and the Change Title button.***

CHOOSING SUITABLE WEB FILE FORMATS *(Continued)*

WEB PAGE, FILTERED FORMAT

The Web Page, Filtered format creates an HTML file that contains the text contents of the document, together with a separate, automatically named folder that contains the graphics for the document. However, this format removes Office-specific tags from the document. Removing these features reduces the size of the file, but the file uses items such as document properties and Visual Basic for Applications (VBA) code, so this format is not useful for round-tripping complex documents (bringing them back into Word and editing them).

Files in the Web Page, Filtered format use the .htm and .html file extensions.

NOTE

Word also offers one other Web-related file format, .xml, which uses the eXtensible Markup Language (XML) to organize and work with data. XML is beyond the scope of this book.

NOTE

You must set the Web options separately for each Office application. The settings you make in Word don't affect the settings in Excel, PowerPoint, or other applications.

9

8. Click **Save**. Word saves the document as a Web page.

9. If you've finished working with the document, click the **Office Button**, and then click **Close**. If you've finished working with Word, click **Close** in the upper-right corner.

Work with Web Pages in Word

Word provides a number of tools and settings that allow you to work with Web pages to give you the features you want on a Web site.

Configure Web Options in Word

Before you start using Word to create Web pages, you must configure the Web options in Word. These options control how Word creates Web pages. Once you've specified the options you want for Web pages, you probably won't need to change them. If you do need to change them for a particular file, you can do so when you're saving the file as a Web page.

DISPLAY THE WEB OPTIONS DIALOG BOX

To configure Web options, first display the Web Options dialog box.

1. If Word is not already running, start it now.

2. Click the **Office Button**, and then click **Word Options**. The Word Options dialog box appears.

3. Click **Advanced** in the left column, scroll down to the bottom of the page, and then click **Web Options**. The Web Options dialog box appears, as shown in Figure 9-2.

4. Choose options, as discussed in the following subsections, click **OK** to close the Web Options dialog box, and then click **OK** to close the Word Options dialog box.

CHOOSE OPTIONS ON THE BROWSERS TAB

Figure 9-2 shows the Browsers tab of the Web Options dialog box for Word. Table 9-1 explains the options and shows for which browsers they're turned on (with the check box selected) or off (with the check box cleared).

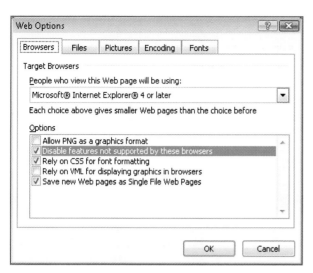

Figure 9-2: *You can create Web pages for specific browser versions.*

The best way to select the options is to click the **People Who View This Web Page Will Be Using** drop-down list and select the earliest browser version that you want to support. The choice you make in this list automatically selects the appropriate check boxes in the Options group box. You can then select or clear check boxes manually to fine-tune the choices you've made:

- Choosing **Microsoft Internet Explorer 4.0, Netscape Navigator 4.0, Or Later** provides a reasonable baseline for most Web sites.

- If you need maximum browser compatibility, choose **Microsoft Internet Explorer 3.0, Netscape Navigator 3.0, Or Later**.

- If your pages don't need support for Netscape Navigator, choose **Microsoft Internet Explorer 4.0 Or Later**.

- If your pages don't need support for Netscape Navigator but need to use features available only in a later version of Internet Explorer, choose **Microsoft Internet Explorer 5.0 Or Later** or **Microsoft Internet Explorer 6.0 Or Later**.

OPTION	EXPLANATION	IE 3, NAVIGATOR 3	IE 4, NAVIGATOR 4	IE 4 OR LATER	IE 5 OR LATER	IE 6 OR LATER
Allow PNG As A Graphics Format	Enables Web pages to contain graphics in the PNG format. All current browsers can display PNG graphics.	Off	Off	Off	Off	On
Disable Features Not Supported By These Browsers	Turns off HTML features the browsers don't support.	On	On	On	On	On
Rely On CSS For Font Formatting	Uses Cascading Style Sheets (CSS) for font formatting.	Off	On	On	On	On
Rely On VML For Displaying Graphics In Browsers	Uses Vector Markup Language (VML) for displaying graphics.	Off	Off	Off	On	On
Save New Web Pages As Single File Web Pages	Uses the Single File Web Page format for saving new files.	Off	Off	On	On	On

Table 9-1: *Options on the Browsers Tab of the Web Options Dialog Box*

TIP

In late fall 2006, Internet Explorer had approximately 70 percent of the browser market (Internet Explorer 7 had 10 percent, Internet Explorer 6 had 55 percent, and Internet Explorer 5 and 5.5 had 5 percent). Mozilla Firefox had approximately 25 percent. Other browsers had 5 percent altogether. Netscape Navigator, once the dominate browser, is now under 1 percent. Firefox is growing rapidly, going from 5 percent to 25 percent in the last two years. These figures show that choosing Microsoft Internet Explorer 5.0 Or Later on the Browsers tab of the Web Options dialog box, and then checking that your Web pages work with Mozilla Firefox will ensure that your pages are viewable by the vast majority of people online.

NOTE

Web documents in Word keep all their text and embedded elements (such as graphics) in the same file. Linked items, such as graphics or automation objects from other applications, are kept in separate files.

NOTE

Keeping the supporting files together in a folder is usually helpful, because you can move the Web page and its supporting files easily to another folder. If you clear the **Organize Supporting Files In A Folder** check box, Word saves the graphics and other separate elements in the same folder as the Web page. This behavior tends to make your folders harder to manage, as you cannot see at a glance which supporting files belong to which Web page. However, if you do not have permission to create new folders in the folder in which you are saving your Web pages (for example on an intranet site), you may need to clear the **Organize Supporting Files In A Folder** check box so that Word does not attempt to create new folders for your Web pages.

CHOOSE OPTIONS ON THE FILES TAB

On the Files tab of the Web Options dialog box, choose options for controlling how Word handles file names and file locations for the Web pages you create, and specify whether to use Office as the default editor for Web pages created by Word. Figure 9-3 shows the Files tab of the Web Options dialog box.

The following options are included in the Files tab:

- Select **Organize Supporting Files In A Folder** if you want the application to save graphics and other separate elements in a folder that has the same name as the Web page plus "_files"—for example, the Web page named "products.html" receives a folder named "products_files." The application automatically creates a file named "filelist.xml" that contains a list of the files required for the Web page.

- Clear the **Use Long File Names Whenever Possible** check box to prevent the application from creating long file names that include spaces, which may not be compatible with the Web server you're using. It's best to keep file names short and to use underscores instead of spaces when you need to separate parts of the file name.

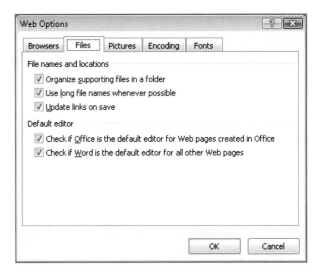

*Figure 9-3: **The Files tab of the Web Options dialog box determines where Web files are stored and how the files are edited.***

QUICKFACTS

UNDERSTANDING HTML AND HOW WORD USES IT

Many Web pages, including those created with Word, use HTML to specify how the page will look and behave in a Web browser.

UNDERSTAND HTML

HTML (Hypertext Markup Language) is responsible for many of the wonders of the Web. It enables you to specify the contents of a Web page and control how it looks and behaves in a Web browser. All modern computer operating systems have browsers, so pages created using HTML can be displayed on almost any computer. An HTML file consists of plain text and pictures with *tags*, or formatting codes, that specify how the text or pictures will look on the page.

For more information on HTML, see *HTML QuickSteps*, published by McGraw-Hill.

UNDERSTAND HOW WORD USES HTML

Word uses HTML to create Web content, automatically applying all necessary tags when you save a file in one of the Web formats. It uses standard HTML tags for creating standard HTML elements (such as headings, paragraphs, and tables) that will be displayed by a Web browser. It uses custom, Word-specific tags for saving Word-specific data in a Web-compatible format.

This combination of standard and custom tags enables Word to save an entire Word document. Saving all the information like this allows what is called *round-tripping*: saving a file with all its contents and formatting so that the application that created the file can reopen it with exactly the same information and formatting as when it saved the file.

Continued . . .

- Click the **Update Links On Save** check box if you want the application to automatically check each link and update any information that has changed each time you save the file. In most cases, this automatic updating is helpful.

- Click the **Check If Office Is The Default Editor For Web Pages Created In Office** check box if you want Internet Explorer to check if Word is your default HTML editor for Web pages created by Word when you click the Edit button in Internet Explorer. Clear this check box if you want to use another application to edit the Web pages you've created with Word.

- Click the **Check If Word Is The Default Editor For All Other Web Pages** check box if you want Internet Explorer to open Word for the editing of all non-Office–created Web pages. Clear this check box if you want to use another application for this function.

CHOOSE OPTIONS ON THE PICTURES TAB

On the Pictures tab of the Web Options dialog box, choose options for the pictures you include in your Web pages:

- In the Screen Size drop-down list, select the minimum resolution that you expect most visitors to your Web site to be using. For most Web sites, the best choice is 800× 600, a resolution supported by almost all monitors manufactured since 2000. If you're creating an intranet site whose visitors will all use monitors with a higher resolution than 800×600, you can choose a higher resolution.

- In the Pixels Per Inch drop-down list, select the number of pixels per inch (ppi) to use for pictures in your Web pages. The default setting is 96 ppi, which works well for most pages. You can also choose 72 ppi or 120 ppi.

CHOOSE OPTIONS ON THE ENCODING TAB

The Encoding tab of the Web Options dialog box lets you specify which character-encoding scheme to use for the characters in your Web pages. Word in North America and Western Europe uses the Western European (Windows)

encoding by default. This works well for most purposes, but you may prefer to choose Western European (ISO) for compliance with the ISO-8859-1 standard or Unicode (UTF-8) for compliance with the Unicode standard.

Select the encoding you want in the Save This Document As drop-down list. Then, if you always want to use this encoding, click the **Always Save Web Pages In The Default Encoding** check box. Selecting this check box disables the Save This Document As drop-down list.

CHOOSE OPTIONS ON THE FONTS TAB

The Fonts tab of the Web Options dialog box (see Figure 9-4) offers the following options:

- Use the Character Set list box to specify the character set you want to use for your pages. Use the **English/Western European/Other Latin Script** item, unless you need to create pages in another character set, such as Hebrew or Arabic.

- Use the Proportional Font drop-down list and its Size drop-down list to specify the proportional font and font size to use for your pages.

- Use the Fixed-Width Font drop-down list and its Size drop-down list to specify the monospaced font and font size.

After you finish choosing settings in the Web Options dialog box, click **OK** to close the dialog box, and then click **OK** to close the Options dialog box.

*Figure 9-4: **Word gives you the capability of choosing a number of different character sets to use on Web pages.***

NOTE

Unicode is a scheme for representing characters on computers. For example, a capital A is represented by 0041 in Unicode, and a capital B is represented by 0042. *UTF-8* is the abbreviation for Universal Character Set Transformation Format 8-Bit. *ISO* is the acronym for the International Organization for Standardization.

QUICKFACTS

UNDERSTANDING HYPERLINKS

Hyperlinks provide the means to switch, or "jump," from one Web page to another or from one location on a Web page to another location on the same page. Hyperlinks can also be used to open files such as pictures and programs. The hundreds of millions of hyperlinks on all the Web pages on the Internet are what give the Web its name. On a Web page, a hyperlink can be a word or words, a graphic, or a picture, which, when clicked, tells the browser to open a new page at another site whose address is stored in the hyperlink. A hyperlink's address is called a *URL*, or Uniform Resource Locator. A URL is used by a browser to locate and open a Web page or file. An example of a URL is http://en.wikipedia.org/wiki/ Hasekurs_Tsunenaga#France:

- The "http://" identifies the site as using Hypertext Transfer Protocol, a set of standards for communication and identification.

- Next, there is often "www," which identifies the site as being on the Internet or World Wide Web; although, frequently, as in this case, the space used by "www" in a URL contains other information used to identify a major segmentation of the Web site. In this case, the "en" identifies the English language area.

Continued . . .

Insert a Hyperlink

There are several different types of hyperlinks. All of them are inserted on a page in Word by first displaying the Insert Hyperlink dialog box, as described here. You then need to follow the steps in the subsequent sections for the particular type of hyperlink you want to create.

1. Start Word and open the file in which you want to insert the hyperlink, as described in "Create a Web Page."

2. Select the text or graphic where you want the hyperlink to appear.

3. In the Insert tab Links group, click Hyperlink. The Insert Hyperlink dialog box appears (see Figure 9-5).

4. Complete the hyperlink by following the steps in one of the following sections, depending on whether you want to create a hyperlink to an existing file or Web page, to a place in the current document, to a new document, or to an e-mail address.

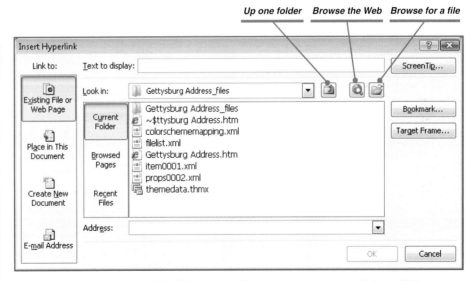

Figure 9-5: **The Insert Hyperlink dialog box enables you to create hyperlinks to Web pages, places within the same file, files, or e-mail addresses.**

UNDERSTANDING HYPERLINKS

(Continued)

- "wikipedia.org" is a *domain name* that is the principle identifier of a Web site.

- "/wiki/" is a folder name identifying a sub-area within a site.

- "Hasekura_Tsunenaga" is a Web page in the wiki folder in the Web site. (Hasekura Tsunenaga was a 17th-century Japanese ambassador first to Mexico and then to Europe.)

- "#France" is a particular location on the Web page, and is called a *bookmark*.

If Internet Explorer is not your default browser, the Browse The Web button may not work correctly. Clicking the button opens your default browser, but when you return to the Insert Hyperlink dialog box, Word may try to get the URL from Internet Explorer rather than from your default browser. Instead, browse to the Web page in your default browser, copy the address from the address bar, and then paste it into the Address box in the Insert Hyperlink dialog box.

CREATE A HYPERLINK TO AN EXISTING FILE OR WEB PAGE

To create a hyperlink to an existing file or Web page:

1. In the Link To column on the left, click the **Existing File Or Web Page** button, if it is not already selected.

2. Navigate to the file or Web page in one of these ways:

   Use the **Look In** drop-down list (and, if necessary, the **Up One Folder** button) to browse to the folder.

   –Or–

   Click the **Browse The Web** button to make Windows open an Internet Explorer window, browse to the page to which you want to link, and then switch back to the Insert Hyperlink dialog box. Word automatically enters the URL in the Address text box (see Figure 9-6).

   –Or–

   Click the **Current Folder** button to display the current folder. Click the **Browsed Pages** button to display a list of Web pages you've browsed recently. Click the **Recent Files** button to display a list of local files you've worked with recently.

   –Or–

   Select the address from the Address drop-down list.

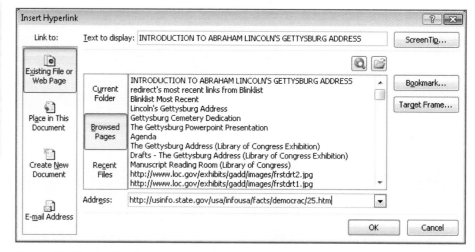

Figure 9-6: **Clicking the Browsed Pages button will give you a list of the Web pages and files that you have viewed so you can select one of them for a hyperlink.**

Set Hyperlink ScreenTip

Scree**n**Tip text:

Gettysburg Address|

Note: Custom ScreenTips are supported in Microsoft® Internet Explorer® version 4 or later.

[OK] [Cancel]

NOTE

Bookmarks cannot have spaces, hyphens, or any other special characters in them, except an underscore (_).

3. Change the default text in the Text To Display text box to the text you want displayed for the hyperlink. (This is the text that the user clicks to access the linked page. If you have selected text on your Web page, it will appear here.)

4. To add a ScreenTip to the hyperlink, click **ScreenTip**, type the text in the Set Hyperlink ScreenTip dialog box, and then click **OK**.

5. To make the hyperlink connect to a particular location in the page rather than simply to the beginning of the page, click **Bookmark**, and choose the location in the Select Place In Document dialog box (see "Create a Hyperlink to a Place in the Current Document").

6. Click **OK**. Word inserts the hyperlink.

Gettysburg Address
Ctrl+Click to follow link

INTRODUCTION TO ABRAHAM LINCOLN'S GETTYSBURG ADDRESS

CREATE A HYPERLINK TO A PLACE IN THE CURRENT DOCUMENT

To create a hyperlink to a place in the current document:

1. In the Link To column, click the **Place In This Document** button. Under Select A Place In This Document, click a heading or a bookmark that is displayed (see Figure 9-7).

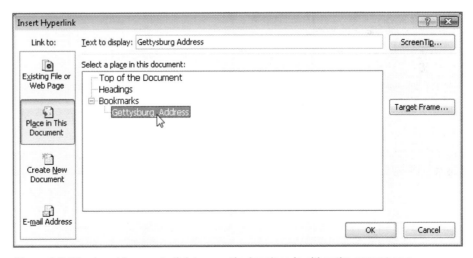

Figure 9-7: Word enables you to link to a particular place in either the current or a destination document—for example, to a heading or bookmark in a Word document.

2. Change the default text in the Text To Display text box to the text you want displayed for the hyperlink. (This is the text that the user clicks to access the linked page and is the text you first selected, if you did so.)

3. To add a ScreenTip to the hyperlink, click **ScreenTip**, type the text in the Set Hyperlink ScreenTip dialog box, and then click **OK**.

4. Click **OK**. Word inserts the hyperlink.

CREATE A HYPERLINK TO A NEW DOCUMENT

To create a hyperlink to a new document:

1. In the Insert Hyperlink dialog box, in the Link To Column on the left, click the **Create New Document** button (see Figure 9-8).

2. Type the file name and extension in the Name Of New Document text box. Check the path in the Full Path area. If necessary, click **Change**; use the Create New Document dialog box to specify the folder, file name, and extension; and then click **OK**.

3. Change the default text in the Text To Display text box to the text you want displayed for the hyperlink. (This is the text that the user clicks to access the linked page and is the text you first selected, if you did so.)

4. To add a ScreenTip to the hyperlink, click **ScreenTip**, type the text in the Set Hyperlink ScreenTip dialog box, and then click **OK**.

5. By default, Word selects the **Edit The New Document Now** option. If you prefer not to open the new document for editing immediately, click the **Edit The New Document Later** option.

6. Click **OK**. Word inserts the hyperlink.

CREATE A HYPERLINK TO AN E-MAIL ADDRESS

To create a mailto hyperlink that starts a message to an e-mail address:

1. In the Link To column, click the **E-mail Address** button (see Figure 9-9).

2. Type the e-mail address in the E-mail Address text box (or click it in the Recently Used E-mail Addresses list box), and type the subject for the message in the Subject text box.

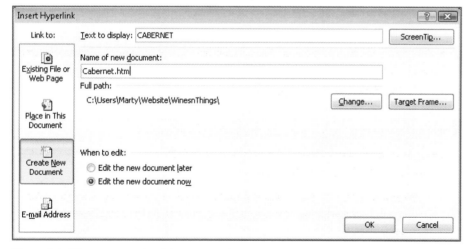

Figure 9-8: When you need to link to a new document, Word lets you create the new document immediately to ensure that it is saved with the correct name and location.

TIP

E-mail addresses you have recently used in other hyperlinks will be in the list of Recently Used E-Mail Addresses at the bottom of the Edit Hyperlink dialog box. If you want to use one of them in another hyperlink, click it instead of typing it again in the E-Mail Address text box.

NOTE

The "mailto:" entry in front of the e-mail address tells a browser to open the default e-mail program, open a new message, and place the address in the "To" line.

NOTE

Word automatically creates a hyperlink when you type a URL, e-mail address, or a network path in a document and then press **SPACEBAR**, **TAB**, **ENTER**, or a punctuation key. If you find this behavior awkward, you can turn it off: Click the **Office Button**, click **Word Options**, click **Proofing** in the left column, click **AutoCorrect Options**, click the **AutoFormat As You Type** tab, clear the **Internet And Network Paths With Hyperlinks** check box, and then click **OK** twice.

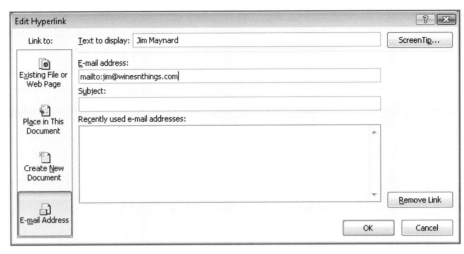

*Figure 9-9: **The Insert Hyperlink dialog box lets you quickly create a mailto hyperlink to an e-mail address.***

3. Change the default text in the Text To Display text box to the text you want displayed for the hyperlink. (This is the text that the user clicks to access the linked page and is the text you first selected, if you did so.)

4. To add a ScreenTip to the hyperlink, click **ScreenTip**, type the text in the Set Hyperlink ScreenTip dialog box, and then click **OK**.

5. Click **OK**. Word inserts the hyperlink.

Verify How a Page Will Look

After you have saved a Word document as a Web page, you'll probably want to check how it looks in your browser.

1. In Windows Vista, click **Start**, click **Computer**, navigate to the folder where the Web page file is stored, and double-click the Web document. It will open in your default browser.

    Figure 9-10 shows an example file in Word on the left and then the file being previewed in the Internet Explorer.

2. After viewing the Web page, click **Close** to close the Internet Explorer window.

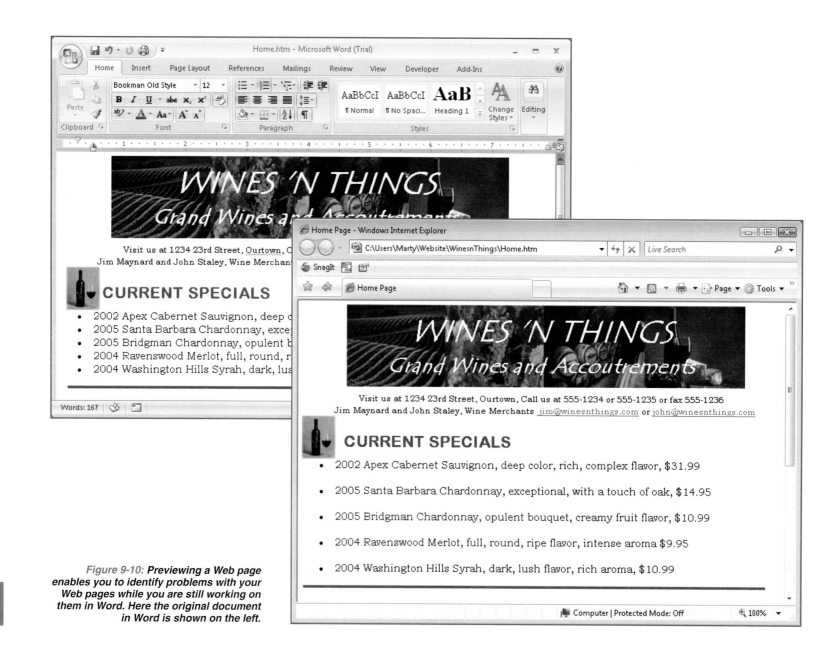

Figure 9-10: *Previewing a Web page enables you to identify problems with your Web pages while you are still working on them in Word. Here the original document in Word is shown on the left.*

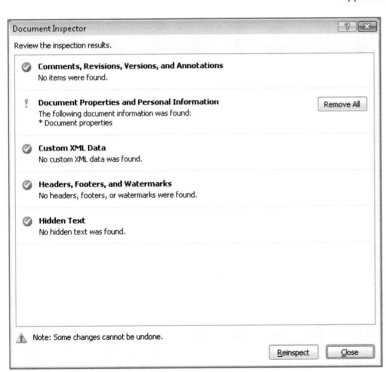

Figure 9-11: *Inspect and remove any personal information in the Web pages you save.*

Remove Personal Information from the File Properties

When creating a Web page that you will place on a Web site (as opposed to a site on a local network), it's a good idea to remove the personal information that Word includes by default in documents. To remove this information:

1. Start Word, if it is not already running, and open the document that will become a Web page.

2. Click the **Office Button**, and then click **Word Options**. The Options dialog box appears.

3. Click **Trust Center** in the left column, and then click **Trust Center Settings** to open the Trust Center dialog box.

4. Click **Privacy Options** in the left column, and click **Document Inspector**. Select the type of data you want to check for (the default is all of the options), and click **Inspect**. The Document Inspector dialog box appears and may show information you want to remove, as shown in Figure 9-11.

5. Click **Remove All** for all the information you want removed. Click **Close** and then click **OK** twice. Save the document, as described in an earlier section of this chapter.

Remove Word-Specific Tags from a Document

As discussed earlier in this chapter, Word uses custom HTML tags to store the Word-specific data required to save the entire Word document in an HTML format. Saving this data is good if you want to be able to again edit the document in Word with all its features present, but you don't need this extra data when you're using Word on a one-time basis to create pages for your Web site.

QUICKSTEPS

USING WORD TO CREATE HTML ELEMENTS

If you choose not to use Word as your main HTML editor, you may still want to use Word to create some HTML elements so that you can include them in your Web pages.

1. Start Word, if it is not already running.

2. Open an existing document, or create a new document that contains the desired content.

3. Save the Word document in one of the HTML formats.

4. View the resulting page in your browser.

5. View the source code of the Web page. For example, in Internet Explorer, click the **View** menu, and then click **Source** (in Internet Explorer 7, you must first turn on the menus by clicking **Tools** and then clicking **Menu Bar**).

6. Select the code for the element you want to copy, and then issue a copy command (for example, press **CTRL+C**).

7. Switch to your HTML editor, position the insertion point, and then issue a paste command (for example, press **CTRL+V**).

8. Close Word and your browser if you have finished working with them.

TIP

Using Word to create HTML elements is a good way to create eBay listings by pasting the HTML code into the eBay selling form. See *eBay QuickSteps*, published by McGraw-Hill.

To remove the Word-specific tags from a document:

1. When you are ready to save the document one final time after you are sure it is the way you want it, click the **Office Button**, click **Save As**, point to **Other Formats**, and click the **Web Page, Filtered** format in the Save As Type drop-down list.

2. Click **Save**. A Microsoft Office Word dialog box appears, telling you that Office-specific tags will be removed. Click **Yes**. (If you click No, the save will not occur. You will be able to change the Save As Type setting.)

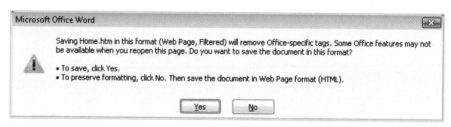

3. Depending on the browser settings you have chosen in the Web Options dialog box, you may also see warnings about features that will be removed from the Word document. Click **Continue** if you want to proceed anyway; click **Cancel** if you want to choose another format.

Chapter 10

Using Word with Other People

In the first nine chapters of this book, we've talked about the many ways you can use Word on your own. In this chapter we'll talk about how you can use Word with other people. Word has a number of features that allow multiple people to work on the same document and see what each other has done. These include marking changes, both additions and deletions that multiple people make to a document; adding comments to a document; highlighting words, lines, and paragraphs of a document; having multiple versions of a document; and comparing documents.

Mark Changes

When two or more people work on a document, it is helpful to see what the other people did without having to read every word and accurately remembering

TIP

By pointing your mouse at a change, you can see who made the change and the date and time it was made.

dow ~~appears~~opens as shown in ~~Figure~~ 6

> Marty, 1/29/2007 5:28:00 PM inserted:
> assists

~~helps~~assists your entering informatio

what it was before it was changed. You can do this in Word by using the Track Changes feature. *Track Changes* identifies the changes (additions or deletions) made to a document by everyone who works on it. Each person is automatically assigned a color, and their changes are noted in that color. For example, Figure 10-1 shows a section of a document in the editing process. After all the changes are made, they can be accepted or rejected, either one at a time or all together.

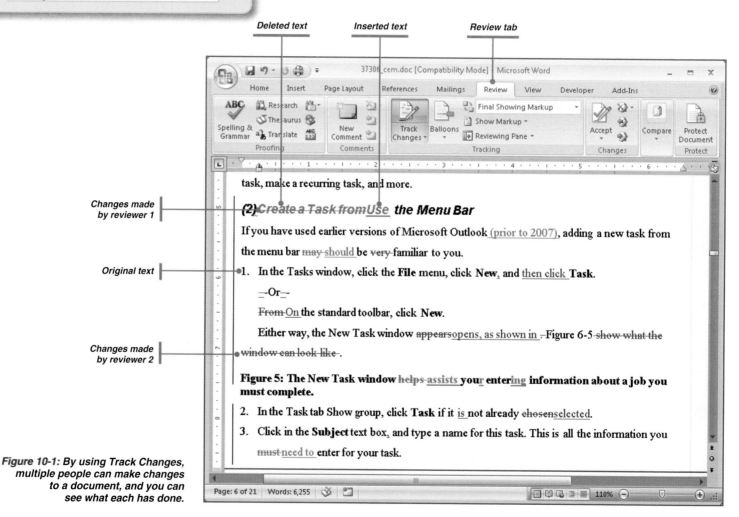

Figure 10-1: By using Track Changes, multiple people can make changes to a document, and you can see what each has done.

Track Changes

To use Track Changes, you must turn it on. Prior to this, anything anyone types looks like ordinary text, and there is no way of telling the difference between the new text and what was on the page before the change was made. Once Track Changes is turned on, however, anything anyone types or does to the document will be shown in the color automatically assigned to that person; furthermore, the changes are fully reversible, if desired. To turn on Track Changes:

1. Start Word and open the document in which you want to track changes.

2. In the Review tab Tracking group, click **Track Changes**.

    –Or–

    Press **CTRL+SHIFT+E**.

USE THE REVIEW TAB

The Review tab provides a number of features that you can use as you and others edit a document, as shown in Figure 10-2.

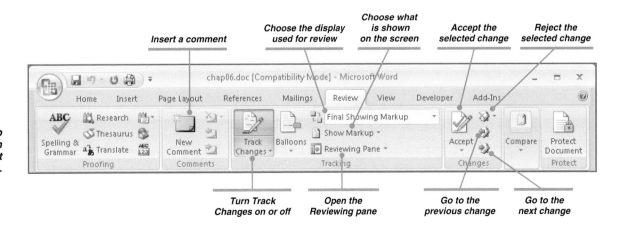

Figure 10-2: The Review tab can be used to go through an edited document and accept or reject changes.

Insert a comment   Choose the display used for review   Choose what is shown on the screen   Accept the selected change   Reject the selected change

Turn Track Changes on or off   Open the Reviewing pane   Go to the previous change   Go to the next change

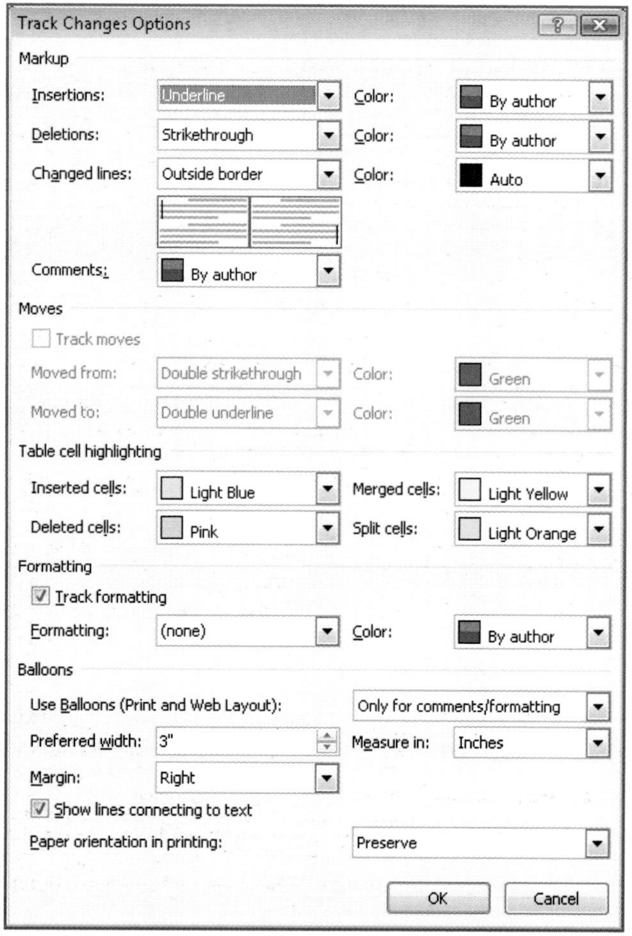

Figure 10-3: *While you can select colors for each type of change, the best practice is to let Word automatically select the color for each reviewer (By Author).*

SET OPTIONS FOR TRACK CHANGES

Word gives you a number of options for how changes are displayed with Track Changes. These are set in the Track Changes Options dialog box, shown in Figure 10-3. To open this dialog box and set the options:

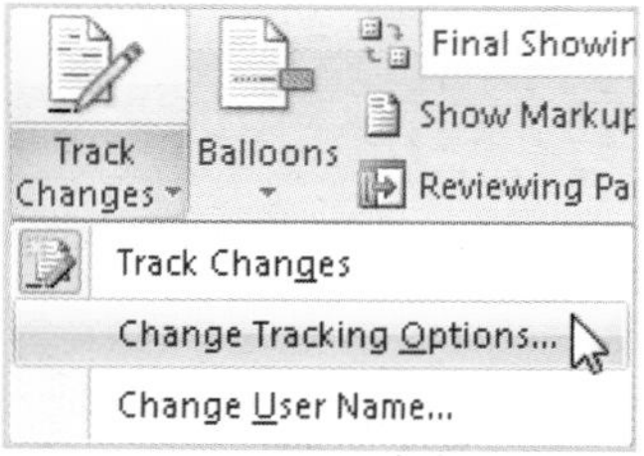

1. In the Review tab Tracking group, click the **Track Changes** down arrow, and click **Change Tracking Options**.

2. Open the drop-down lists next to **Insertions**, **Deletions**, **Changed Lines**, and **Comments** to review and change the options for displaying each of these items. Also, you can change the colors used for each of these.

3. Review and consider how moving text, changing tables, and revising formatting are handled, and make any changes you want. (Balloons are discussed in the following section.)

4. When you are done, click **OK**.

PUT CHANGES IN BALLOONS

Word gives you two ways of viewing changes, both on the screen and when you print out the document. One is an inline method, where the changes are made within the original text, as shown in Figure 10-1. The other is to put changes in balloons to the right of the text, as shown in Figure 10-4. What is in the balloon and what is in the text depends on your choice in the Display For Review area. The default option, shown in Figure 10-4, is Final Showing Markup, which shows the text with the final wording and the balloons with primarily deletions. The options available in Display For Review are described in Table 10-1.

You can quickly turn the balloon changes on or off.

In the Review tab Tracking group, click the **Balloons** down arrow, and click **Show Revisions In Balloons** or **Show All Revisions Inline**.

10

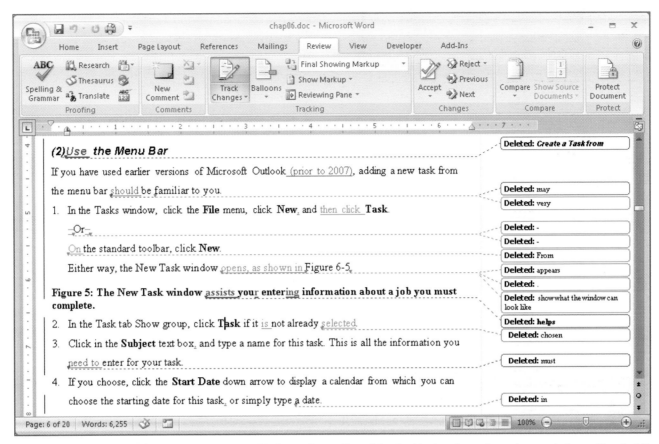

Figure 10-4: Using balloons for changes can provide for easier reading of the final text and can show changes in formatting, but it can be harder to see what has been changed.

DISPLAY OPTION	WHAT IS IN THE TEXT	WHAT IS IN THE BALLOON
Final Showing Markup	Final text with insertions	Deletions and format changes
Final	Final text without markings	Nothing
Original Showing Markup	Original text with deletions	Insertions and format changes
Original	Original text without markings	Nothing

Table 10-1: Display For Review Options

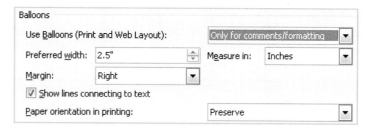

You can also turn balloons on and off and set other balloon-related options.

1. In the Review tab Tracking group, click the **Track Changes** down arrow, and click **Change Tracking Options**.

2. Under Balloons, opposite Use Balloons (Print And Web Layout), click **Never** to turn off balloons, click **Always** to turn on balloons, or click **Only For Comments/Formatting** (the default) to use balloons in that way.

3. If you choose to turn balloons on, you can:

   - Set how wide you want the balloons to be, along with the unit of measure to use.

   - Determine which margin the balloons should be on.

   - Determine whether there are connecting lines between the balloons and the text.

   - Determine whether to pint a document with balloon changes in its normal portrait orientation or force it to be printed in landscape orientation to better keep the original text size.

4. When you are done setting balloon-related settings, click **OK**.

Review Changes

Changes are made to a document by simply adding, deleting, and reformatting the text. If Track Changes is turned on, the changes appear either in the text or in balloons in the margins. Once all changes have been made to a document, you will want to go through the document, look at the changes, and decide to accept or reject each one.

1. With the document you want to review, as well as the Review tab open in Word (see "Use the Review Tab" earlier in this chapter), click **Track Changes**, if it is turned on, to turn it off.

TIP

If you want to accept all changes or reject all changes in a document, click the down arrow below Accept or next to Reject Change in the Review tab Changes group, and click **Accept All Changes In Document** or **Reject All Changes In Document**.

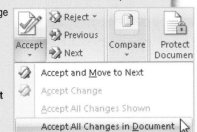

QUICKSTEPS

CREATING REVIEWING SHORTCUTS

If you are going through a large document, looking at each change and accepting or rejecting it, clicking the mouse repeatedly on **Accept** or **Reject** can become tedious. A partial solution for this is to make keyboard shortcuts.

To assign shortcut keys to each of the three functions—Next, Accept Change, and Reject Change:

1. Click the **Office Button**, click **Word Options**, click **Customize** in the left column, and, opposite Keyboard Shortcuts at the bottom of the dialog box, click **Customize** again. The Customize Keyboard dialog box appears.

2. Click **Review Tab** in the Categories list, click **AcceptChangesOrAdvance** in the Commands list, click in the **Press New Shortcut Key** text box, and press the key(s) you want to use. For example, press **ALT+A** for Accept Change (see Figure 10-5). Click **Assign**.

Continued . . .

2. Press **CTRL+HOME** to position the insertion point at the beginning of the document, and click **Next** on the Review tab to select the first change.

3. Click **Accept** on the Review tab if you want to make the change permanent.

   –Or–

   Click **Reject** on the Review tab if you want to remove the change and leave the text as it was originally.

4. Repeat step 3 for each of the changes in the document. Each time you click **Accept** or **Reject**, you automatically move to the next change. (See the QuickSteps "Creating Reviewing Shortcuts" for creating keyboard shortcuts for these reviewing tasks.)

5. When you are finished, click **Save** on the Quick Access toolbar to save the reviewed document.

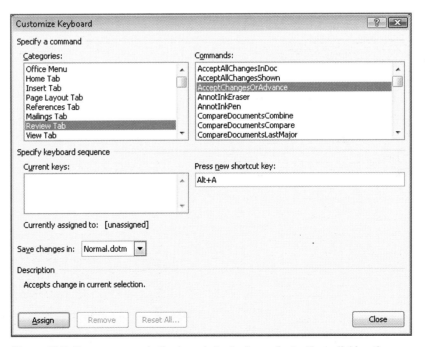

Figure 10-5: For some people, keyboard shortcuts are faster than clicking the mouse, especially if you use two hands.

QUICKSTEPS

CREATING REVIEWING SHORTCUTS
(Continued)

3. Repeat step 2, first for Next by clicking **NextChangeOrComment** in the Command list and assigning, for example, **ALT+N**; and then for Reject by clicking **RejectChangesOrAdvance** and assigning, for example, **ALT+R**, and clicking **Assign** for each.

4. When you are done, click **Close** and then click **OK**.

5. Open a document for which you want to review changes.

6. Press **ALT+N** to go to the first change. Then press either **ALT+A** to accept the change or **ALT+R** to reject the change and automatically move on to the next change. Repeat this for the remainder of the changes.

NOTE

When you use Accept Changes Or Advance or Reject Changes Or Advance, you are automatically moved to the next change. You only need to use Next to move on without accepting or rejecting a change.

USE THE REVIEWING PANE

Word provides another way to look at changes using the Reviewing pane, shown in Figure 10-6. This pane opens at left or at the bottom of the Word window and lists each individual change, with its type, the author, and the date and time the change was made (the latter is included only if the column is wide enough).

1. With the document you want to review, as well as the Review tab open in Word, click **Reviewing Pane** in the Tracking group to open it.

2. Scroll through the changes in the Reviewing pane, and/or use the **Next** and **Previous** buttons on the Review tab (or your shortcut keys) to display each change in the Reviewing pane, as well as to highlight them in the document pane.

3. When you are finished making changes, click **Save** on the toolbar.

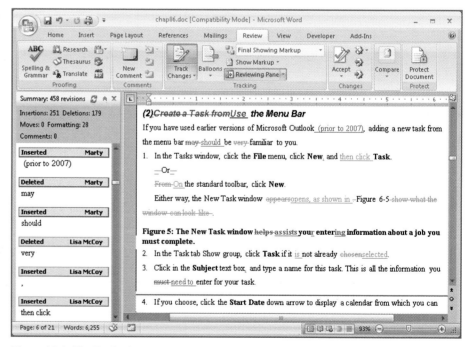

Figure 10-6: The Reviewing pane provides a detailed way of looking at each individual change.

E-MAIL A DOCUMENT FOR REVIEW

Often, when several people are working on a document, they exchange the document using e-mail. Word makes using e-mail with the reviewing process easy. You can both send out a document for review and return it with your changes.

To send out the currently opened document for review:

1. Click the **Office Button**, click **Send**, and click **E-mail**. The E-mail Message window opens with the Word document you want reviewed attached and shown as the subject (see Figure 10-7).

2. Fill in the name of the addressee, plus those who are to get copies, make any desired changes to the Subject line, and add a message. Then, when you are ready, click **Send**.

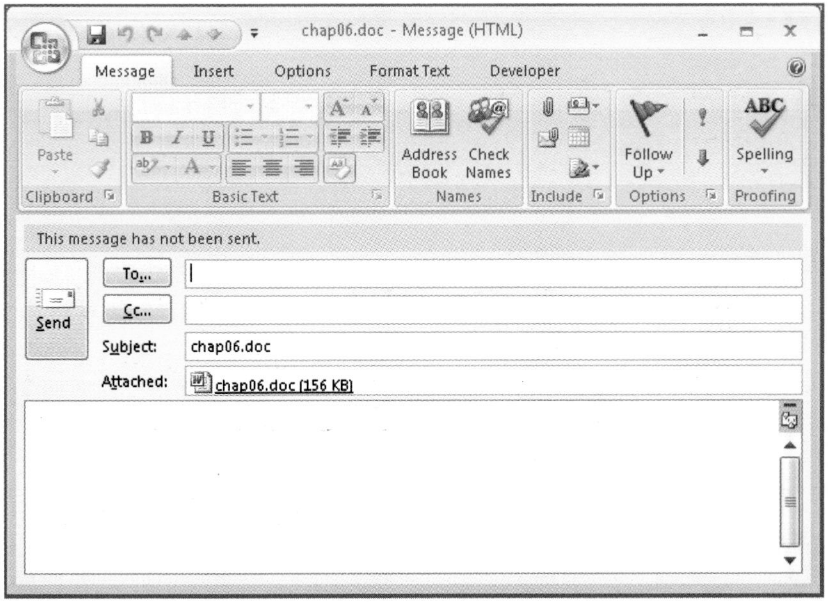

E-MAIL A REVIEWED DOCUMENT

When a document has been e-mailed to you for review and you have finished making the changes you want, you can e-mail it back in the same way you received it. With the document open in Word:

1. Click the **Office Button**, click **Send**, and click **E-mail**. The E-mail Message window opens with the Word document you have reviewed attached and shown as the Subject line.

2. Add the addresses for those who are to receive copies, add a message if desired, make any desired changes to the Subject line and then, when ready, click **Send**.

Add Comments

When you review or edit a document, you may want to make a comment instead of or in addition to making a change. To add a comment:

1. With the document to which you want to add a comment, as well as the Review tab open in Word, place the insertion point at the location you want the comment to refer to.

Figure 10-7: When you use the Send option in Word, the Subject and Attachment lines are filled in for you.

2. Click **New Comment** in the Review tab Comments group. An annotation with your initials will appear where the insertion point was in the text, and the Reviewing pane will open (if it isn't already open), with a new comment area, as you can see in Figure 10-8.

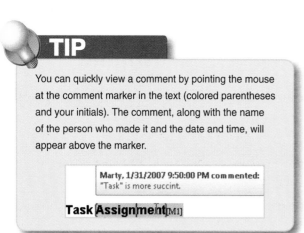

3. Type the comment you want to make (it can be of any length), and then click in the document pane to continue reviewing the document.

4. If you wish, you can close the Reviewing pane by clicking **Reviewing Pane** on the Review tab or clicking **Close** in the upper-right area of the Reviewing pane.

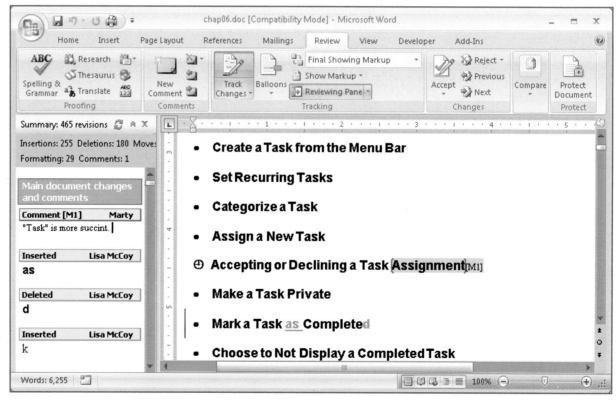

Figure 10-8: Comments allow you to explain why you made a change.

NOTE

A comment can be deleted by locating it using the **Next** or **Previous** button on the Review tab Changes group and then clicking **Reject**.

NOTE

On a Tablet PC, you can use the tablet pen to handwrite comments (called "ink comments"). These are similar to the comments entered on a regular PC, except that they are handwritten instead of typed. In addition, you can use the tablet pen to directly mark in the document pane, not just in the comment areas (called "ink annotations"). For example, you might circle an incorrect phrase and write "Fixed?".

NOTE

You can remove highlighting by selecting the highlighted text, clicking the **Highlight** tool down arrow, and clicking **No Color**.

CAUTION

Highlighting shows up when you print a document that contains it. This is fine with a color printer, but if you print on a black-and-white printer, the highlighting will be gray, which will make black text under the highlighting hard to read.

Highlight Objects

As you review and change a document, you may want to highlight some text so you can discuss it in a comment or otherwise call attention to it. You do this using the Highlight tool in the Home tab Font group.

The highlighting that is placed on a page can be one of 15 different colors, so you first need to select the color.

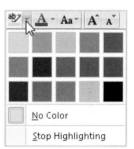

1. In the Home tab Font group, click the **Highlight** tool down arrow. The highlighting color palette will open.

2. Click the color you want to use. Remember: you want whatever color text you are using to show up well on the color you choose (yellow is the most common).

When you set out to highlight, you can select the Highlight tool first and then drag over the text to highlight it, or you can select the text to be highlighted first and then click the Highlight tool.

SELECT THE HIGHLIGHT TOOL FIRST

To highlight several sections of text, it is easiest to first select the Highlight tool.

1. With the document you want to highlight open in Word, click the **Highlight** tool in the Review tab Font group. The mouse pointer becomes a highlighter superimposed on the I-beam.

2. Drag over as much and as many separate pieces text as you want to highlight, also entering comments as needed (you will need to reselect the Highlight tool after you type comments). See Figure 10-9.

3. When you are done with the Highlight tool, you can either press **ESC** or click the **Highlight** tool down arrow in the Review tab Font group, and click **Stop Highlighting** to return to the normal I-beam insertion point.

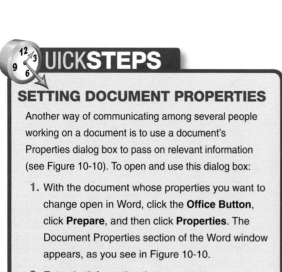

UICKSTEPS

SETTING DOCUMENT PROPERTIES

Another way of communicating among several people working on a document is to use a document's Properties dialog box to pass on relevant information (see Figure 10-10). To open and use this dialog box:

1. With the document whose properties you want to change open in Word, click the **Office Button**, click **Prepare**, and then click **Properties**. The Document Properties section of the Word window appears, as you see in Figure 10-10.

2. Enter the information that you want to communicate into the various fields. None are required, and most are self-explanatory.

3. To view additional properties of the document, click the **Document Properties** down arrow, and click **Advanced Properties**. The Properties dialog box appears.

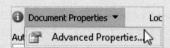

The **General** tab tells you where the document is stored and its relevant dates. The **Summary** tab repeats the information you saw in the Word window. The **Statistics** tab repeats the dates, tells you who last saved the file, and gives you various length statistics. The **Contents** tab repeats the title and may show the headings.

Continued . . .

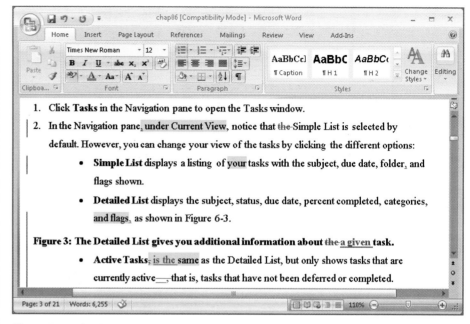

1. Click **Tasks** in the Navigation pane to open the Tasks window.
2. In the Navigation pane, under Current View, notice that the Simple List is selected by default. However, you can change your view of the tasks by clicking the different options:
   - **Simple List** displays a listing of your tasks with the subject, due date, folder, and flags shown.
   - **Detailed List** displays the subject, status, due date, percent completed, categories, and flags, as shown in Figure 6-3.

Figure 3: The Detailed List gives you additional information about the a given task.
   - **Active Tasks, is the same** as the Detailed List, but only shows tasks that are currently active, that is, tasks that have not been deferred or completed.

Figure 10-9: Highlighting is often used to identify a piece of text about which a reviewer has a question.

SELECT THE TEXT FIRST

To highlight a single piece of text, it is easiest to first select the text.

1. With the document you want to highlight open in Word, drag across the text that you want highlighted.

2. Click the **Highlight** tool in the Review tab Font group. The selected text will be highlighted.

Work with Multiple Documents

As you are going through the reviewing process with several people, it is likely that you will end up with multiple copies of a document. Word gives you a way of comparing these versions.

SETTING DOCUMENT PROPERTIES

(Continued)

4. The **Custom** tab allows you to attach a value to a category. Click a category in the Name list, click a type of information, and enter the information in the Value text box.

5. Click **OK** when you are done with the Properties dialog box, and then click **Close** to close the properties section of the Word window.

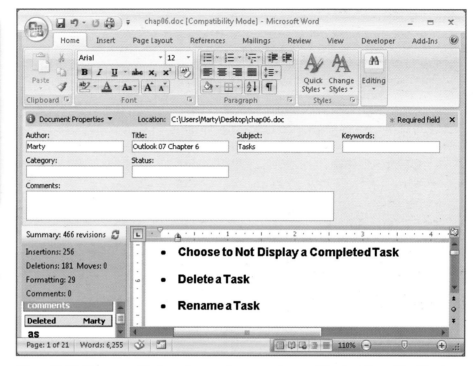

Figure 10-10: The properties for a document are seen in an optional section of the Word window and in a Properties dialog box.

Save Several Copies of a Document

First, you want to separately save each copy of the document with a unique name, giving you the ability to compare two copies of the document, as explained in the next section.

SAVE A UNIQUE COPY

With the document for which you want to create different versions open in Word, click the **Office Button**, click **Save As**, select the format you want to use, select the folder in which you want the file saved, enter a unique name, and click **Save**.

OPEN A DIFFERENT COPY

With a document for which there are multiple copies open in Word, to open another copy, click the **Office Button**, click **Open**, select the folder in which the file is stored, select the file, and click **Open**.

Compare Documents

If changes have been made to a copy of a document without using Track Changes, Word has the ability to compare the two and then merge them into a single document, with the differences shown as they would be with Track Changes.

1. In Word, open the first or original document.

2. In the Review tab Compare group, click **Compare** and, unless the window is maximized, click **Compare** two more times. The Compare Documents dialog box will appear.

3. Click **More** to first select the types of differences you want to see and have reflected in the final document. Second, select whether you want to show changes at the character or word level. Finally, select whether you want the combined changes in the original document, the revised document, or a new document (the default).

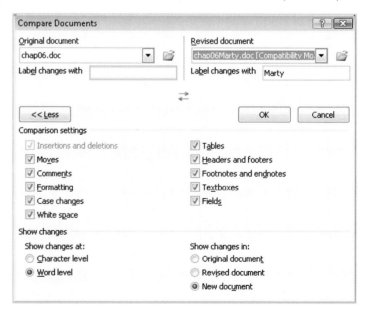

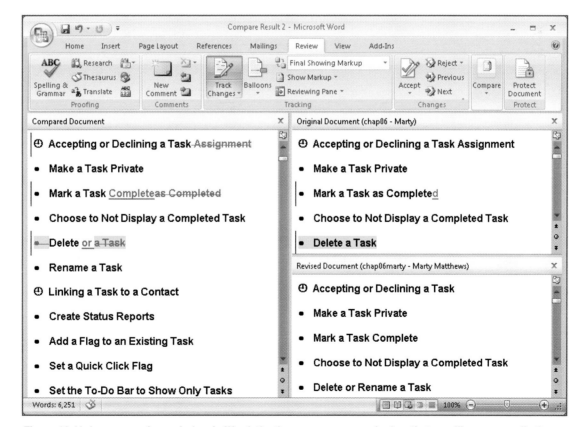

NOTE

If you still have Track Changes turned on, Word will ask you if, for the purposes of the conversion, it can consider all the changes accepted.

4. Select the original document and the revised document you want to compare and merge into the original document, make any changes to the settings that you want, and click **OK**.

5. With the default settings, a three-document window will open and display the original, the revised, and a compared document, with the changes the revised document makes to the original document, as you can see in Figure 10-11.

6. Scroll through the compared document pane, and accept or reject the changes that have been made.

7. If you want to save the compared document under a new name, click the **Office Button**, click **Save As**, select a folder, enter a name, and click **Save**.

Figure 10-11: In a comparison window in Word, the three panes are synched so that scrolling one scrolls the other two.

C

cameras, troubleshooting, 155
capitalization, changing, 51
caps formatting, keyboard shortcut for, 46
captions, adding to pictures, 159
case, changing, 51
[cc] wildcard character, using with Find
   command, 39
[c-c] wildcard character, using with Find
   command, 39
cell margins, changing in tables, 147.
   See also margins
cell references, relationship to formulas, 141
cells. *See also* tables
   adding to tables, 132–133
   changing text wrapping in, 144–145
   creating spacing between, 147
   merging in tables, 144
   orienting text direction in, 145
   removing from tables, 134
   selecting in tables, 134
   sorting in tables, 137–138
   splitting in tables, 144
cent (¢) symbol, keyboard shortcut for, 27
center formatting, keyboard shortcut for, 46
Center icon, identifying, 45
change case formatting, keyboard shortcut
   for, 46
Change Case icon, identifying, 45
Change Styles function, using, 72
changes. *See* Reviewing pane; Track
   Changes feature
character formatting
   applying, 49
   applying with mini toolbar, 45
character sets, using with Web pages, 206
character spacing, setting, 50–51

characters
   counting, 101–102
   replacing, 39
   selecting, 29
   shortcut keys for, 27
chart items
   formatting, 196–197
   selecting, 194–195
chart templates
   creating and using, 193
   deleting, 195
chart titles, adding, 194
charts
   adding axis titles to, 195
   components of, 190
   creating, 191
   data series and axes in, 196
   formatting text in, 197
   moving legends in, 195
   showing data labels in, 195
   types of, 193
   using data tables with, 198
Clear Formatting icon, identifying, 45
clicking with mouse, 6
clip art. *See also* image properties; pictures
   adding, 153, 156
   using shapes with, 163
Clip Art Organizer
   deleting clips with, 157
   moving and copying clips in, 156–157
   opening, 156
Clipboard. *See* Office Clipboard; Windows
   Clipboard
clips. *See also* pictures
   deleting, 157
   editing keywords and captions for, 158
   moving and copying by dragging, 157
   moving and copying in dialog boxes, 156–157

Close button, location of, 3–4
color effects
   removing, 171
   selecting colors for, 169
   setting gradients for, 169–171
colors
   changing for fonts, 48
   changing for highlighting, 102
   changing for themes, 76–77
   restoring for themes, 79
   selecting for highlighting, 225
   selecting for Track Changes feature, 218
column chart, function of, 193
column dimensions, viewing in tables, 135
column widths
   changing in tables, 135–136
   spacing in tables, 136
columns
   creating and using, 82–83
   inserting in tables, 133
   moving and copying, 139
   removing from tables, 134
   selecting in tables, 133–134
   separating, 140
   sorting, 138–139
   sorting by, 138
Columns dialog box, displaying effects of
   changes in, 83
command groups, identifying in tabs, 5
commands
   accessing with Quick Access toolbar, 8–9
   changing keyboard shortcuts for, 10
   selecting, 7
comments
   adding to documents, 223–224
   deleting, 225
   viewing, 224
   writing on Tablet PCs, 225

Compare feature, using with documents, 228–229
context menus, using with tables, 132
controls, using with forms, 185
copies of documents, saving, 227–228
copy format formatting, keyboard
  shortcut for, 46
copying
  formulas, 140
  and moving text, 30–32
  tables, columns, and rows, 138–139
copyright symbol, keyboard shortcut for, 27
corrections. *See* AutoCorrect feature
curves
  adjusting, 165
  creating, 164
  opening and closing, 165
  using edit points with, 163
Cut icon, identifying, 32

D

data labels in charts
  examples of, 190
  showing, 195
data series, using in charts, 196
data source in Mail Merge, explanation of, 117
data tables, using with charts, 198
date separators, using, 138
decrease font size formatting, keyboard
  shortcut for, 46
Decrease Indent icon, identifying, 45
Decrease Indent option, using, 55
deleted text, recovering, 33
desktop shortcut, creating to start Word, 3
diagrams
  creating, 166–168
  deleting elements of, 168

Dialog Box Launcher, displaying options in, 5
display elements, selecting, 11
.doc extension, file type associated with, 25
Document Inspector, using with Web pages, 213
document pane
  gaining working space in, 6
  identifying, 18
  location of, 4
document properties, setting, 226–227
documents
  adding comments to, 223–224
  adding identifying information to, 10–12
  applying style sets to, 72
  applying templates to, 81
  assigning themes to, 75
  changing display of, 35
  checking pagination for indexing, 90
  comparing, 228–229
  creating, 19
  creating hyperlinks to, 210
  deleting styles from, 76
  displaying information about, 23
  e-mailing for review, 223
  entering text in, 26
  hyphenating, 103–104
  importing, 25–26
  locating, 11, 23
  navigating, 33
  placing hyperlinks in, 209–210
  removing Word-specific tags from, 214
  reviewing via e-mail, 223
  saving, 41–42
  saving as templates, 42
  saving as Web pages, 200–202
  saving automatically, 42
  saving copies of, 41, 227–228
  searching text, 38

selecting, 29
translating, 14, 187–188
translating to other languages, 14
types of, 16
viewing in full-screen mode, 111
.docx and .docm extensions, file types
  associated with, 25
domain name, example of, 208
.dot extension, file type associated with, 25
.dotx extension, file type associated with, 25
double-clicking with mouse, 6
double-spacing, setting, 57–58
doughnut chart, function of, 193
Draft view, description of, 8, 94
dragging with mouse, 6
drawing canvas, opening, 162
drawings
  creating, aligning, and arranging precisely, 173
  filling with pictures, 171
drop caps, creating and removing, 51–52

E

em (—) dash, keyboard shortcut for, 27
e-mail
  reviewing edited documents by means of, 223
  sending Word documents in, 117
e-mail addresses, creating hyperlinks to, 210–211
en (–) dash, keyboard shortcut for, 27
Encoding tab, Web options on, 205–206
endnotes
  changing, 88
  converting to footnotes, 88–89
  deleting, 88
  going to, 88
  inserting, 87

importing documents, 25–26
increase font size formatting, keyboard
    shortcut for, 46
Increase Indent icon, identifying, 45
indent paragraph formatting, keyboard
    shortcut for, 46
indentation, using, 54–57
indenting first line, 56
indents, using ruler for, 57–58
index entries, tagging, 89
indexes, generating, 89–90
inline positioning, using with graphics, 175
INS key capability, turning on, 28
Insert Hyperlink dialog box, opening, 207
Insert Picture dialog box, displaying, 152
Insert Table dialog box, options in, 128, 130
insertion point
  determining text placement with, 27
  displaying, 33
  identifying, 18
  moving, 27–28, 30, 35
  moving to beginning of documents, 221
Internet Explorer
  browser market for, 204
  Web options for, 203
italic formatting, keyboard shortcut for, 46
italic style, applying, 47
Italics icon, identifying, 45

J

justification, setting for paragraphs, 52–54
Justify icon, identifying, 45
justify paragraph formatting, keyboard
    shortcut for, 46

K

kerning, using, 50
keyboard
  copying formats with, 68
  entering special characters from, 26–27
  navigating documents with, 35
  selecting chart items with, 194
  selecting text with, 30
keyboard shortcuts
  for accepting track changes, 221
  for Apply Styles dialog box, 73
  for applying bold style, 47
  for bullets, 27
  for cent (¢) symbol, 27
  for changing font size, 47
  changing for commands, 10
  for changing left indents, 54
  for converting formula results to plain text, 140
  for copying formatting, 68
  for copying text, 31
  for copyright symbol, 27
  for cutting text, 31
  displaying for special characters, 27
  for em dash, 27
  for en dash, 27
  for Euro symbol, 27
  for Find Next option, 36
  for finding remaining occurrences of words, 36
  for formatting, 46
  for hanging indents, 56
  for italic bold style, 47
  for marking index entries, 89
  for moving insertion point to beginning of
    documents, 221
  for navigating documents, 35

for page breaks, 59
for paragraph alignment, 53
for pasting text, 31
for pound (£) symbol, 27
for registered (®) symbol, 27
for rejecting track changes, 222
for removing left indents, 55
for resetting paragraph formatting, 57
for selecting documents, 29
for table navigation, 136
for tagging table of contents entries, 92
for Thesaurus, 14, 104
toggling ribbon size with, 6
for trade mark (™) symbol, 27
for turning on Track Changes feature, 217
for underlines, 48
for undoing move and paste actions, 32
using for common characters, 27

L

labels
  merging to, 125–126
  printing, 114–117
landscape page orientation, applying, 68
Language Settings options, selecting, 12
languages. See also translating
  translating between documents, 13
  translating documents into, 187–188
  translating phrases between, 13
  translating words and phrases into, 187
language-supported software, installing, 187
Layout tab, selecting chart items from, 194
leaders, setting tabs with, 84
left alignment, setting, 53

left indent
changing, 54
removing, 55
setting with ruler, 57
Left Tab icon, identifying, 83
legacy forms controls, using, 185
legends, moving in charts, 195
line breaks, inserting, 28, 59
line chart, function of, 193
Line formatting option, using with
chart items, 196
line space formatting, keyboard shortcuts for, 46
line spacing
overlapping of, 58
setting, 57–58
Line Spacing icon, identifying, 45
Line Style formatting option, using
with chart items, 196
lines
creating horizontal lines while typing, 63
indenting, 56
selecting, 29
links, creating between objects, 170
lists. *See* bulleted lists; numbered lists
logos, laying out in tables, 145

M

Magnifier, using, 109
Mail Merge feature
description of, 117
using, 118–119
mailto: entry, meaning of, 211
main document in Mail Merge,
explanation of, 117
margins. *See also* cell margins
changing for printing, 110
setting, 66
using mirror margins, 68

Match Case search option, using, 37
Match Prefix Or Match Suffix search
option, using, 37
Math AutoCorrect feature, using, 100–101
Maximize button, location of, 4
menus, opening, 5–7
merge documents
creating, 118–121
inserting variable fields into, 122
merge fields in Mail Merge
explanation of, 117
using rules with, 121–122
merge recipients, sorting, 120
merges
completing, 122–123
previewing, 121–122
merging
to envelopes, 123–124
to labels, 125–126
.mht and .mhtml extensions, file type
associated with, 25
Microsoft Office Online forms. *See* form
templates
mini toolbar
applying character formatting with, 45
clarifying, 8
using and hiding, 7
Minimize button, location of, 4
mirror margins, using, 68
modified styles, 74
More option in Find And Replace
dialog box, using, 37
mouse
navigating documents with, 33
selecting text with, 29–30
using, 5–6
move actions, undoing, 32
moving
and copying text, 30–32

items relative to position, 36
tables, columns, and rows, 138–139
Mozilla Firefox, browser market for, 204
Multilevel List icon, identifying, 45

N

{n,} wildcard character, using with Find
command, 39
{n,m} wildcard character, using with Find
command, 39
{n} wildcard character, using with Find
command, 39
name and address list, setting up, 119–120
Netscape Navigator, browser market for, 204
Normal style, advisory about making
changes to, 75
normal style formatting, keyboard
shortcut for, 46
Normal template, changing, 79–80
Number Format option, using with formulas, 140
Number formatting option, using with chart
items, 196
numbered lists
converting to bulleted lists, 63
creating before typing text, 61–62
creating with AutoCorrect, 60–61
numbering
applying to typed lists, 62
customizing, 62–63
removing, 63
Numbering icon, identifying, 45, 61

O

objects
adding from other programs, 169–170
aligning, 163
manipulating in documents, 170

Office button, location of, 4
Office Clipboard
  adding items to, 30
  closing and reverting to Windows Clipboard, 32
  copying and moving text with, 31
  deleting items on, 31
  displaying items on, 32
  opening, 30
  pasting items from, 30–31
  setting options for, 31–32
  showing, 32
  using, 31
Office online templates, using, 20–21
Open dialog box, accessing file search from, 23
operations, undoing, 33
Order option, using with graphics, 178
organization charts
  creating in SmartArt, 166–167
  redesigning, 168
Original display option, using with Track
    Changes, 219
Original Showing Markup display option, using
    with Track Changes, 219
Outline view, description of, 8, 94
outlines, creating and using, 92–93
Outlining tab, using for table of contents, 91
overtype mode, switching to, 28

P

page borders, adding, 65
page breaks, inserting, 28, 59
page formatting, advisory about, 66
Page Layout dialog box, formatting
    pages with, 67
page orientation, determining, 68
Page Setup dialog box, editing section
    breaks from, 82
page splits, handling, 60

pages
  formatting, 66–69
  moving between, 110
  navigating, 36
  reducing number of, 110–111
  viewing multiple pages, 110
paper size, specifying, 68
paragraph alignment, setting, 52–54
paragraph borders, adding, 65
Paragraph dialog box, opening, 54
paragraph formatting
  resetting, 57
  retaining, 59
paragraph spacing, setting, 58–59
paragraphs
  adding horizontal lines to, 63
  controlling splitting of, 60
  formatting, 52–54
  indenting, 54–57
  selecting, 29
paste actions, undoing, 32
Paste All option, using with Office Clipboard, 31
paste format formatting, keyboard
    shortcut for, 46
Paste Options smart tags, using, 32
phrases
  translating, 15, 187
  translating between languages, 13
Picture Tools Format tab, using, 158
pictures. *See also* clips; graphics; image
    properties
  adding, 154–155
  adding captions to, 159
  browsing for, 152
  changing paragraph formatting behavior
    of, 172
  cropping, 159
  filling drawings with, 171
  formats for, 153

linking, 152
moving, 162
positioning, 161–162
reducing size of, 159–161
selecting, 33
Pictures tab, Web options on, 205
pie chart, function of, 193
plain text, converting formula results to, 140
pointing with mouse, 6
points, font size measured as, 47
Popular options, setting preferences for, 12
portrait page orientation, applying, 68
pound (£) symbol, keyboard shortcut for, 27
preferences, setting, 11–12
Print icon, adding to Quick Access toolbar, 112
print jobs, customizing, 112–113
Print Layout view, description of, 7, 93, 108
Print Preview feature
  exiting, 111
  using, 109
printers
  defining properties for, 107–108
  installing, 106
  setting default for, 107
printing
  envelopes, 113–114
  labels, 114–117
Properties dialog box
  opening and using, 226–227
  opening for printers, 107–108

Q

Quick Access toolbar
  adding to, 8–9
  adding Print icon to, 112
  location of, 4
  moving, 10
Quick Launch toolbar, starting Word with, 3

Quick Parts feature, using with
building blocks, 97–98
Quick Styles, saving, 73
QuickFacts topics
data series and axes, 196
graphic positioning, 175
HTML (Hypertext Markup Language), 205–206
hyperlinks, 207–208
indentation, 54
linking picture files, 152
resource center, 15–16
ribbon, 5–6
tables, 128
themes, styles, and templates, 72
Web file formats, 201–202
wildcards, 39
QuickSteps topics
adding objects from other programs, 169–170
copying formatting, 68–69
creating reviewing shortcuts, 221–222
curves, 164–165
data tables, 198
deleting a style, 75–76
e-mailing, 117
entering information in tables, 136–137
entering special characters, 25–27
exiting Word, 3
faxing, 115–118
font dialog box, 50
formatting content, 144–145
formatting marks, 66
forms, 186
formulas, 141–142
graphics, 177–178
html elements, 214
left and right headers, 86–87
mini toolbar, 7
moving and copying tables, columns,
and rows, 138–139

Office Clipboard, 30–32
picture tools format tab, 158
positioning pictures, 161–162
ruler for indents, 57–58
rules for merge fields and static text, 121–122
saving documents, 41–42
selecting chart items, 194–195
selecting tables, rows, columns, or cells, 133–134
setting document properties, 226–227
setting preferences, 11–12
table alignment, 146
thesaurus, 104
tracking inconsistent formatting, 69
view buttons, 93–94
window color, 10

R

radar chart, function of, 193
Reading Highlight option, using
with searches, 37
Recent Pages down arrow, finding
folders with, 24
Redo icon, identifying, 32
registered (®) symbol, keyboard shortcut for, 27
RejectChangesOrAdvance option, using, 222
relative positioning, using with graphics, 175
Repeat Header Rows feature, using, 142
Repeat option, appearance of, 33
research, conducting, 13
Research task pane, displaying, 13
reset character formatting, keyboard
shortcut for, 46
reset paragraph formatting, keyboard
shortcut for, 46
resource center, accessing, 15–16
Review tab, using with Track
Changes feature, 217

reviewed documents, sending via e-mail, 223
reviewers, identifying in Track
Changes feature, 220
Reviewing pane, checking changes with, 222
reviewing shortcuts, creating with Track
Changes feature, 221–222
ribbon
adding commands to Quick Access
toolbar from, 9
commands and tools on, 5
features of, 3–4, 5–6
location of, 4
minimizing size of, 6
tabs on, 4
ribbon groups, locations of, 4
right indent
changing, 56
setting with ruler, 57
right-clicking with mouse, 6
round-tripping feature, using with
Web pages, 205–206
row heights
changing in tables, 135
spacing in tables, 136
rows
adding at bottom of tables, 133
inserting in tables, 133
moving and copying, 139
removing from tables, 134
selecting in tables, 133–134
separating, 140
.rtf extension, file type associated
with, 25
ruler
displaying, 57, 83
setting tabs with, 83–84
using for indents, 57–58
rules, using with merge fields, 121–122

S

save interval, default for, 42
scatter (XY) chart, function of, 193
ScreenTips, showing and hiding, 10
Scribble action, using with curves, 164
scroll arrow
  identifying, 34
  location of, 4
scroll bars
  location of, 4
  navigating documents with, 33
scroll button
  identifying, 34
  location of, 4
search criteria, entering for research, 13
search items, moving between, 36
search results, sorting files in, 23–24
searches
  highlighting items in, 37
  limiting, 36
  modifying with filters, 24
  specifying direction of, 37
  using wildcards in, 39
searching
  files, 23–24
  text, 36
section breaks, inserting, deleting, and
    displaying, 81–82
selecting areas, 30
selection group, selecting chart items from, 194
Send option, using, 223
sentences, selecting, 29
separators, formatting text with, 141
serif versus sans-serif fonts, 47
shading
  adding to text, 64–66
  applying to tables, 147–148

Shadow formatting option, using with chart
    items, 196
shapes, choosing, 163
Shapes feature, options for, 164
shortcut icon, creating to start Word, 3
shortcut keys. *See* keyboard shortcuts
Show Markup option, using with Track
    Changes feature, 220
Shrink font, identifying, 45
Single File Web Page format, using, 201–202
single-spacing, setting, 57–58
slider, location of, 4
small caps formatting, keyboard shortcut for, 46
smart tags, using with Paste Options, 32
SmartArt, creating diagrams with, 166–168
Sort icon, identifying, 45
sort order, explanation of, 138
sorting
  columns, 138–139
  files, 23–24
  merge recipients, 120
  by multiple fields in columns, 139
  by table columns, 138
  tables and selected cells in, 137–138
Sounds Like search option, using, 37
special characters
  displaying shortcut keys for, 27
  entering, 25–27
  inserting sequentially, 28
  rules for bookmarks, 209
Special search option, using, 37
spelling and grammar, checking, 38–41
split pages, handling, 60
Start menu, starting Word with, 2
static text in Mail Merge, explanation of, 117
status bar, location of, 4
stock chart, function of, 193

Strikethrough icon, identifying, 45
style sets, applying to documents, 72
styles. *See also* table styles
  changing for default Normal template, 79–80
  deleting, 75–76
  explanation of, 72
  identifying text with, 72
  modifying, 74–75
  saving Quick Styles, 73
  updating automatically, 75
subdocument commands, using with table of
    contents, 91
submenus, opening, 7
subscript formatting, keyboard shortcut for, 46
Subscript icon, identifying, 45
superscript formatting, keyboard shortcut for, 46
surface chart, function of, 193
Symbol dialog box, selecting special characters
    from, 25–26
symbol font formatting, keyboard shortcut for, 46
symbol fonts, examples of, 47
syntax, relationship to formulas, 141

T

table attributes, determining, 130
table of contents
  generating, 92
  placing in sections, 92
  placing text in, 90–91
  tagging entries for, 90, 92
  using Outlining tab for, 91
  using subdocument commands with, 91
table position, locking, 146
table styles. *See also* styles
  applying and modifying, 149–150
  deleting, 150

tables. *See also* cells
   adding cells to, 132–133
   aligning and indenting, 146
   aligning cell content in, 144
   applying shading and border effects to, 147–148
   changing column width and row height in, 135
   components of, 129
   converting text to, 141
   converting to text, 142
   drawing, 130–131
   formatting automatically, 148–150
   formatting content in, 144–145
   inserting, 128, 130
   merging cells in, 144
   moving and copying, 139
   moving content around in, 137
   navigating, 136
   navigation shortcuts for, 136
   organizing forms with, 183
   removing, 143
   removing parts of, 135
   resizing, 133
   selecting, 133
   selecting rows, columns, and cells in,
      133–134
   sorting, 137–138
   sorting cells in, 137–138
   spacing column widths in, 136
   splitting, 134
   typing text above, 136
   using, 128
   using context menus with, 132
   using contextual tabs with, 131
   using Eraser with, 135
   viewing column dimensions in, 135
   wrapping text around, 145–146
Tablet PCs, writing comments on, 225

tabs
   displaying, 83
   displaying text formatting for, 84
   groups and commands in, 5
   opening, 6–7
   setting using measurements, 84
   setting with leaders, 84
   setting with ruler, 83–84
   types of, 83
templates. *See also* form templates
   applying to documents, 81
   basing on different documents, 80
   changing default Normal template, 79–80
   creating, 80
   creating for charts, 193
   explanation of, 72
   saving documents as, 42
   saving forms as, 186
   using, 19–22
   using with charts, 193–194
Templates pane, options in, 19
text. *See also* building blocks; fonts
   adding borders and shading to, 64–66
   converting tables to, 142
   converting to tables, 141
   copying and moving, 30–32
   copying to Clipboard, 31
   cutting, 31
   deleting, 32
   determining placement of, 27
   entering in documents, 26
   finding with advanced search, 37
   finding with search, 36
   formatting in charts, 197
   formatting with separators, 141
   highlighting, 226
   hyphenating, 103–104

   identifying with styles, 72
   inserting, 27–28
   pasting, 31
   placing in table of contents, 90–91
   replacing, 37–38
   resetting, 49
   selecting, 29–30
   typing above tables, 136
   typing over, 27–28
   underlining, 48
   wrapping around tables, 145–146
text boxes, coloring text in, 171
text changes, identifying in Track Changes
      feature, 216
text effects
   adding, 163–166
   adding through Font dialog box, 50
text formatting, displaying when using tabs, 84
Text Highlight Color icon, identifying, 45
text toolbar, displaying, 7
text tools, using, 7
text wrapping in table cells, changing, 144–145
theme font sets, creating, 77–78
theme fonts, changing, 77
themed graphic effects, changing, 78
themes
   assigning to documents, 75
   changing colors of, 76–77
   customizing, 78–79
   explanation of, 72
   restoring colors for, 79
thesaurus, using, 14, 104
title bar, location of, 4
TOC (table of contents). *See* table of contents
Track Changes feature
   accepting and rejecting changes with, 221
   creating reviewing shortcuts with, 221–222

display options for, 219
explanation of, 216
hiding changes with, 220
identifying reviewers with, 220
moving to changes with, 222
navigating to changes with, 222
reviewing changes with, 220–223
setting options for, 218
turning on, 217
using balloons with, 218–220
using Review tab with, 217
using Reviewing pane with, 222
trade mark (™) symbol, keyboard shortcut for, 27
translating. *See also* languages
documents, 187–188
words and phrases, 187
.txt extension, file type associated with, 25

U

underline formatting, keyboard shortcut for, 46
Underline icon, identifying, 45
Underline Style drop-down list, using, 48
Undo option, using, 32
un-hang formatting, keyboard shortcut for, 46
unicode, explanation of, 207
un-indent formatting, keyboard shortcut for, 46
URL (Uniform Resource Locator),
    example of, 207
Use Wildcards search option, using, 37

V

vertical alignment, setting, 69
vertical scroll bar
identifying, 34
using, 33

View buttons
changing document display with, 35
locations of, 4
using, 93–94
views, using, 7–8

W

Web file formats, choosing, 201–202
Web Layout Reading view, description of, 94
Web Layout view, description of, 8
Web options
choosing on Browsers tab, 202–203
choosing on Files tab, 204–205
on Encoding tab, 205–206
on Fonts tab, 206
on Pictures tab, 205
Web pages
character sets available to, 206
creating, 200
creating hyperlinks to, 208–209
managing folders for, 204
previewing, 211–212
saving Word documents as, 200–202
Widow/Orphan Control, options for, 60
wildcard characters, using, 39
window color, changing, 10
Windows Clipboard
copying and moving text with, 30
reverting to, 32
using, 30
Windows Vista, using filters in, 24
Word
exiting, 3
starting, 2–3
updating, 15–16
use of HTML by, 205–206

Word documents. *See* documents
Word Help dialog box, displaying, 13
Word window
changing background color for, 10
features of, 4
WordArt effects, applying, 164–166
words
counting, 101–102
replacing beginnings and endings of, 39
selecting, 29
translating, 15, 187
Word-specific tags, removing
    from documents, 214
word-wrap option, using, 145
WorldLingo machine translation,
    performing, 14, 188–189
.wpd extension, file type associated with, 25
.wps extension, file type associated with, 25
wrapping
changing in table cells, 144–145
default for, 174
www in hyperlinks, meaning of, 207

X

XE (Index Entry) fields, hiding and showing, 90
.xml extension, file type associated with, 25
XY (scatter) chart, function of, 193

Z

zoom buttons, locations of, 4
Zoom dialog box, displaying, 109